BILLY WALKER
Once, Twice, Three Times a Winner
THE FA CUP
Villa 1920, Wednesday 1935, Forest 1959

BILLY WALKER

Once, Twice, Three Times a Winner
THE FA CUP
Villa 1920, Wednesday 1935, Forest 1959

Series Editor: Clive Leatherdale

Edward Giles

DESERT ISLAND BOOKS

First published in 2008
by
DESERT ISLAND BOOKS LIMITED
7 Clarence Road, Southend-on-Sea, Essex SS1 1AN
United Kingdom
www.desertislandbooks.com

© 2008 Edward Giles

The right of Edward Giles to be identified as author of this work has been
asserted under The Copyright Designs and Patents Act 1988

British Library Cataloguing-in-Publication Data
A catalogue record for this book is available from the British Library

IBSN 978-1-905328-42-0

Printed in Great Britain
by
Biddles Ltd, King's Lynn

Illustrations reproduced courtesy of Colorsport

Contents

DEDICATION

To Bob Parker, who for many years travelled from his home near Wolverhampton to broadcast running commentaries on the home matches of Notts County and Nottingham Forest to patients in local hospitals.

CHAPTER ONE

Cup Winner in his First Season

Billy Walker enjoyed considerable success with each of his three Football League clubs in a senior career that lasted from the first season after the 1914-18 War until his death towards the end of 1964. As a player, he took part in two FA Cup finals, the first of them as a winner, and his aggregate of 244 League and Cup goals set an Aston Villa record that still stands. As a manager, he won the Cup with both Sheffield Wednesday and Nottingham Forest, and also guided Forest from the Third Division back to the First.

William Henry Walker was born at Wednesbury in Staffordshire on 29 October 1897. His father, George, had been a strong and uncompromising defender with Wolverhampton Wanderers during the first five years of the twentieth century, and then with Crystal Palace in the Southern League for the next two. It seemed reasonable to expect, therefore, that he would give his son every encouragement to follow him as a professional footballer, yet at the outset he did the exact opposite.

Maybe his view was jaundiced by having been in a Wolves team that never aspired to the game's honours, invariably in mid-table and swiftly knocked out of the Cup. Perhaps he feared that the physical demands of top-level football would be too great for an offspring who had often suffered from ill health as a child and almost died from consumption. At any rate, no parental support was forthcoming in that direction at that time, and, on leaving King's Hill School at Wednesbury after playing once for England Boys, young Billy was found employment with an engineering firm in the hope that.he would be diverted from trying to make a living from kicking a football about.

How forlorn that hope was. And how fortunate for Aston Villa that his enthusiasm for soccer was undiminished. It was even said that he deliberately failed a scholarship to a grammar school so that he could concentrate on developing an aptitude for the game he demonstrated by scoring 80 goals in the Walsall Boys' League during the 1910-11 season. After that, George Walker realised it was pointless persevering with his attempt to block his son's soccer ambitions, and from then onwards he gave him his unreserved backing. Freed from disapproval, Billy progressed to playing for Fallings Heath, Hednesford Town, Darlaston, Wednesbury Old Park and Wednesbury Old Athletic, then was taken on as an amateur by Villa in the spring of 1915 after scoring nine times in a spell of 40 minutes in one match for the Athletic. Wolves were found wanting there, for he would almost certainly have signed for them if they had given him the chance. He had been an ardent follower of his father's old club.

With war soon afterwards closing down League football for four years, it was not until May 1919 that Walker, a well-built six-footer, was taken on as a professional at Villa Park. In the meantime, his work at a factory manufacturing nuts and bolts kept him close enough on hand to gain some experience in the Midland wartime competitions.

His first-team appearances for Villa while the League was in limbo were limited to five, none of them any portent of what was to come. On his debut, away to West Bromwich Albion in a match in aid of the War Fund on Boxing Day 1916, Villa's only reply to the five goals they let in was made by 36-year-old Joe Bache, occupier for most of his fourteen seasons before the war of the inside-left position Walker was to make his own for a similar length of time after it. Villa were also beaten, twice more giving away five goals, in the four other games Walker played for them before the League got under way again. Three of them were in the Midland Victory League, all in April 1919; the other in aid of charity early the following month.

Walker scored two of the five goals Villa mustered against the twenty they conceded in those five matches. He opened his account with their lone response as Albion again went nap at the Hawthorns, and obtained his first at Villa Park in a Charity Fund defeat by Birmingham by the odd goal of three. In the Midland Victory League, Villa were far removed from their pre-war power. Only four clubs competed, and they finished a poor last behind West Bromwich, Derby and Wolves, who each gained seven points from their six matches to Villa's three.

Promising though some of Walker's displays had been, it was hardly surprising in those disappointing circumstances that he was not chosen to continue at centre-forward, his regular position in those days, when Aston Villa started up again in the First Division on the last Saturday of August in 1919. Indeed, no fewer than six other players were tried there before his recall for a first-round FA Cup-tie at home to Queen's Park Rangers just over four months later.

Once in, he was in no mood to be left out. From the day, the tenth of January 1920, on which he marked his full debut by scoring both the goals that took Villa into the next round, he was a regular first choice until he played the last five of his 531 League and Cup games in the opening weeks of the 1933-34 season. With his deceptive body swerve, ready eye for goal, and the accurate long passes he swept out to either wing, he stands high in the list of truly great players who have graced Aston Villa teams ever since the club lifted their first trophy, the Birmingham Senior Cup, way back in 1880. A legendary figure, a superb tactician as well as a sharp and consistent finisher, he was an icon if ever there was one. The many years he spent with Villa have been named after him in the club's annals, known as 'the Walker period.'

Seriously as he took his soccer, Walker was not averse to some light-hearted leg-pulling or practical joking. In that respect he particularly remembered one jape concerning a slim outside-left named Reg Chester: 'One day we painted his back with lipstick. We told him later that the breathing exercises he used to do had been too much. It took us half-an-hour to convince him that it was lipstick, and not blood.'

A week after being a Cup winner against QPR, Walker made the first of his 478 League appearances, all for Villa and all in the First Division, in a scoreless draw at Burnley. Two weeks later, he scored the first of his 214 League goals in a 1-1 draw away to Everton. His final total of games, both in the League and overall, broke the respective records Joe Bache had set with 431 and 473, and stood until nearly 40 years after he had retired. Full-back Charlie Aitken overtook his League tally in December 1973, going on altogether to amass 561 matches, two of them as a sub-stitute, over nearly sixteen years up to the middle of January in 1976. With the inclusion of cup-ties, the Edinburgh-born Aitken forged to a new peak of 659, three as a sub, before leaving for a last stint with New York Cosmos. On his return from the United States, he ran a jewellery and antiques business in Birmingham and resumed some connection with Villa as a member of their Old Stars team for a few more years.

Walker's number of League goals left him just one short of Harry Hampton's club record, but in the aggregate he ended two ahead of Hampton, a centre-forward who specialised in charging both ball and goalkeeper into the net, with the addition of the 30 he scored in creating another Villa record by taking part in 53 FA Cup-ties. Hampton's 27 Cup goals gave him an overall total of 242 to Walker's 244.

The first half-dozen of Walker's Cup games culminated in his achieve-ment in his first season as a professional of what was then a player's most coveted club honour, a winner's medal in the national knock-out compe-tition. He scored three more goals on the way to the final – one in the second round against Manchester United at Old Trafford (it was not until the 1925-26 season that the third round became the starting point for the big clubs), and the two others in the 3-1 defeat of Chelsea in the semi-final at Bramall Lane, Sheffield. In between, Sunderland, at Villa Park, and Tottenham Hotspur, at White Hart Lane, were both beaten by an only goal – in Spurs' case an own goal by their captain, full-back Tommy Clay.

That year of 1920 was the first of three in which the final was staged at Stamford Bridge before Wembley became the venue, so Villa's defeat of Chelsea averted the possibility of the West London club's taking part in it on their home ground. The scorer of Villa's other goal in the semi-final was Harold Edgley, a former Crewe outside-left who had the cruel misfortune to miss the final after playing in each of the previous rounds. On Good Friday, just under three weeks before the big occasion at the Bridge, he suffered a double fracture of the left leg while playing there in a First Division game against Chelsea only six days after helping to end the Cup hopes of the Pensioners, as they were then known. Edgley never appeared in the Villa first team again, but after the final the club obtained permission from the FA for him to be presented with a special souvenir medal. Following a move to QPR, he returned to Cheshire with Stockport and was later a Notts County director.

As successor to Edgley on their left wing, Aston Villa had a ready-made replacement in Arthur Dorrell, who was to be Walker's partner for most of eight successive seasons during the 1920s after Billy's switch from centre-forward to inside-left. Dorrell, son of a former Villa player, was noted for the speed he had shown as a sprinter in the French athletics championships while serving in the Army in the First World War. Although fortunate, because of a clubmate's bad luck, to be a Cup winner, like Walker, in his first season, he maintained such a high level of consistency that he missed only five matches in four successive seasons and was not far short of 400 appearances by the time he left for a final year with Port Vale in 1931.

Another change Villa had to make before the 1920 final brought in Frank Moss, the only Aston-born player in the side. He, too, was in to stay. Fair-haired Moss, naturally nicknamed 'Snowy', played for the club in a couple of League games before the First World War. After it, having recovered from a serious wound to his left knee that had threatened his career while on Army service, he took part in nearly 300 more before his transfer to Cardiff City in 1929. His sons Amos and Frank also played for Villa, Frank Junior exceeding 300 games – the first two of them before the Second World War.

The player from whom Frank Moss Senior took over on the left flank of the half-back line was Jimmy Harrop, who dropped out through injury a week before the semi-final with Chelsea. Harrop had joined Villa from Liverpool in May 1912, in one of the best of double deals in company with Sam Hardy, by common consent the outstanding goalkeeper of his day. Hardy was the man Villa had mostly to thank for so luckily edging dominant Spurs out of their quarter-final, bringing off a series of superb saves. He had also been a key figure in Villa's defeat of Sunderland in the 1913 final, despite the handicap of an injury that had kept him off the field for some ten minutes during which Harrop had moved back from centre-half to deputise. That had been a match missed, because of a broken leg, by Andy Ducat, Harrop's successor as captain for the 1920 final. Ducat, signed from Woolwich Arsenal the month after the arrival of Hardy and Harrop at Villa Park, was a member of the select band capped by England at both cricket and football. To his six soccer caps he added just one Test appearance, ill-fated for its coinciding with Australia's decisive third successive victory of the 1921 series at Leeds in the considerable absence of Jack Hobbs. England's top batsman, taken ill, was unable to bat in either innings. It was also an ill-fated match for Ducat personally. He totalled only five runs in his two innings, and in the first one he had the shoulder of his bat knocked off onto the wicket by a ball from fast bowler Ted McDonald. The ball was caught by Jack Gregory, the other intimidating half of Australia's opening attack, and it was that form of dismissal which went into the scorebook.

Ducat died playing cricket. He collapsed while batting for Surrey against Sussex in a Home Guard match at Lord's in 1942, at the age of 56. McDonald, who qualified to play for Lancashire after returning to England to play in league cricket, also came to an untimely premature end. Early one July morning in 1937 he was killed in a road accident near Bolton after stopping to help another motorist.

Aston Villa's opponents in the 1920 FA Cup final were Huddersfield Town, a club that only the previous November had been declared 'to all intents and purposes extinct'. A financial crisis, arising from lack of support in an area much more enthusiastic about Rugby League than soccer, had almost resulted in an amalgamation with the new Leeds United that had arisen from the Football League's expulsion of the Leeds City club accused of illegal payments to players during the 1914-18 War. Not until 17 June 1920, nearly two months after the Cup final, were terms for Huddersfield Town's security finally settled. In those traumatic circumstances, it was incredible that the Terriers, as they were so aptly nicknamed, not only won through to the final but also climbed into the First Division for the first time as runners-up to Tottenham.

And that was far from all. Although beaten by Villa at Stamford Bridge, the Town were on the brink of the most successful era in their history under the dynamic and far-seeing management of Herbert Chapman, later also to wield his magic wand over Arsenal. Within two years Huddersfield were back at the Bridge for a final in which they defeated Preston North End, and two years after that they completed the first leg of a League title treble. Ironically, Aston Villa were the providers of the main on-field schemer of those successes. Their transfer of Clem Stephenson created the vacancy at inside-left that Billy Walker was switched from the head of Villa's attack to fill, and provided Huddersfield with an inspiring captain who led them to another Cup Final (though lost to Blackburn) after the three consecutive seasons as champions that were immediately followed by two as runners-up.

Having played in four finals from 1913 to 1928, the first three as a winner, Stephenson piloted Huddersfield to two more in his thirteen years as their manager, and to another second place in the First Division. They were also runners-up, however, on both their visits to Wembley under his direction, losing in 1930 to Arsenal, who gained the first of their many major trophies, and in 1938 to Preston, who exactly reversed the result of their defeat by Huddersfield in the 1922 final by triumphing with a penalty. It was also to Arsenal that Town were second in the League in 1934 – just a few months after the sudden untimely death of Herbert Chapman while the Gunners were in the middle of their own title hat-trick.

Huddersfield's defeat in the 1920 final gave Aston Villa the Cup for a then record sixth time, overtaking the Wanderers and Blackburn Rovers, but it was a mighty close thing. The only goal of the match did not come until the first period of extra time, in the 100th minute, and it was not clear who had scored it as the heads went up in a crowded goalmouth to meet a corner kick taken by Dorrell. One source says that the referee, Jack ('Jimmy') Howcroft, of Bolton, thought that the ball glanced into the net off a defender, another that he later confirmed inside-right Billy Kirton as the scorer, and yet another that Kirton's header was deflected home by Tommy Wilson, the Huddersfield centre-half. At any rate, Kirton, a full-back turned forward who was the most impressive member of the Villa attack that afternoon, has officially been given the credit.

So it was in such confusing circumstances that Huddersfield narrowly failed to overcome the handicap of being without their star turn, left-winger Billy Smith, who in the very week of the final was suspended for an incident in a League game a few weeks earlier. Neither did they find the good fortune they hoped for from their lucky charm, a lamp from a local production of the pantomime Aladdin that each of their players rubbed before the kick-off.

Billy Kirton joined Villa, along with Clem Stephenson's younger brother George, in the humiliating auction of Leeds City players, plus the sale of nets, goal posts, boots, kit and physiotherapy equipment, that resulted from the Yorkshire club's expulsion. The entire squad fetched only just over £10,000, with Kirton priced at £500 and Stephenson £250. Both those bargains for Villa went on to play for England. Kirton scored the goal that earned a draw when he won his one cap against Ireland in Belfast; George Stephenson outdid Clem, who surprisingly also played just the once for England, by gaining two caps after leaving Villa for Derby County and another while with Sheffield Wednesday. George did not play in Villa's first team with Clem and another brother, Jimmy, but he later provided the first case of two brothers managing the same League club when he was also in charge at Huddersfield.

Left-back Tommy Weston was the only member of Villa'a Cup-winning team of 1920 not to play for his country, but, after overcoming early criticism that he was too impetuous, he gave the club excellent service either side of the 1914-18 War before moving to Stoke in 1922. He was one of three survivors from the side successful in the 1913 final, and at Stamford Bridge in 1920 it was his leg that ensured victory by deflecting wide a goalbound shot from Huddersfield's Frank Mann, a former Villa player. From forming one efficient full-back partnership before the war with Tom Lyons, Weston struck up another after it with Tommy Smart, a barrel-chested fierce tackler who, along with Barson, Dorrell, Moss, Kirton and Walker, was a Cup winner in his first season with Villa – a distinction all the more remarkable for the fact that he picked up his medal only three months after being signed from Halesowen. Smart's 452 League and Cup games also included the 1924 Cup Final and put him third to Billy Walker and Joe Bache for Villa appearances by the time he left for Brierley Hill Alliance in 1934.

The other Villa player besides Sam Hardy and Tommy Weston who took part in the finals of 1913 and 1920 was right-winger Charlie Wallace. Fifteen minutes into that pre-war match with Sunderland, Wallace became the first to fail with a penalty in an FA Cup Final, but fifteen minutes from the finish he took the corner kick from which Tommy Barber made a Clem Stephenson dream come true by heading the winning goal. Both clubs, the top two in the First Division, went into the game with a chance of doing the League and Cup double Villa had completed in 1897. Having denied Sunderland that distinction, Villa were themselves foiled on the following Wednesday, when the pair met again in a drawn League match at Villa Park that dashed the home team's faint hopes of overtaking the Wearsiders.

The member of Villa's team for the 1920 final from whom the young Billy Walker drew most inspiration was centre-half Frank Barson, a hard man of Yorkshire who was a diamond of a defender, but a rough-cut one, the most suspended of his day. 'Frank did more than any other player to help me when I started with Villa,' Walker once said in looking back on his career, 'but he had no friends on the field. He was much maligned, the greatest of all the characters I came across in football.' Barson, a former blacksmith, was signed by Villa from Barnsley in October 1919 after upsetting the Oakwell club's directors, and sold to Manchester United in August 1922 after being banned for refusing to move his home from Sheffield to Birmingham. In between, he revitalised flagging Villa as the power of his personality brought out the best in those around him, and just over a week before giving a typically dominant display in the final against Huddersfield he was awarded his one England cap alongside Andy Ducat against Wales at Arsenal's ground. Sam Hardy was the third Villa player in a side beaten by the odd goal of three.

These were the teams in the final, watched by a crowd of 50,018 (receipts £9,722), at Stamford Bridge on 24 April 1920:

Aston Villa: Hardy; Smart, Weston; Ducat, Barson, Moss; Wallace, Kirton, Walker, Stephenson (C), Dorrell.

Huddersfield Town: Mutch; Wood, Bullock; Slade, Wilson, Watson; Richardson, Mann, Taylor, Swann, Islip.

For Villa, however, the golden era was over. Their sixth winning of the Cup equalled the number of League titles they had acquired up to that time, but not for 37 years were they to chalk up another major success – and then it was a controversial victory that gave them a lucky thirteenth trophy, and cost Manchester United the first League and Cup double of the twentieth century, at Wembley on 4 May 1957. Controversial because that was the final in which United's goalkeeper, Ray Wood, was carried off as early as the sixth minute with concussion and a fractured cheek-bone suffered in a challenge by Peter McParland, Villa's Irish international outside-left, that referee Frank Coultas termed 'just a bit too robust.'

Wood resumed as a right-wing 'passenger' before half-time, and took over in goal again from his deputy, Jackie Blanchflower, for the last eight minutes after United had halved the lead gained with two McParland goals, but there was to be no equaliser.

CHAPTER TWO

Last England Cap after Six-Year Gap

To the Cup winner's medal he had gained in his first season as a professional, Billy Walker soon added a first England cap in his second. Having
scored 14 goals in Aston Villa's first eleven games of 1920-21, he led
England's attack against Ireland at Roker Park, Sunderland, on 23
October 1920. Again he was a scorer, along with Burnley's Bob Kelly, in
a 2-0 victory.

The first four of the 32 goals Walker was to score that season – a personal best – came on the opening day in a 5-0 crushing of Arsenal at Villa
Park. He was also on target in each of Villa's next four games, including
the goal that completed a double over the Gunners, and a couple when
Tottenham were the losing visitors. Only twice in the opening sequence
that led to his England call-up did he fail to score – in a five-goal defeat
at Bolton, and when Spurs were again beaten in the return at White Hart
Lane. On the Saturday before made his international debut he was
Villa's only scorer when they were hit for six by Preston, who a week earlier had been unable to reply to his lone goal at Villa Park (for the first
five post-war seasons clubs met each other, home and away, on successive weekends.)

Billy Walker wore an England shirt for the first time in the company
of Andy Ducat, who was winning the last of his six caps. This was the
team:

Mew (Manchester United); Downs (Everton), Bullock (Huddersfield
Town); Ducat (Aston Villa), McCall (Preston North End), Grimsdell
(Tottenham Hotspur); Chedgzoy (Everton), Kelly (Burnley). Walker
(Aston Villa), Morris (West Bromwich Albion), Quantrill (Derby
County).

For John Mew, 'Dicky' Downs and Fred Bullock it was to be their only
England appearance – as professionals, that is. Bullock, Huddersfield's
captain, whose career was ended by cartilage trouble that season, had
skippered the amateur international side in Belfast while with Ilford nearly ten years earlier. Two others besides Ducat were not to be chosen again
– Joe McCall, also gaining his sixth cap, and Fred Morris, who had made
his debut in England's previous match, a Sheffield spectacular in which
Scotland had been defeated by the odd goal of nine. That game had
brought down the curtain on Sam Hardy's distinguished international
career, starting a search for his successor for which Mew was one of half-

a-dozen goalkeepers tried before Huddersfield's Ted Taylor was given an extended run in the side.

Despite his scoring debut, Billy Walker missed England's next three matches, a scoreless draw with Wales in Cardiff, a 0-3 defeat by Scotland at Hampden Park in Glasgow, and a 2-0 win against Belgium in Brussels. He had to wait another year, almost exactly to the day, before being awarded his second cap, this time at inside-left, in the drawn game in Belfast in which his clubmate Billy Kirton scored England's goal in his only international. Frank Moss was the third Villa player in that team, for the first of his five caps.

The player from whom Walker took over on his recall was Harry Chambers, of Liverpool, who had scored one of the goals in Belgium. The centre-forward position from which Walker had by then been switched by Villa was filled by another of those who turned out only the once for England – Ernest Simms of Luton Town, a then Third Division club that also supplied Ireland's left-wing pair, Alan Mathieson and Louis Bookman. No other Luton player appeared in the long-defunct British Championship until Bobby Brennan was in the Irish attack against Wales in Belfast nearly 28 years later.

Walker kept his place for England's next match, won against Wales in Liverpool with a Kelly goal in March 1922, but he was again omitted after a defeat by Scotland, also by only one goal, in Birmingham the following month. Aston Villa again had three players in the England line-up for that clash with the Scots at their own ground. Walker and Moss were joined by Dicky York, whose exceptional pace made him a natural successor to Charlie Wallace on the club's right wing. York was born almost directly opposite where, in 1874, Villa had come into existence at a meeting in Heathfield Road, on the fringes of the Birchfields and Lozxells districts of Birmingham. He had preferred rugby to soccer while at school, but was soon snapped up by Villa after guesting for Chelsea as a wing-half during the First World War, in which he served in the Royal Flying Corps. Although chosen just once more for England – and again in defeat by a lone Scotland goal, at Old Trafford, Manchester, in 1926 – he was within ten games of 400 for Villa by the time he moved to Port Vale with Arthur Dorrell.

With the bow-legged 'Smiler' Chambers, possessor of a fierce left-foot shot who helped Liverpool to two successive League titles in those years, reclaiming England's inside-left spot, Walker was overlooked by the international selectors until two games with Sweden in Stockholm after the 1922-23 season. He celebrated another cap comeback with two goals in a 4-2 win in the first of them, but was kept off the scoresheet when a

3-1 victory was gained in the second one, and again had to give way to Chambers for England's next visit to Belfast that autumn. The ending of Chambers' international career was one outcome of defeat by the Irish, yet Walker found two more rivals in his way before he was brought back in April 1924 for Scotland's first visit to Wembley the year after the opening of the Empire Stadium. One was the Corinthian A G Doggart, who added a single cap among the professionals to the four he gained as an amateur in captaining the team that drew with the Belgians in Antwerp; the other, Walker's former Villa team-mate Clem Stephenson, whose overdue, but solitary, cap came in a defeat by Wales at Blackburn.

Billy Walker became the first to score for England at Wembley in getting the goal that earned a draw with Scotland. It was a dull game, watched by a crowd of only about 60,000 that was well below the capacity set for the stadium after the frightening pitch invasion by spectators at the first FA Cup final staged there between Bolton and West Ham. Once more, two other Villa players were in the England team, Frank Moss having Tommy Smart behind him at right-back.

After missing a win against France in Paris, Walker was back for England's next eight matches, in half of which he was partnered by Arthur Dorrell. They were first together for their country against Belgium at West Bromwich Albion's ground, where both netted twice in a 4-0 victory. Dorrell, also a scorer when France were again beaten in Paris, was never on the losing side in his four games for England, yet lost his place after a scoreless draw in Belfast in which Tommy Smart made up another Villa trio in collecting his fourth cap. Four more years went by before Smart was given his final one, in a 6-0 drubbing of Wales at Stamford Bridge.

The 3-2 victory in the French capital was gained with the aid of an own goal, but with only ten men. Goalkeeper Fred Fox, who was transferred from one Third Division club, Gillingham, to another, Millwall, between being selected and winning his one cap, was unable to resume for the second half after being accidentally kicked in the face. The man who took over from him was none other than Walker, though his choice for that role was not altogether surprising considering that he was also Villa's deputy when a similar emergency arose.

For Billy Walker there was to be an even longer wait than Smart's for his last England game. His sequence of eight caps ended when a defeat by Wales at Selhurst Park was followed by another setback against Scotland at Old Trafford in which Tommy Mort, successor to Weston as Smart's full-back partner with Villa, made the last of his three England appearances as York completed another Villa threesome. Although recalled after just one more match, Walker really did appear at last to be at the end of his international road when he was again omitted in the wake of 3-3 draws with Ireland and Wales. No fewer than 31 fixtures were fulfilled by England before his surprise return for his farewell eighteenth cap after an interval of nearly six years.

Tommy Mort, a Lancastrian master of the sliding tackle, did not quite match Dorrell, Smart and Walker by being with Villa all through the League's first decade after the First World War, but his signing from Rochdale in April 1922 gave the club a bumper dividend of nearly 370 League and Cup games before his retirement in 1935. The great majority of those games were played alongside Smart, in a resourceful pairing dubbed 'Death and Glory' by Villa fans.

Walker scored one of the goals, his ninth for England, in the drawn match with Wales at Wrexham on 12 February 1927 that became accepted as his international swan song as the years rolled by. Ten players were tried in the inside-left position he vacated before his unexpected one-off reinstatement. George Stephenson was among them, but those most in favour for that role during his absence were Joe Bradford (Birmingham), Arthur Rigby (Blackburn Rovers), Tom Johnson (Manchester City and Everton) and Harry Burgess (Sheffield Wednesday). Burgess, later to come under Walker's management at Hillsborough, featured prominently in Wednesday's second consecutive season as champions in 1929-30.

Those players provided formidable competition indeed for Walker, who was getting into the veteran stage for a top-class footballer. Another factor that conspired to keep Villa's star man out of the international reckoning was that there were some big wins among those England gained while he was away. Nine goals were scored against Belgium, six against France, Wales and Ireland, five against Luxembourg, France, Belgium, Scotland and Ireland.

Much of the impetus for those successes was supplied by Everton's Bill ('Dixie') Dean and George Camsell, of Middlesbrough. Dean, scorer of the two other goals when he first led the England attack in the 3-3 draw with Wales, totalled a dozen in also finding the net in each of his next four internationals. Among them were the brace that beat the Scots, in Glasgow, for the first time in five meetings, and hat-tricks at the expense of Belgium and Luxembourg. Camsell, whose 59 goals in Boro's runaway promotion from the Second Division in 1926-27 set a League record Dean broke the very next season with 60 in the First Division, scored four goals against Belgium in Brussels and three against Wales at Chelsea's ground. He altogether notched eighteen in finding the net in each of his nine England appearances.

But it was not all-conquering for England while Walker was out of their team. Their seven defeats during that period included the infamous 1-5 lesson handed out in pouring rain by Scotland's 'Wembley Wizards' of 1928. Humiliation on such a scale had hardly been anticipated considering the Scots' controversial exclusion of several tartan titans, most notably Celtic's free scorer Jimmy McGrory. The high number of eight players in their team who were with Football League clubs included the one Aston Villa player afield – Jimmy Gibson, whose father Neil had also been capped.

Jimmy's transfer from Partick Thistle the year before that Wembley upset cost Villa their then record fee of £7,500, an outlay he repaid in style for the best part of nine seasons up to his retirement in 1936. Around the turn into the 1930s, he formed with Alec Talbot and Joe Tate the club's formidable half-back line known as 'Wind, Sleet and Rain'. Talbot, perversely nicknamed 'Tiny' because, like Gibson, he was more than six feet tall, turned professional with Villa straight after a ten-hour shift down the pit at West Cannock Colliery and played 141 of his 263 League and Cup games in succession before his move to Bradford in 1935. Tate, the youngest of five brothers, ended a wait of more than two years in the Reserves by filling the vacancy left by Frank Moss's departure, then held his place for five more years until dogged by a series of niggling injuries. Off he went to Brierley Hill as player-manager, but broke his neck during a match with Moor Green and on his recovery was forced to give up the game to concentrate on his tobacconist business.

Shattering as that hammering by the Scots was, another of those seven setbacks was to have far more significance as far as Billy Walker was concerned. Just over a year later, on 15 May 1929, England lost for the first time to a foreign team, defeated 3-4 by Spain on a bone-hard pitch in the torrid heat of Madrid. There was some excuse because the match was their third in a week, and Spain's coach, the former Middlesbrough and England winger Fred Pentland, had made sure it was played when the sun was at its height. Furthermore, England were without not only Dean, who did not make that close-season tour, but also Camsell, out with an injury suffered during his four-goal spree against the Belgians.

Spain, however, had already given fair warning that they were a cut above the level of Continental opposition England were accustomed to facing. Only recently they had scored five goals without reply from Portugal, and then, in trouncing France 8-1, doubled the tally England managed against that country before the Camsell-inspired beating of Belgium. Even so, England led in Madrid at half-time, and they went ahead again at 3-2 after the Spaniards had recovered to equalise. Not until well into the second half did England finally tire to the accompaniment of mounting vocal support for the home side from a crowd of 30,000.

England extracted emphatic revenge when they next met Spain in an eagerly awaited match at Highbury two years later, winning 7-1, but by then there had been further signs that other countries in Europe were no longer push-overs. France defeated England at the seventh attempt, 5-2 in Paris, Germany equally shared six goals in Berlin, and Austria, thrashed 1-6, 1-11, and 1-8 on England's previous visits, forced a scoreless draw in Vienna. So it was regarded as something of a showdown when Austria's much-vaunted 'Wunderteam,' hailed as the 'unofficial champions of the Continent' after an 18-match unbeaten run embellished by a 5-0 humiliation of a Scotland side devoid of Celtic and Rangers players, turned up at Stamford Bridge on 7 December 1932. That was the game for which the England selectors gave Billy Walker his final cap by ending his long absence from the international stage. They drew upon his wide experience as a player newly into his 36th year by bringing him back as captain.

Team: Hibbs (Birmingham); Goodall (Huddersfield Town), Blenkinsop (Sheffield Wednesday); Strange (Sheffield Wednesday), Hart (Leeds United), Keen (Derby County); Crooks (Derby County), Jack (Arsenal), Hampson (Blackpool), Walker (Aston Villa), Houghton (Aston Villa).

Eric Houghton, who also played county cricket for Warwickshire, was an admirable successor to Arthur Dorrell as Walker's left-wing partner with Villa. His 392 League and Cup games for the club exceeded Dorrell's total by just two, and he was far ahead of him as a scorer with 170 goals to 65. Indeed, in all his Villa appearances, including the second and third teams, Houghton netted almost 350 times. As packer of an exceptionally powerful shot, especially with dead-ball kicks, he was an automatic taker of penalties – right from his very first League match at home to Leeds United on the first Saturday of 1930. Ironically, he failed to convert that one, in a 3-4 defeat, but there were to be only six more misses among the 78 other penalties he took for Villa, ending with a successful one with his last kick for the club in a Central League game against Huddersfield Reserves on Boxing Day in 1946 – the day before his transfer to Notts County after eighteen years at Villa Park.

Another year later, Notts embarked upon the Tommy Lawton era with the sensational signing of the England centre-forward from Chelsea. When Houghton was named manager in May 1949 he took over a team that Lawton's goals spurred to the Third Division South title. Having rejoined Villa as manager in September 1953, Houghton was at the helm when the FA Cup final victory was gained against Manchester United in 1957, but within eighteen months he was sacked as relegation loomed.

Even then, however, Villa had not seen the last of Houghton. After being Forest's chief scout while Billy Walker was manager, then Rugby Town's secretary-manager and a scout for Walsall, he organised a fund-raising lottery in his third spell at Villa Park. He also served Villa as a director, and in 1983 became the club's senior vice-president, completing a connection with the club that stretched across more than 50 years.

The match with Austria at Chelsea was Houghton's seventh and last in an England shirt. He scored, too, his fifth international goal, in a 4-3 win that was hard earned against a team coached by Jimmy Hogan, formerly an inside-forward with various English clubs and within a few years destined to become Aston Villa's second manager. Not until the summer of 1934 was that post first held by Jimmy McMullan, the former Manchester City player who captained Scotland's 'Wizards' in their big win at Wembley. Hogan, who also coached in Hungary and Germany after being interned in Budapest during the 1914-18 War, possessed the technical knowledge that combined with the astute management of the legendary Hugo Meisl to make that Austrian team such a force to be reckoned with, but in the early stages at Stamford Bridge there were scant signs of the struggle England were to have to overcome them.

Play had been in progress for only a few minutes when England took the lead, and just before the half-hour they increased it. Both goals were scored by Jimmy Hampson, the Blackpool sharpshooter whose death so shocked the soccer world just over five years later, when, aged only 32, he was drowned in an accident while on a fishing expedition off the Fleetwood coast. His body was never recovered.

A half-time pep talk by Meisl spurred the Austrians into a second-half display more in keeping with their growing reputation, with centre-forward Matthias Sindelar causing the England defence particular problems. Sindelar's appearance – tall, pale and so thin that he was nicknamed Der Papierener (the Man of Paper) – belied his status as arguably the greatest Austrian footballer of them all. According to one account, 'his brilliance at times baffled description.' His clever footwork, baffling body swerve, and accurate passes made him a masterly maker, as well as taker, of goals. Sadly, however, like Hampson, he came to a tragic end. A Jew, he was persecuted by the Nazis and gassed himself in 1939.

Though given a scare by Austria's three-goal revival, Walker's England hung on to win, their other goal coming from Sammy Crooks, the speedy Derby winger who was second only (just) to Arsenal's Eddie Hapgood for the number of England caps won between the world wars. Job done, Billy Walker dropped out of the international limelight – and soon after reached the end of his long and eventful career with Aston Villa.

CHAPTER THREE

An Epic Villa-Arsenal Encounter

Billy Walker took part in another FA Cup final in 1924, but this time on the losing side, and in the First Division he was twice in a team that also finished runners-up. Even when Villa scored a record 128 goals in the 1930-31 season they had to settle for second place. Champions Arsenal chalked up only one fewer and headed them by seven points.

Aston Villa's opponents on their first visit to Wembley for the second final to be played there were Newcastle United, against whom Walker had done the hat-trick in a 6-1 League victory at Villa Park only five days earlier. Villa, winners of all but one of their seven previous finals, were therefore installed as firm favourites against a club that had triumphed in only one out of five – and that after being taken to a replay by Second Division Barnsley.

But that big League win for Villa was no true guide to form for the final. Far from it. Whereas Walker was in an unchanged line-up, only one Newcastle player turned out in both games. It was not the first time United had been below strength in the First Division on their way to the final, especially after a second-round tie with Derby County that stretched to three replays, and the League determined to stamp out what was by no means a new ploy by fining them £750 – a not inconsiderable amount for those days. Left-half Willie Gibson was the only member of Newcastle's Wembley team to play in that heavy defeat at Villa Park. The stylish Gibson, one of the three sons of a former Glasgow Rangers player who all made good in top football, figured prominently not only in the first of the five wins Newcastle were to gain at the Wembley of the Twin Towers, but also in the fourth League title they claimed four years later.

The result of the 1924 final exactly reversed that of 1905 between Villa and Newcastle at the Crystal Palace, though not until the last eight minutes was the stalemate broken. Villa had won the earlier clash with goals by Harry Hampton after two and 76 minutes. This time, the delayed breakthrough was achieved by another centre-forward, Neil Harris, whose powerful shot so shocked Villa that they were in disarray when left-winger Stan Seymour raced in to put the outcome beyond doubt three minutes later. Harris, who was said by one football writer to possess 'the quintessence of dash,' had won what was to be his one Scotland cap at Wembley a fortnight earlier, in the drawn match in which Walker scored England's goal.

Harris's son John, a League champion with Chelsea in their Golden Jubilee year of 1955 and later a long-serving manager of Sheffield United, also played just the once for Scotland – but not when caps were awarded. Neither was it a happy experience for him. In April 1945, while a Wolves player, he was at centre-half in the side against which England gained their biggest win, by 6-1, at Hampden Park. For Tommy Bogan the experience that day was the unhappiest of all. The Hibernian inside-right's international debut was only 40 seconds old when he collided with Frank Swift and was carried off to the touchline by the England goal-keeper. On being conveyed to hospital, he was found to have broken a leg, never to play for his country again. Clyde's Leslie Johnstone, who was sent on in his place after sixteen minutes' play, scored Scotland's goal. There could have been another, but Swift saved a penalty taken by Matt Busby, who had given the big keeper a good insight into his spot-kick methods during training while they had been Manchester City clubmates.

In 1905, the conditions for the final had been perfect, with gloriously sunny weather tempered by a pleasant breeze. In 1924, the first half was free from rain and the sun came out a few times, but later it became the wettest of all the 48 finals staged up to that time. On both occasions Villa thrived – until the conditions at Wembley deteriorated. An injury to Walker, shaken up in a collision, also had a bearing on the loss of the initiative that led to Newcastle's late and irretrievable double strike. Before that he was the mainspring of incisive attacks that could have put the result beyond all doubt but for an inspired display by Bill Bradley in the Newcastle goal. Bradley, signed from Jarrow, had taken over a position for so long filled by Glaswegian Jimmy Lawrence, holder of United's record of just over 500 appearances, but he had recently lost it to 'Sandy' Mutch and was back in the team at Wembley only because Mutch had a knee injury.

Some indication of how prominent a part Billy Walker played against Newcastle at Wembley before his injury can be gained from this extract from the recollections of Roland Allen, a national newspaper journalist who was at the match: 'I went to Wembley this time with an American newspaper man, who was new over here and anxious to get the "gen" about this English craze for football. He was not exactly thrilled with it all until Billy Walker did one of the cleverest of the many clever things in the game. Then he murmured "That guy's good." It was almost his only comment on the entire game.'

Allen himself described Walker as 'one of the greatest soccer person-alities it was my privilege ever to watch and know.' He added: 'He was, in the manner of most of the great artists of the game, rarely in a hurry. His cunning feet looked – oh so deceptively – as if they were encased in leaden boots, so deliberately did he move. Ask the footballers who played with him, and they will tell you that he actually was one of the fastest movers in the game.'

At Wembley in 1924, Walker's expertise brought out the best in his wing partner Arthur Dorrell in a team that showed six changes in personnel from that fielded in the 1920 final. The three others who played in both games were Tommy Smart, Frank Moss, who had crossed over to the right flank of the half-back line, and Billy Kirton. These were the teams:

Aston Villa: Jackson; Smart, Mort; Moss, Milne, Blackburn; York, Kirton, Capewell, Walker, Dorrell.

Newcastle United: Bradley; Hampson, Hudspeth; Mooney, Spencer, Gibson; Low, Cowan, Harris, McDonald, Seymour.

Compare that Newcastle side with the one that lost so heavily at Villa Park in their final League match of the season at the beginning of that week: Mutch; Curry, Hunter; McKenzie, Finlay, Gibson; Aitken, Clark (R), Keating, Clark (J), Mitchell.

Tom Curry, who, as Manchester United's trainer, was among those who would lose their lives in the disaster at Munich airport in 1958, did not play the last of almost 250 League and Cup games for Newcastle until early in the 1928-29 season, but his unfortunate exclusion at Wembley in 1924 made Billy Hampson, his replacement at right-back, the oldest FA Cup finalist at the age of 41 years and eight months. And even then Hampson was not finished. Not until three years later did he finally stand down from League football.

Two of the players who had been brought into the Villa team since the 1920 final had professions outside football. Tommy Jackson, who hailed from a village near Newcastle, was a schoolteacher, Vic Milne a doctor. Jackson, originally signed as an amateur while still at Durham University, had to contend with strong competition for a first-team place from Cyril Spiers after Sam Hardy's departure, but he still got near a double century of appearances before going back to teaching. Spiers also kept goal in more than 100 League and Cup games for Villa, then did the same for Tottenham before guiding Cardiff City back to the First Division as a manager. Milne's medical studies at Aberdeen University, interrupted by the First World War, were completed during the three seasons he spent with the Aberdeen club before Villa signed him to fill the gap left by Frank Barson's move to Manchester United. He retired from playing six years later to concentrate on his practice, though he also served Villa again as their official doctor in the early 1930s.

Birmingham-born Len Capewell, who for much of Milne's reign at the hub of the defence spearheaded the attack alongside Billy Walker, totalled exactly 100 goals before staying in the Midlands with Walsall. He scored five of them in a 10-0 home win against Burnley on the opening day of the 1925-26 season, four in 7-2 FA Cup defeat of Port Vale at Villa Park the previous January, and, under the handicap of a dislocated shoulder, completed a hat-trick as Villa turned a 2-3 deficit into a 5-3 victory over their Everton visitors on the first Saturday of December in 1926.

Walker, as usual, was the brains behind each of those successes, also finding the time to contribute three goals to both the first two. The swamping of Burnley, which Capewell took only 25 seconds to start, was an immediate outcome of the change in the offside law whereby, on the proposal of the Scottish FA, the number of defenders needed to be goal-side of an onside attacking player was reduced from three to two. But there was another important influence. As the fourth goal went in on the half-hour George Stephenson and Frank Hill, the Burnley centre-half and captain, collided heavily head-on. Hill was carried off to have a deep cut above his left eye stitched and was unable to return, leaving his disorganised defence to be run ragged. Stephenson not only groggily carried on, his head swathed in a blood-stained bandage, but also joined Dicky York as one of the other scorers.

Burnley, whose record League defeat was equalled against Sheffield United just over three years later, ended that 1925-26 season with the leakiest defence in the whole League, conceding 108 goals. Even so, they narrowly escaped dropping into the Second Division with Notts County instead of Manchester City, who let in 100. They even indulged themselves with a 7-1 away win against Birmingham in which six of the goals were scored by Louis Page, a left-winger tried for the first time at centre-forward.

George Blackburn, for whom the 1924 Wembley final came at the end of his third and final full season as Villa's left-half after skipper Moss's move to the opposite flank, had his disappointment of the Cup defeat lessened to some extent by being on the winning side against France in Paris when he was given his lone England cap during one of the breaks in Billy Walker's international career the following month. He also did not go short of a cup winner's medal, later twice helping Cardiff City to lift their national trophy.

Aston Villa were almost back at Wembley five years after losing there to Newcastle. In the 1928-29 season, during which they had hopes of repeating their League and Cup double of 1896-97 until the last few weeks, they swept aside Cardiff 6-1 and Clapton Orient 8-0 (in a replay after being held goalless at home) on their way to a semi-final they lost to Portsmouth at Highbury by an only goal. That was a penalty converted by Jack Smith, a former miner whose brothers Bill, a Pompey team-mate, and Sep (Leicester City) were also players of considerable League experience.

Walker, the schemer, but not a scorer, in the defeat of Cardiff, was kept out of the eclipse of Orient by injury. Only two years before Cardiff had taken the Cup out of England for the first time but were heading for relegation from the First Division; Orient were booked for last place in the Second. The scoring in those two big wins was spread among seven players, with most of it done by Tom ('Pongo') Waring, who did the hat-trick against Orient, and Joe Beresford, a stocky foraging forward whose outstanding form for Mansfield Town persuaded Billy Smith he was worth signing in preference to the goalkeeper the Villa secretary had gone to watch in a match at Stockport.

Waring was the most lethal of the centre-forwards Walker played alongside in the First Division. Villa had to beat off strong competition from Arsenal, Bolton Wanderers and Manchester United to sign him for £4,700 from Tranmere Rovers, and he repaid them with 167 goals in 216 games before, much to many fans' displeasure, he was sold to Barnsley. Fifty of those goals, all but one of them in the League, set the Villa record for one season – that of 1930-31 in which the club's Division One record total of 128 (Walker was their second highest scorer with 15) would surely have made them champions in normal circumstances. These, though, were anything but normal. It was Villa's misfortune to be pushed into second place by the new force that was arising on the English soccer scene and was to dominate it for much of the 1930s.

The season before, Arsenal had carried off the FA Cup for the first time. Now they were winners of their first League title, an achievement they were to repeat in three successive seasons from 1932-35, and again in 1937-38 during their pre-war dominance. Never during that decade did they finish outside the top six, and twice more they were Cup finalists, once successfully. Villa were again runners-up to them, four points behind, in 1933 as Billy Walker's long and distinguished playing career was finally approaching its end. With Waring rarely available that season because of injury, the main impetus for their challenge came from the 33 goals (plus two in the Cup) scored by his replacement, George ('Bomber') Brown, Huddersfield's top marksman in their title treble of the Twenties. In successive games the previous year, Brown scored five goals in an 8-3 win at Leicester and four in a 6-1 home victory over Liverpool.

Villa were comfortably on the credit side in their League meetings with Arsenal while Walker was with them, but had only one win to show in their six Cup clashes during that time. The most memorable of all those matches, just over 30 of them, was played at Villa Park on 19 November 1932, with nearly 60,000 packed inside for the tussle between the First Division's top two in which only five of the 22 players on the field were not internationals. Arsenal, who in their previous away game had followed an 8-2 home win against Leicester with a 7-1 victory at Wolverhampton, arrived as leaders by two points. They and Villa, twice scorers of six goals in a match – against visitors from Bolton and Blackpool – had lost only once in fourteen outings, both of them to West Bromwich Albion.

Anticipation of another scoring spree was therefore high, and the big crowd was not to be disappointed. Even though Arsenal conceded five of the eight goals scored, their record signing David Jack said it was 'almost a pleasure to lose', such was the exceptional standard of play in a real thriller. Jack himself set the tone soon after the start with a blockbuster of a shot that threatened to burst the net. Jimmy Gibson, the man of the match, quickly smashed in an equaliser after going up for a corner, and although Eric Houghton promptly put Villa ahead with one of his spectacular specials, Jack Lambert countered with a piledriver for the fourth goal in thirteen minutes. Early in the second half Arsenal regained the lead through Cliff Bastin, whose 33 goals that season set a League record for a winger, only for Houghton (a 30-goal man two seasons before) to bring the scores level again almost on the hour with another hefty swing of his trusty left boot.

And that was how it stood until eighteen minutes from time, when right-winger Jack Mandley, a former haulage hand at a Staffordshire pit, raised the roof by firing home following a free kick. Four minutes later, George Brown put the issue beyond doubt by bustling through to complete an epic win that hoisted Villa level on points with their big rivals, but still behind them on goal-average. During the next fortnight, however, two victories for Arsenal while Villa tumbled to two heavy defeats opened up the four-point gap that was to be between the clubs at the season's end. Frustrating though that second title miss in three years was for Villa, nothing could detract from the sublime satisfaction of their 5-3 defeat of such formidable opponents as Arsenal – not even the five-goal beating they suffered in the return game at Highbury on the first day of the following April.

These were the teams for those two matches, with changes for the second one shown in brackets:

Aston Villa: Morton; Blair, Mort; Kingdon (Wood), Gibson, Tate (Simpson); Mandley, Astley, Brown, Walker, Houghton.

Arsenal: Moss; Male, Hapgood; Hill, Roberts, John; Hulme (Jack), Jack (Bowden), Lambert, James, Bastin.

Billy Walker averaged a goal every two games against Arsenal, his 15 in 31 including the four on the first day of the 1920-21 season – a feat he equalled at home to Sheffield United nine years later. Of all his dozen hat-tricks, however, there was one that stood out for being the first of its kind in the Football League. All three of his goals in a 7-1 trouncing of Bradford City at Villa Park in November 1921 came from penalties. The only previous spot-kick treble in a league game in Britain had been performed by David Lindsay for St Mirren in a 5-4 defeat of Glasgow Rangers in 1904 – the first match in which four penalties were converted.

It was during a bleak period for the Yorkshire city of Bradford in the soccer sense that Walker registered his penalty hat-trick. The Park Avenue club had dropped out of the First Division the season before, and their Valley Parade neighbours were now also on their way down. Both eventually sank as low as the Fourth Division, Bradford PA out of the League altogether. It took City 74 years to get back into Division One, and although they soon afterwards rose to the Premiership they were swiftly on the downward spiral again.

In only one of Billy Walker's thirteen full seasons as an automatic choice did Aston Villa fail to finish in the top half of the First Division. That was in 1924-25, when they slipped to fifteenth and, as holders, went out of the FA Cup competition in the third round – beaten at home by West Bromwich Albion in a replay. The club's most successful spell in the League while Walker was a first-team regular was spread across the last five of his seasons with the club, during which they were third, fourth, second, fifth and second again. For the first two of those seasons Sheffield Wednesday were the champions. Then, either side of Everton's title year of 1932 (straight after their promotion from Division Two), came the two seasons in which Villa were runners-up to Arsenal, who in 1933 completed the first leg of their championship hat-trick.

Coincidence or not, Villa's fortunes began to wane after Walker's last appearance in their first team in a narrow defeat at Portsmouth on the last Saturday of September in 1933. They ended both that season and the next in thirteenth place, then in 1935-36 were relegated from the First Division for the first time. Down with them went Blackburn Rovers, who had also been in unbroken membership of the top flight ever since becoming founder members of the Football League in 1888.

The sudden slump in Villa's League form in 1933-34 following Walker's departure was offset by their first run to the FA Cup semi-finals for five years. Dai Astley, a Welsh sharpshooter from Charlton Athletic, scored seven of the goals that took them there – four in a 7-2 defeat of Sunderland, who were to be First Division runners-up and champions in the next two seasons – but hopes of a return to Wembley crumbled in the ruins of a 1-6 beating by Manchester City at Huddersfield's Leeds Road ground. Fred Tilson, who that summer won his first England cap, scored four of those goals, and in the final he made up for missing City's defeat by Everton at Wembley the previous season, through injury, by getting the couple that snatched the trophy in the last quarter of an hour after Portsmouth had led at half-time. With the winner not coming until three minutes from time, the tension was so great that teenager Frank Swift, fourteen years later a goalkeeper who captained England, fainted at the final whistle.

Serious defensive flaws were Aston Villa's undoing when they finally surrendered their first Division status. Of the 110 goals scored against them, 56 were conceded at home. Three times they let in seven goals at Villa Park, including the famous occasion on which Ted Drake did all Arsenal's scoring with eight shots (the other one came down off the underside of the crossbar for a defender to clear).

There were four survivors that day, 14 December 1935, from the team Villa had fielded in Billy Walker's final match – Eric Houghton, Harry Morton, Danny Blair and Astley. The Oldham-born Morton had also been beaten seven times, but still impressed sufficiently to be signed, when he had played against Villa for the Army in a friendly match while a corporal in the Welch Fusiliers. His entry into Villa's League side was unusual too. He was a spectator in the stand at Maine Road when he was summoned to make his debut against Manchester City as deputy for Fred Biddlestone, who was injured during the pre-match limbering-up. The points were shared in a 3-3 draw.

Blair, very lightly built for a full-back in comparison with the burly Smart he was bought from Clyde to replace, was a Scottish international who had played in Ireland and Canada while in those countries to study agriculture and farming. Although he took time to please a good many of Villa's supporters, he settled down to give good value for the £7,500 paid for him before leaving for Blackpool in 1936, the year before Morton moved back to Lancashire with first Everton, then Burnley.

These were Villa's teams in Billy Walker's first and last League games for the club: 17 January 1920, at Burnley (0-0): Hardy; Blackburn, Thompson; Ducat, Barson, Harrop; York, Kirton, Walker, Stephenson

(C), Edgley. (Thompson joined the club from Nantwich Victoria and was afterwards with Brighton). 30 September 1933, at Portsmouth (lost 2-3): Morton; Blair, Nibloe; Gibson, Talbot, Simpson; Houghton, Astley, Waring, Walker, Cunliffe.

Joe Nibloe crops up in a later chapter as one of the players Walker signed while manager of Sheffield Wednesday; Alec Talbot, a six-footer known at 'Tiny' who was a centre-half fixture for some six seasons, played for Walker's old club Hednesford Town before joining Villa straight after completing a ten-hour shift as a miner; 'Jock' Simpson came from Clyde and returned to Scotland with Cowdenbeath; Arthur Cunliffe, Walker's last wing partner, was transferred from Blackburn Rovers along with Ronnie Dix, the former Bristol Rovers 'Boy Wonder' who in 1928 had become the youngest scorer in a League game at the age of 15 years and 180 days.

Walker was recalled for his final five League matches in Dix's absence through injury, but failed to add to his club record haul of goals. He had become more of a schemer than a scorer in his last few seasons as a regular choice, having fallen short of double figures in both the last two. In 30 games in 1932-33 he had his lowest seasonal total of five goals – the last two of them when he supplied his own fireworks in a 6-2 home win against Blackpool on the fifth of November.

His retirement from playing came just over a year later when, in December 1933, he left Villa to embark upon a managerial career that was no less distinguished.

CHAPTER FOUR

Into Management at Sheffield

Billy Walker was not Sheffield Wednesday's first choice as secretary-manager in succession to Bob Brown, the Hillsborough club's first professional holder of that dual office. The job was originally accepted by Tom Muirhead, manager of St Johnstone, but it became available again when, after his appointment had been officially announced, Muirhead could not obtain release from his Perth post. It was not until then that Walker decided to apply.

For most of the years in which he played against them, the club with which Walker set out on management went under the name of The Wednesday – formed in 1867 to keep a cricket club's players fit over the winter, and so named because the cricketers, mostly self-employed cutlers, played on their half-day off in midweek. As far back as 1905 the name Sheffield Wednesday was used in the programme for a home match, but it was not until June in 1927 that the club's directors expressed a wish to adopt it officially. The legal change of title was formally approved by the Football League two years later.

Although Bob Brown never played at the top level, or professionally, after having his hopes of doing so dashed by an injury suffered while with Hebburn Argyle in his native North-East, he achieved excellent credentials as a manager. Before that, however, he was first employed by Sheffield Wednesday as a scout, paid all of ten shillings (50p) a week, plus expenses, and also had a spell assisting honorary secretary Arthur Dickinson in the club's office at Owlerton, as Hillsborough was then known (and from which the Owls took their nickname). On then obtaining his first managerial post in the summer of 1911, Brown dispelled Portsmouth's financial worries by guiding them to promotion from the Second Division of the Southern League at his first attempt, and to the championship of its First Division in 1919-20, the first season after the First World War. But he did not stay on for Pompey's entry into the Football League a few months later as founder members of the Third Division. He resigned, along with chairman George Lewin-Oliver, over a difference of opinion about future policy.

Gillingham, the Kent club originally known as New Brompton, promptly provided Brown with another opportunity to manage a team admitted to the new Division Three from the Southern League – but again he was on his way out before its inaugural season got under way.

Arthur Dickinson, weighed down by having to shoulder much of the responsibility for signing new players since joining Wednesday in 1891, finally persuaded his directors to engage a professional manager. Brown was the man to whom they turned, and the offer to rejoin the club in that role was too tempting to resist even though it presented him with a formidable task. Wednesday had just been relegated from the First Division with the wretched record of only seven wins, 28 goals and 23 points from their 42 games.

With a £5,000 deficit on transfers and an overall loss of more than £1,600 on the past season, drastic action was certainly needed – and the belated acceptance of Dickinson's advice was only part of it. Wednesday had resumed after the war with all but two of the senior players they had possessed before it – many of them by then well past their sell-by date – and their new manager had quickly to bolster a playing staff from which twenty men had now either been released or placed on the transfer list.

Dramatically successful though Brown was eventually to become, there were precious few signs of the triumphs in store during his first five seasons at the helm. After that, promotion from the Second Division was won as champions in 1925-26, but only two seasons later Wednesday went desperately close to going down again. Ten games from the finishing line they were seven points adrift in last place, but then pulled off an astonishing escape with an unbeaten run in which the only points dropped were from three draws. A first glance at the final table gives the misleading impression of a comfortable fourteenth place. On closer inspection, it is seen that they were only one point clear of the drop zone – the first, on goal-average, of no fewer than seven clubs with 39 points. Then came the relegated pair, Tottenham (38) and Middlesbrough (37).

Wednesday would have been relegated instead of Spurs if they had lost their final match, at home to Aston Villa (and Billy Walker). As it was, they won 2-0, though a draw would have been sufficient because their goal figures were superior to Tottenham's. There were many anxious moments for the Owls in a scoreless first half, a good number of them caused by Walker, before goals from Jack Allen and Jimmy Trotter sent relieved fans into the rhapsodies of a pitch invasion at the final whistle. How great the tension had been can be gathered from the fact that at the start of the matches played on that final day, 5 May 1928, only two points separated Liverpool, in twelfth place, from Manchester United, who were at the bottom of the table. Liverpool were the visitors to Old Trafford that afternoon, and United climbed clear by thrashing them 6-1.

Ironically, Jimmy Seed was the inspiration of Spurs' downfall after they had transferred him to Sheffield Wednesday. He had been unable to regain the place in Tottenham's attack he had lost to Eugene ('Taffy') O'Callaghan, a coming Welsh international, but that was not the reason why he had asked for his release. That came about because Billy Minter, a former Spurs forward who had taken over as manager following the move to Middlesbrough of Peter McWilliam (thrice a League champion and four times an FA Cup finalist as a player with Newcastle United), decided to reduce Seed's weekly wage from the then maximum of £8 to £7. Minter, in the record books as a player for finishing on the losing side despite scoring seven goals for St Albans City in an FA Cup qualifying tie against Dulwich Hamlet, unwisely considered that Seed, at 32, was over the hill.

Even then, Seed would have gone to Aldershot as manager, instead of to Wednesday, if Spurs had not insisted on using him as the part-exchange makeweight in the deal with the Sheffield club by which they obtained Arthur ('Darkie') Lowdell, a forward they had rejected for being too small after he had played for London Boys. So it was under Seed's captaincy that Wednesday launched their Great Escape – under, ironically, the early impetus of a 3-1 win at Tottenham. Spurs went into that Good Friday match tenth in the table with 35 points from 36 games; Wednesday were down at the bottom with 25 from 34.

From flirting so dangerously with relegation, Seed-led Wednesday went straight into their transformation as First Division champions for two successive seasons, 1928-30. And in the second of those title years they went very close to the Cup and League double, controversially beaten by Huddersfield Town in a semi-final at Old Trafford. The Yorkshire club's equalising goal was allowed despite a clear handling offence, and after going behind Wednesday were denied an equaliser of their own when the final whistle blew, two minutes early it was claimed, as the ball was on its way into the net.

In each of the next three seasons, the last two of them after Seed's departure to manage Clapton (now Leyton) Orient, Wednesday finished third in the table, but that period of prosperity then ended as abruptly as it had begun. And with it went Brown. He never really recovered from the tragedy of his wife's death while they were on holiday at Blackpool during the summer of 1933, and when he was himself suddenly taken ill during a poor start to the following football season he was ordered by his doctor to take a complete rest. Within two weeks he resigned.

As Keith Farnsworth, an old friend of mine who is an authority on Sheffield soccer, remarked in his Sheffield Football History, 'it was a sorry conclusion to the managerial career of a man who had achieved so much for the club.' This was especially so, considering that Brown's

departure was not even mentioned in the Wednesday's official programme. 'Perhaps,' observed Farnsworth, 'the fact that the Owls had
made their worst start in eight seasons had something to do with the
oversight. Even then, directors lived for the present; past achievements
counted for nothing. The Hillsborough board accepted his resignation
with what seems to have been surprising haste.'

If many of the club's supporters had had their way, the choice of successor would have fallen on Jimmy Seed. This was hardly surprising. His
experience and leadership had been so valuable as skipper of the double
champions before a succession of injuries had confirmed it was at last
time for him to give up playing at the end of his fourth season with
Wednesday, 1930-31. But by the time of Brown's sad exit Seed had not
long left Clapton Orient to manage Charlton Athletic. And he was to stay
at the Valley for nearly two dozen years, during which he guided that hitherto unsung London club to promotion from the Third Division to the
First in successive seasons, and to four finals at Wembley in five years –
the last two of them in the FA Cup, which they won for the first time in
1947.

So, with Wednesday foiled in their quest in the opposite direction, to
Scotland for Muirhead, the path to the manager's chair at Hillsborough
opened up for Billy Walker. For Bob Brown there was one last role in
football after his rest cure. Chelsea engaged him as a scout, but in March
1935 he collapsed while boarding a train on his way to watch a potential
recruit. He died in hospital the next day.

In giving up his playing career with Aston Villa to take the Wednesday
post shortly before Christmas in 1933, two months after his 36th birthday, Billy Walker was under no illusions about the size of the task his initial venture into management entailed. It was daunting enough to follow
a manager who had supervised so much success, but on top of that
Walker had to satisfy fans who were thirsting for more of it at a time
when the club's fortunes were in worrying decline.

After five seasons of never finishing outside the top three, Wednesday
were struggling near the foot of the First Division, having won only two
of their last eleven games. They had recently conceded six goals at
Wolverhampton, four at Sunderland, and were in dire need of a new
injection of confidence.

Under Walker, the rot was swiftly stopped. Off the mark with four
victories in a row, his new charges surged into an unbeaten sequence of
sixteen matches that included four FA Cup-ties. Its end in late February
came at Maine Road, where Manchester City, who were on their way to
winning at Wembley on their second consecutive appearance there,

gained a 2-0 fifth-round replay victory after a hard-fought 2-2 draw in front of Hillsborough's record crowd of 72,841.

City's Frank Swift had more than 400 matches to choose from when he described that fifth-round tie at Sheffield in 1934 as 'one of the most amazing games I have ever played in – it brought all the sights, scenes and sounds that are only provided by a cup-crazy mob.' He added: 'After we had changed, and were ready for the field, we found that the narrow tunnel from the dressing room to the pitch was blocked by ambulance men tending groaning casualties. After forcing my way through with the other players, I had to stand aside to let pass a stretcher bearing a man crushed to death against the railings on Spion Kop.'

Ellis Rimmer, of whom more shortly, gave Wednesday a fifth-minute lead from a pass by Neil Dewar, Billy Walker's first big signing for the club (more about him in the next chapter) after Sam Cowan, the City centre-half and captain, had missed his kick. But that lead did not last long. Alex Herd equalised by crowning a mazy dribble with a blistering shot from some 25 yards as defenders backed off expecting him to pass. Dewar regained the lead after the interval, only for Herd to bring the scores level again with just under half-an-hour left. There were no further goals in what City's players considered to be their toughest match on the way to Wembley.

The replay, watched by 68,614, was also a tense affair, but Cowan, who steered City to promotion back to the First Division as their manager in the first season after the Second World War, led his men to a victory gained with two goals that both followed long free-kicks from the home half. Fred Tilson nipped round Walter Millership to score the first after waiting for the ball to bounce in front of the centre-half. Bobby Marshall got the second after half-time by heading in a free kick that full-back Billy Dale delivered from fully 40 yards.

Wednesday won only four, and lost seven, of their remaining thirteen League games after that Cup defeat, but finished in the middle of the table, seven points clear of the drop. Their biggest beating during that period was suffered where they and their supporters least wanted it – across the city at Bramall Lane. Sheffield United trounced them 5-1, yet tailed off to fall into the Second Division three points worse off than their relegation companions from Newcastle.

Two of the first important decisions Billy Walker took on the Owls' behalf were to restore Ronnie Starling to their attack, and give him the captaincy. Starling, a Bob Brown signing from Newcastle for £1,500 less than the £4,000 the Geordies had paid Hull City for him, had been left out by caretaker manager Joe McClelland after losing form during the slump in Wednesday's fortunes, but the faith Walker placed in him provided just the boost he needed. From that point he was a model of consistency, leading the team to victory in an FA Cup final and adding almost 200 appearances to his career total before his next move, to Aston Villa, early in 1937. His value had by then increased to £7,000, an outlay he repaid by not missing a match when Walker's old club regained First Division status the following season. A schemer rather than a scorer, Starling was most unfortunate to be awarded no more than two England caps – and those four years apart, in defeats by Scotland at Hampden Park.

Another significant early step taken by Billy Walker as Wednesday's manager was to renew his connection with the Austrians whose footballing tactics had greatly impressed him from the day he had experienced them at first hand in his last game as an England player. On that occasion he had taken the trouble to discuss with the coaches the methods employed by their 'Wunderteam', and he now invited them over to Sheffield to have further talks about their ideas with the object of putting them into practice. The Austrians, however, had possessed players of exceptional technical ability to make the most of their smooth and speedy inter-passing game, whereas Walker soon made it evident, to the displeasure of not a few Wednesday followers, that he was not all that taken with some of the players he had inherited (more about that in the next chapter).

One member of the staff to win the discerning Walker's particular approval was not a player. He was one Bob Brown had appointed in making arguably his most prescient decision in Wednesday's metamorphosis from relegation candidates to table-toppers. A vacancy as trainer-coach cropped up when George Utley, a former Sheffield United captain, left to join Fulham. To fill it, Brown brought in from Aberdare a Scot, Chris Craig, who had impressed him as a guest player at Portsmouth while stationed there in the Royal Army Medical Corps. Craig was wanted for his expertise in the treatment of injuries and, even more importantly, his ability to deal with people. He proved himself just the man for the job in both respects, also instilling discipline and building up team spirit, but, sadly, he was suddenly taken fatally ill not long after Walker had taken over.

Craig was especially appreciated while Brown was manager because of Brown's rather withdrawn attitude. Brown did not help himself by failing to co-operate readily with journalists who could have made life a little less difficult for him as he strove to improve results. To quote Keith Farnsworth again, Brown was 'decidedly distant with the Press and never welcomed personal publicity.' Moreover, and more disquieting, he was also somewhat of a remote figure to his players, and not closely involved with them in training. His strength was as an administrator with a nose for talent that he augmented to telling effect, eventually, by moving some players into positions for which they were best suited. Alf Strange, Tony Leach and Billy Marsden were signed as inside-forwards (Leach after failing a trial with Liverpool), but for Brown they formed a half-back line still widely regarded as the best the club have ever fielded. The switching to centre-forward of Jack Allen, an inside-forward of average ability from Brentford, was another master stroke, rewarded with 74 goals during the two seasons from 1928-30 in which Wednesday equalled their consecutive championships of 1902-04.

By the time Walker took over, however, Allen had left, and injuries had broken up the celebrated half-back line. Of the players in the first Wednesday team put out by Walker, for a League match they won 3-1 at Liverpool on 9 December 1933, only four would be in the side that defeated West Bromwich Albion 4-2 in the Cup final at Wembley nearly eighteen months later, on 27 April 1935. They were goalkeeper Jack Brown, centre-half Walter Millership, and wingers Mark Hooper and Ellis Rimmer. Hooper, who stood less than 5ft 6in and wore size-four boots, was regarded by many as the best uncapped right-winger of his day. He and the contrastingly tall Rimmer, another outstanding signing who was snapped up from Tranmere Rovers after eluding the attention of neighbouring Everton, formed one of the most dangerous wing pairings in an era when several other clubs were not lacking in that respect either. Hooper was at first considered by Bob Brown to be too small to make the grade, but this nippy little North-Easterner brought about a rapid change of mind with a brilliant display in Darlington's 5-1 defeat of Wednesday after helping his home club to the Third North championship in the 1924-25 season.

Hooper repaid the £2,000 spent on him several times over. He had already played in nearly 300 League and Cup games for Wednesday when Walker took over. He was still at Hillsborough when Walker left, although no longer sure of a first-team place, and it was not until April in 1939 that he himself departed to join Rotherham United. He became the Millmoor club's coach, but the FA Cup had not yet seen the last of him as a player. In his 45th year, he was the oldest to turn out in the competition during the 1945-46 season in which it was first started up after the war. Later, up to his death in 1974, he ran a tobacconist's shop close to Hillsborough.

Hooper and Rimmer between them piled up 276 goals for Wednesday – 136 in 423 games for Hooper, 140 in 418 for Rimmer. Both also played (against Arsenal each time) in the FA Charity Shield matches between the League champions and Cup winners in 1930 and 1935. Rimmer, who died in 1965, moved to Ipswich Town in 1938, then returned to Merseyside to take over a pubic house.

It was not only with changes to Wednesday's team that Billy Walker sought to improve the club's fortunes. He also had some novel ideas when it came to training. From the vantage point of the broadcasting box in Hillsborough's main stand, he watched the players in practice games and told them through loudspeakers where they were going wrong. Tactical moves he had worked out were tried in the strictest secrecy, though some of the training sessions were conducted in public. All this provoked accusations of 'stunts' from the diehards, but it was results that counted, and in Walker's first full season with Wednesday they finished third in the First Division in addition to winning the FA Cup.

CHAPTER FIVE

Mixed Reaction in Transfer Market

If he had had his way, Billy Walker's early attempts to recruit new talent would have taken to Hillsborough a couple of young players who were quickly to become legendary figures in the game – Stanley Matthews and Tommy Lawton, no less.

There was never any real chance that Matthews could then have been lured away from Stoke City, his home club for which he had signed as a 15-year-old amateur a few years before, but Lawton might well have been tempted but for his mother's intervention. 'Mr Walker was very nice to me,' he recalled. 'He offered to find me lodgings and to give me ten shillings a week pocket money.' There was also the offer of a job outside football until he was old enough to turn professional, but, as Lawton put it, 'my mother thought I was too young to go so far away on my own, so the matter was dropped.'

Ten days later, Lawton gave up the work he had only recently started since leaving school, at a tannery where golf clubs were made, and signed for Burnley. Just over three years after that, the centre-forward regarded by many as one of England's best, if not the best, was with Everton, and with Matthews in an England team for the first time. Both scored, Lawton entrusted with a penalty on his international debut, but they were on the losing side against Wales in Cardiff.

Just over a decade after his unsuccessful overtures for Matthews and Lawton, Billy Walker was also foiled in the quest for another famous England forward while manager of Nottingham Forest. When the time came for Raich Carter to leave Derby County he was seen by Walker as Forest's perfect counter-attraction to Lawton at Notts County, but Carter wanted to be an assistant manager as well as a player, with an eye to future management, and he considered his prospects in that direction much brighter at Hull City. So it proved – far sooner, indeed, than Carter could have expected. Within a couple of weeks the veteran Major Frank Buckley suddenly resigned as Hull's manager to take over at Leeds, and Carter was appointed player-manager of the Humberside club.

For his first successful venture into the transfer market as manager of Sheffield Wednesday, Billy Walker looked to Manchester United for Neil Dewar, a Scottish international centre-forward who was well-known as a public speaker in his home country. Dewar, a tall former hotel porter with a soldierly bearing, had helped Third Lanark to promotion from the

Second Division of the Scottish League before his £6,000 departure to Old Trafford. Although temporarily out of the first-team reckoning at the time Wednesday won the FA Cup in 1935, he found his stay at Hillsborough much more enjoyable than his brief time in Lancashire, having become embroiled in United's struggle for survival in the Second Division.

Before returning to Third Lanark during the 1937 close season, Dewar showed a good many signs of the form that had earned him a hat-trick against France in Paris, scoring 50 goals in 95 games for Wednesday, but it was in order to sign him that Walker first gave supporters cause to grumble by transferring Jack Ball back to the Manchester club as part of the deal. Ball was a firm favourite of those fans right from the first few months of the 1930-31 season that followed his arrival from Old Trafford. During that period up to early December he scored 17 goals in his first 14 games, including hat-tricks against Sunderland and Leicester City.

Ball's immediate success meant there was no longer any room for Jack Allen, Wednesday's master marksman of the past two seasons, so off he went to Newcastle – and to a Cup winner's medal as scorer of both their goals, the first of them controversially from the notorious 'over the line' centre, in the defeat of Arsenal at Wembley. Referee Harper ruled that the ball had not gone out of play as Jimmy Richardson, Newcastle's inside-right, crossed it for Allen to equalise Bob John's early goal for the Gunners, and he stuck to that view even though photographic evidence afterwards indicated otherwise. 'As God is my judge,' he said, 'the man was in play.' The man yes, but it was the ball that mattered. Mr Harper (given the mode of address that applied to all referees, and managers too, in those days) was also quoted as saying that he was only eight yards away, yet the photograph of the incident showed him to be outside the penalty area. Richardson crops up again later for spotting the potential of a player who was one of Billy Walker's most successful signings for Nottingham Forest.

Although understandably unable to maintain the high ratio of goals to games with which he had started out, Jack Ball was not all that far short of it in totalling 94 in 135 League and Cup appearances before being traded away. His 23 in 1931-32 included eleven penalties, then a record for one season. In 1932-33 he had a personal best of 35 goals, four of them in an away win over Wolves. No wonder his discarding by Billy Walker was so unpopular. Back with Manchester United, a yo-yo club of the 1930s, Ball was in the team, though not a scorer, which squeezed to safety by a single point. On the final day of the season, 5 May 1934,

United swapped places with Millwall by bearding the Lions in their Den, a 2-0 victory sending the London club down with Lincoln City. For those who took such things seriously, United owed it all to the change of colours, to a design of cherry hoops on white, that they had made in an attempt also to change their fortunes.

Two years later, just a few weeks after Ball, by then with Luton Town, had been alongside 'Ten-Goal' Joe Payne in the Hatters' Easter demolition of Bristol Rovers, United climbed out of the Second Division to which they had been relegated in 1931. Over the next two seasons they descended again (with Walker's Wednesday), but bounced straight back up (with Aston Villa, the club where Walker had made his name).

As if the sale of Jack Ball was not quite enough to make Wednesday's faithful wonder where Billy Walker was leading them, there was soon another exit that aroused even more concern. For nearly a dozen years dating back to the last Saturday of January in 1923, former miner Ernest Blenkinsop had been a pillar of the club's defence, rated by many as the best left-back ever to wear Wednesday's blue and white stripes – and as one of the best anywhere between the two world wars.

Stylish and assured, Blenkinsop was immaculate in ball control, unruffled under pressure, and both accurate and perceptive in his distribution. An ideal defender, yet he was signed by Hull City as an inside-forward – from Brierley Colliery for £100 and, so the story goes, 80 pints of beer – and the Humbersiders tried to convert him into a half-back before he found his rightful place at full-back. Bob Brown spotted him there in Hull's reserve side, and had no hesitation in agreeing a fee of £1,000 even though Blenkinsop was out of action at that time, suffering from influenza. Neither did Brown have any qualms about putting him straight into Wednesday's first team after his recovery. For more than 400 League and Cup games it was to prove a highly astute judgment.

From 1928 to 1933, Blenkinsop also played in all 26 of England's games. That made him Wednesday's most-capped player until the autumn of 1962, when Ron Springett guarded the England goal for the 27th of 33 times in a Belfast victory paradoxically achieved through a couple of goals from a player with the Irish-sounding name of O'Grady. Springett has since been overtaken by Nigel Worthington, who made 50 of his 66 appearances for Northern Ireland while with Wednesday.

In 1930, Blenkinsop was one of four Wednesday players, along with Alf Strange, Billy Marsden and left-winger Ellis Rimmer, in the England team whose 5-2 defeat of Scotland at Wembley (their first success at the stadium at the third attempt) avenged the shock 5-1 victory gained at the same ground by the 'Wizards' of two years before. Rimmer scored twice on his international debut in that trimming of the tartans, but the man of the match was Derby's Sammy Crooks, another newcomer on the opposite wing. He made four of England's five goals. Rimmer was awarded the last of his four caps against Spain at Arsenal's ground towards the end of the following year, but, unusually for a winger who was so often a scorer, he was not among the goals even though England chalked up seven of them to their visitors' one.

Blenkinsop twice captained his country in other games against the Scots, but then had to give way to Eddie Hapgood only ten months before Billy Walker decided that he was also surplus to his club's requirements. So it was that, in March 1934, Blenkinsop was sold to Liverpool for £6,500. Although then almost 34, he showed that he still had much to offer in striking up a distinguished full-back partnership with Tommy Cooper, a fellow ex-England captain who had also been thought past his best in being discarded by Derby County. After giving up playing Blenkinsop became a licensee. It was while serving a customer in his public house in Sheffield that he collapsed and died on 24 April,1969 – four days after his 69th birthday.

Sad as many Wednesday supporters were to see Blenkinsop leave the club, Billy Walker soon provided them with another full-back of international standard to admire. He went back to Aston Villa to sign Joe Nibloe, another erstwhile forward, in part exchange for George Beeson, a former Chesterfield full-back who had been kept in the Wednesday background for the best part of three seasons before earning selection for the Football League during a good run as Blenkinsop's partner. Nibloe, briefly a playing colleague of Walker's when transferred to Villa from Kilmarnock soon after winning the last of his eleven Scotland caps, gave Wednesday good value over more than 100 games – notably in harness with Ted Catlin, who so soundly shouldered the unenviable task of filling the vacancy left by Blenkinsop. Nibloe had gained a Scottish Cup-winner's medal with Kilmarnock in 1929, and was to collect an FA Cup one with Wednesday six years later.

Catlin, missed by Middlesbrough while with South Bank, overcame the early unsettling experience of being in a Wednesday team humiliated 3-9 by Everton at Goodison Park (five goals for Dean) to exceed 200 League and Cup appearances, and then to make nearly 100 more during the Second World War. Having made his First Division debut as far back as late March in 1931, in the absence of Blenkinsop on England duty in Glasgow, he did not finally bow out until October 1944 – and that after a comeback from a serious injury suffered during the first leg of the 1943 League North Cup final in which Wednesday lost to Blackpool on aggregate by the odd goal of seven. He could have been as excellent a successor to Blenkinsop for his country as he was for his club but for the misfortune of having his career coincide with that of Eddie Hapgood, As it was, he had to be content with five caps, and one game in the Football League XI, while the Arsenal and England captain was out injured.

After Blenkinsop, the next England international with whom Walker parted company was Tony Leach (he was always known as Tony, but his given first name was Thomas). Leach, who played his two games for England in big wins against Ireland and Wales, had consistently dominated at the heart of Wednesday's defence after being switched there for most of his 260 appearances, but he was allowed to leave, for Newcastle, because of the strong claims for his place being pressed by Walter Millership, yet another forward to benefit from Bob Brown's realisation of his true position. After two seasons at Newcastle, Leach helped Stockport County to promotion as champions of the Third Division's Northern Section, then rounded off his career with Carlisle United and Lincoln City.

Millership, whose nickname 'Battleship' perfectly reflected his formidably tough attitude, so typical of someone who had worked at the coal face, was allowed only limited opportunities in Wednesday's attack after costing nearly £3,000 from Bradford. Even his four goals in a 7-0 Cup defeat of Bournemouth could not make him the regular choice he became once his career was uplifted by his conversion to centre-half. He still turned out up front from time to time, and also at wing-half, but it was as the bulwark in central defence that he played the great majority of his games for Wednesday – not far off 400 of them with the inclusion of some 150 in wartime competitions. And to all that fine service he added one last big favour after leaving to play for Denaby United when peace returned. He had so much difficulty dealing with the awkward amateur centre-forward he faced in a game against Lincoln City Reserves that he tipped Wednesday off about him. That lanky, red-haired youth, a sharpshooter with size 12 boots, was Derek Dooley.

Alongside Millership in Wednesday's half-back line for much of Billy Walker's time with the club was another of the prime assets left by Bob Brown. This was Horace Burrows, a Nottinghamshire man (as also was Millership) whose polished, creative style made him the club's most efficient left-half since the untimely loss of Marsden through injury. Burrows had to wait two years after joining Wednesday from Mansfield Town before establishing himself, but he then made up for lost time with a sequence of 136 League and Cup appearances up to March 1936 – a period during which he played his three games for England on a close-season tour of Hungary, Czechoslovakia and the Netherlands. Although injuries interrupted his progress on several occasions subsequently, he was a season's ever-present for the third time in the last full pre-war campaign of 1938-39, and he played on for two more years before stepping down to run a sports outfitting business.

Billy Marsden was a naturally right-footed player who became equally adept with his left through constant practice in so efficiently switching to left-half with Wednesday from the inside-forward position in which he had understudied the legendary Charlie Buchan at Sunderland in his native North-East. Marsden played more than 200 games for Wednesday before suffering damage to his spine during his third game for England, against Germany in Berlin in May 1930. The collision that caused it was with not an opponent but, ironically, a team-mate, Roy Goodall, as he and the Huddersfield full-back both went for the ball.

Marsden received £750 in compensation (Wednesday £2,000) on having to abandon an attempted comeback after just a few games with the Reserves, and he was Gateshead's trainer before obtaining coaching posts with the Dutch FA. The outbreak of war in 1939 brought him back to England, where he combined being a publican with managing Doncaster Rovers part-time for almost two years before League football resumed in 1946. Later he also managed Worksop Town.

Worksop was the first club of another Wednesday player who was injured on England duty – though, thankfully, not with such dire consequences. Jack Brown, a goalkeeper Billy Walker was thankful to have available when he took over as manager, collected five more caps, and also twice represented the Football League, after being a casualty on his international debut in the 3-3 draw of 1927 with Wales at Wrexham in which Walker was among the scorers. Brown, who had been a centre-forward in junior football, arrived at Hillsborough in 1923 as the star turn of a recent scoreless draw with which Midland League Worksop, his home club, had shocked First Division Tottenham in an FA Cup-tie at White Hart Lane. There was no fairy-tale ending, Spurs scoring nine goals without reply in the replay, but Brown performed more heroics behind his overrun defence and promptly became a target for his namesake in Wednesday's managerial chair.

Bob Brown was as delighted to complete, for £300, what became in many eyes the biggest of all his bargains as Jack Brown was to give up his work at Manton Colliery, where he had first made his mark in the pit lads' team, to enter the Football League as a full-time professional. Wednesday's goalkeeper at the time, Teddy Davison, was a Bob Brown discovery who, at 5ft 7in, had become the smallest to play in that position for

England in winning his one cap (and keeping a clean sheet) against Wales only a year earlier. But, having made his League debut as far back as October 1908, Davison was nearing the end of eighteen years with Wednesday, and Jack Brown dislodged him as a firm first choice for the season of 1925-26 that ended in the club's promotion back to the First Division.

Off Davison went to Mansfield as player-manager, a short prelude to further distinction during a managerial career in which he spent twenty years with Sheffield United between two spells at Chesterfield. He guided Chesterfield to the Third Division North title in 1930-31, and although United were relegated in 1934, soon after he had joined them, he took them to the FA Cup final of 1936 (but as losers to Arsenal), and back to the First Division in 1938-39. Failure to stave off another relegation in the early post-war years led to his return to Chesterfield, where the youth scheme he developed unearthed Gordon Banks, rated by many as the best goalkeeper ever to play for England. And even when Davison finally stood down as manager in 1958 the Derbyshire club had still not seen the last of him. In his early seventies, he carried on a little longer as their chief scout.

Remarkably consistent as Davison was in protecting Sheffield Wednesday's net for 424 games (397 in the League, 27 in the Cup), he was outdone by Jack Brown, whose total of 507 (465 and 42) is the second highest in the club's history. The only man ahead of Brown is Andrew Wilson, the burly Scottish international forward who from 1900, when he was signed from Clyde, to 1920, when he went into management, made 545 appearances (501 and 44) for Wednesday and scored 216 goals. Wilson and Brown also had the edge over Davison for club honours as players. Both helped the Owls to two First Division championships and one victory in an FA Cup final. Davison was left wanting at that level, but he earned selection for the Sheffield FA and augmented his lone England cap by going on an FA tour of Australia after the 1924-25 season in which he finally had to give way to Brown.

Brown's vice-like grip on a first-team place with Wednesday was not broken until towards the end of the 1936-37 season that was to be Billy Walker's third and last full one as the club's manager. It culminated in relegation, and in the following September Brown left for Hartlepools United – but stayed there for only a fortnight. Walker was to follow him out of Hillsborough two months later, only just over two years since he had guided Wednesday to the heady heights of FA Cup glory at Wembley the season after Manchester City had foiled his expressed hopes of getting them there at his first attempt.

The Maine Road club, who had been knocked out at Tottenham in their first defence of the Cup, were Wednesday's main rivals for third place in the final First Division table of the 1934-35 season, behind Arsenal and Sunderland. Wednesday had two games left to City's one after succeeding the Maine Road club as Cup holders, and they took three points from them with a draw at Everton and a narrow home win against Grimsby Town. That lifted them one point clear of City, who ended a run of four defeats by scoring five goals without reply from Wolves in their remaining match. Grimsby, 3-0 home winners against West Bromwich four days after Albion's defeat by Wednesday at Wembley, finished fifth, three points further away. These were the final leading positions:

Season 1934-35	P	W	D	L	F	A	Pts
1 Arsenal	42	23	12	7	115	46	58
2 Sunderland	42	19	16	7	90	51	54
3 Sheffield W	42	18	13	11	70	64	49
4 Manchester C	42	20	8	14	82	67	48
5 Grimsby	42	17	11	14	78	60	45
6 Derby	42	18	9	15	81	66	45
7 Liverpool	42	19	7	16	85	88	45

Rimmer's 26 goals that season, eight of them in the Cup, broke his own record of 24 in 1930-31 for a Wednesday winger.

CHAPTER SIX

Late Horseshoe 'Luck' at Wembley

Sheffield Wednesday's defeat of West Bromwich Albion in the 1935 FA Cup final, after one of Wembley's most sensational finishes, took the trophy back to their part of the steel city for the third time, and the first since 1907.

Only the month before that overdue triumph, Billy Walker had again upset a good many Wednesday fans by selling another of their favourites, Harry Burgess, to Chelsea. This forceful, long-striding inside-forward had been a consistent scorer from the time he had entered League football with Stockport County in the March of 1926, benefiting greatly from playing alongside Joe Smith, the former Bolton and England forward, as the Cheshire club maintained a high position in the Northern Section of the Third Division.

In 1928-29, Burgess's last season with them before Bob Brown signed him for Wednesday, Stockport went desperately close to the climb into the Second Division for which they would have to wait eight more years. With 62 points they were runners-up, only one point away, as Bradford City secured the single promotion place – and ten clear of the next club, Wrexham. (In the following season Stockport accumulated their then record number of points, 63, in those days of two for a win and one for a draw, but were second again – thirteen points ahead of third-placed Darlington, but four behind Port Vale's champions.)

Burgess wasted no time impressing Wednesday supporters. From his scoring debut in an away win against an Aston Villa side containing Billy Walker, he was regularly among the goals in playing an important part as the First Division championship was won for a second successive year. Wednesday totalled 105 goals in the League in that 1929-30 season, getting into three figures for the first time, and Burgess made the openings for quite a few of the 33 Jack Allen contributed besides being the team's second highest scorer with 19. The success Burgess continued to enjoy in his schemer-scorer role, which made him an equally fine foil for Jack Ball, inevitably brought him to the attention of the England selectors – but with deliberations that had puzzling outcomes.

In October 1930, Burgess scored twice on his international debut in the company of three other Wednesday players, Blenkinsop, Strange and Leach, in a 5-1 defeat of Ireland – in Sheffield, but at Bramall Lane, not on their home ground. It was to be expected that such a promising start would ensure his retention, but of that Wednesday quartet he was the only one to be excluded from England's next match the following month. While Wales were being beaten 4-0 at Wrexham, Burgess was at Leicester, bolstering a Ball hat-trick with two more goals in a 5-2 win for Wednesday's below-strength side. Burgess was then brought back for games England lost in Glasgow and Paris, kept his place despite failing to score in those defeats, and was again omitted, never to be capped again, after netting twice in a 4-1 victory over Belgium in Brussels. Although Leach had dropped out after the Wrexham match, Wednesday also had four players in the team defeated 5-2 by France with the inclusion, for his third and final cap, of George Stephenson, the former Villa forward newly signed from Derby.

Burgess's appearances in Wednesday's senior side suddenly fell away through the combination of Billy Walker's reinstatement of Ronnie Starling and the new manager's acquisition of Jack Surtees, a North-Easterner who was taken on from Bournemouth after a successful trial. Burgess was recommended by Bob Brown to Leslie Knighton, then Chelsea's manager, and he moved to the London club with 77 goals in 234 League and Cup games for Wednesday to his credit, plus another in the 1-2 defeat by Arsenal in the FA Charity Shield match of 1930. He stayed at Stamford Bridge right through to the outbreak of another world war, making 155 appearances, and although his scoring rate slackened there were some crucial goals among the 37 he added to his account. The steadying influence his considerable experience brought to bear was never more appreciated than during the 1938-39 season that Chelsea ended on the brink of relegation to the Second Division.

Jack Surtees was one of three players Billy Walker introduced into the Sheffield Wednesday team during the month before the club embarked upon what was to be a run to Wembley. On 8 December 1934, Wilf Sharp, a wing-half from Airdrieonians, made his debut in a win at Leicester gained with a Burgess goal. A week later, Jack Palethorpe, a well-built centre-forward from Preston North End, made his first appearance in a scoreless home draw with Everton. Following a defeat away to Grimsby, Surtees became the third newcomer in four matches in a Christmas Day victory over Birmingham at Hillsborough. Burgess was again on target that afternoon, and he also scored, in a win at Liverpool, when he played his final first-team game for the club the following February.

Wednesday's other goal against Birmingham came from Bernard Oxley, a versatile forward Walker had signed from Sheffield United just in time for him to make a scoring start in a draw at Stoke on the last day of the previous season. Oxley failed to establish himself, however, and within a year he was on his way out to Plymouth. Neither was Palethorpe destined to be at Hillsborough for long. It was in November 1935, two months after Oxley's departure, that Aston Villa made him one of their purchases in their unsuccessful attempt to avoid relegation. Palethorpe, whose departure enabled Neil Dewar to be reinstated at the head of Wednesday's attack, had helped Stoke to promotion before going to Preston, but he played only six times in the League for doomed Villa, netting twice, before returning to the Crystal Palace club he had first joined as an amateur. For Wednesday he averaged a goal every two games, 17 in 34. Three of those goals were scored along the path to Wembley; another gave them an early lead in the final.

The first hurdle on the Cup trail was negotiated comfortably enough, by 3-1 with goals by Palethorpe, Rimmer and Surtees, at home to an Oldham side labouring under the distraction of waging a battle against relegation from the Second Division they were fated to lose. But a discordant note was struck before the more demanding tie in the next round – away to Wolverhampton Wanderers, fellow members of the First Division. Billy Walker made another of his controversial decisions by dropping his namesake, the unrelated Tommy Walker, in favour of Joe Nibloe. It was the only change he was to make throughout that season's competition.

The unfortunate Tommy Walker, who was in his tenth season since his £1,900 signing by Bob Brown from Bradford City, and had missed only one of Wednesday's previous 30 Cup games, claimed he did not learn he would not be required until he was in the dressing room getting ready to play. The manager certainly left it late to decide that Nibloe, who had missed a few games after playing in both full-back positions, would make a better partner for Catlin after the defence had leaked five goals in the previous League match at Middlesbrough. Tommy Walker played only three more times in Wednesday's first team after that, taking him to a League and Cup total of 287, but he remained at Hillsborough as a member of the training staff until the late 1960s.

Wednesday, thankful for Jack Brown's brilliance in goal, squeezed through against Wolves, Rimmer scoring their winner after 'Artillery Billy' Hartill had wiped out a lead gained by Palethorpe. The draw for the fifth round then took them to Norwich – and to another example of Billy Walker's close attention to detail. To familiarise his players with the conditions they would encounter at the Second Division club's tight little ground in Rosary Road known as The Nest (from which they were to move to Carrow Road after that season), he arranged a public practice match on a Hillsborough pitch reduced in width by five yards. And, making it all the more realistic, some 8,000 supporters answered his call by crowding along the touchlines. This thorough preparation paid off, but only just. Wednesday were made to struggle all the way for another slender success, Rimmer grabbing the only goal to the dismay of most in the packed attendance of a little more than 25,000. Brown was again the barrier.

So to the quarter-finals, and to a daunting visit from Arsenal, leaders of the First Division who were heading for the completion of their title treble. Wednesday were among the Gunners' closest challengers in the League, but they had been well beaten by them at Highbury only a month before. And thereby hung the tale of how Billy Walker had been outsmarted. This was how Bernard Joy, the Arsenal centre-half who, while with Casuals, was the last amateur to play for England in a full international, recalled it in his book Forward, Arsenal:

'Wednesday manager Billy Walker had been so often shadowed by Alex James when he was an inside-forward for Aston Villa that he told his team not to worry about the little Scottish wizard as a goal scorer. The plan was to let him dribble and weave to his heart's content, and to cover the men to whom he could pass. James spotted the plan and went through on his own, with an impish grin on his puckered face, to score three times.'

It was James's only hat-trick in first-class football, and he scored just one other goal that season – back in September in a 4-3 home win against West Bromwich Albion. His team-mates ribbed him after the game with Wednesday, saying that he would not have scored at all but for two deflections off defenders and one off another Arsenal player, but James was quite content to tell them that his sudden scoring spree settled a question of parental dignity. His 13-year-old son had returned home at lunch-time after scoring four goals in a school match that morning and taunted him by saying: 'That's more than you've scored all season.'

Billy Walker was not a man to repeat his mistake when Arsenal paid their Cup visit to Hillsborough. For that match James was back to the familiar creative role he had been required to adopt, very reluctantly at first, after having been primarily a scorer with Raith Rovers and Preston, and this time he was carefully watched. Consequently, the threat from that source was greatly reduced, yet Wednesday still needed some good luck to progress. A bad bounce thwarted Ted Drake, and Brown brought off a spectacular finger-tip save in fortunately going the right way by flinging himself to his right as Cliff Bastin flicked a hard cross goalwards from close range. A draw looked likely with the teams deadlocked at 1-1, but a rare misunderstanding in the Arsenal defence then led to the winner. Mark Hooper, scorer of Wednesday's first goal, sent over a fast low centre, and Ellis Rimmer cut in from the opposite wing for a typically opportunist strike. Hesitation cost George Male, Arsenal's right-back, the excellent chance he appeared to have to intercept the cross before the left-winger could get to it as he stood well positioned at the far post.

The bitterness of defeat was intensified for Arsenal when they travelled back by train to London knowing they were no longer at the top of the League table. From having been one point ahead of Sunderland they were now one point behind them. Sunderland, whose own Cup hopes had been dashed in an epic 6-4 defeat by Everton in a fourth-round replay at Goodison Park, took advantage of the reigning champions' absence from First Division action with a convincing home win against Blackburn Rovers at Roker Park. Arsenal, however, then had three games in hand, and they still had two when, with ten more to play, they kept the point lead they had wrested back from Sunderland by drawing with them in a grim goalless game watched by Highbury's record crowd of 73,295.

The Gunners' only defeat in those last ten matches was suffered at home to Derby County on the final day of the season, but by then the pressure was off them. As already recalled, they finished four points ahead of Sunderland, with Wednesday five points further behind in third place. Sunderland were to have their turn as champions, for the first time since 1913, a year later – and then to win the Cup, for the first time in their first final since 1913, the season after that.

Sheffield Wednesday's hard-earned victory over Arsenal on the second day of March in 1935 brought them a semi-final back on Billy Walker's familiar territory at Villa Park. Up against them were Burnley, a mid-table Second Division club that had only narrowly avoided the plunge into the Third North in two of the past three seasons. An appearance at such a late stage of the competition was therefore a welcome bright spot during the slump into which Burnley had slipped since winning the Cup just before the First World War, and the First Division championship shortly after it, but Wednesday were in no mood to jeopardise their obvious rating as clear favourites. Form did indeed run true, though not as smoothly as the 3-0 result might indicate. Despite an early headed goal by Rimmer, Wednesday had some anxious moments before the same player scored again a dozen minutes into the second half – and that increasing of the lead would not have come about but for the persistence of Hooper, whose charge so surprised Bob Scott that the former Liverpool goalkeeper dropped the ball for Rimmer to pounce. Palethorpe completed the scoring.

Preoccupation with the Cup put paid to Wednesday's prospects of pressing home a serious challenge for the First Division title during the six weeks between the semi-final and final. Of the seven games they played in that period they won only two – both at home, against Billy Walker's old club Aston Villa and the team that finished at the bottom of the table, Tottenham Hotspur. Two of the others were lost, and three drawn – the last of them, by 1-1, away to West Bromwich Albion, the other finalists, on the Monday before the big day at Wembley. Neither club revealed a full hand for the Hawthorns 'rehearsal'. Wednesday rested Nibloe, Sharp and skipper Starling; Albion fielded only six of their players who took part in the final. Tommy Walker and Alf Strange both made their last League appearance for the Owls that afternoon. Starling's place was taken by debutant Jackie Robinson, Billy Walker's biggest discovery for the club.

Robinson, spotted in a junior match in his native North-East, got off to a scoring start, and he was such an outstanding talent, one of the finest forwards ever to play for Sheffield Wednesday, that within weeks of gaining a regular place late the following year he was chosen for an international trial despite being in a team heading for relegation. He also scored when he won the first of his four England caps, against Finland in Helsinki in May 1937, and a year later he netted twice in the 6-3 defeat of Germany in Berlin – a famous victory also remembered for the Nazi salute the team reluctantly had to give before the kick-off to avoid an international incident.

But for the war that soon afterwards broke out Robinson would surely have left an indelible mark on the game. He had everything that makes an inside-forward of the highest class – exceptional speed, superb ball control, a deceptive body swerve, and a ready eye for goal. He was past his best by the time the war ended, but still cost £7,500, a sizeable fee for the time, when he was transferred to Sunderland in the autumn of 1946. Three years later he moved to Lincoln City, but was forced into retirement when he broke a leg in only his eighth game for them.

In 1935, West Bromwich were unbeaten in the seven League matches they played between their Cup semi-final, in which they were taken to a replay by Bolton, and the final, winning three and drawing four. Although below Wednesday in the table (they finished ninth), they were generally looked upon as favourites to lift the trophy – mainly because all but two of their team had previous Wembley experience from the 1931 final in which Albion had beaten Birmingham and gone on to become the first (and still only) club to lift the Cup and gain promotion to the First Division in the same season. A week after winning at Wembley they had beaten Charlton at the Hawthorns to make sure of going up as runners-up to Everton.

The Throstles were also thought to have the edge over Wednesday in attack for the 1935 final, though they caused some surprise by omitting Arthur Gale from it in favour of Tommy Glidden, and took another gamble in recalling Joe Carter in the month of his 34th birthday. Gale, a schoolteacher, had played in every previous round, scoring in each of the first four up to the semi-final. His diving header for the only goal of the quarter-final against Preston had been a particularly brilliant effort. Glidden, the captain, and Carter had been out of action for several weeks, but Glidden had made a comeback a week ahead of the final, scoring in a defeat of Derby, before missing the home League game with Wednesday two days later. He and Carter were called the 'twins' by fans, so often, in more than 350 senior matches, were they partners on Albion's right wing.

These were the teams for the final, watched by a crowd of 93,204 (receipts £24,856) on 27 April 1935:

Sheffield Wednesday: Brown; Nibloe, Catlin; Sharp, Millership, Burrows; Hooper, Surtees, Palethorpe, Starling, Rimmer.

West Bromwich: Pearson; Shaw, Trentham; Murphy, Richardson (W), Edwards; Glidden, Carter, Richardson (W G), Sandford, Boyes.

It was soon evident that neither Glidden nor Carter was back to the full fitness necessary to cope adequately with such a demanding occasion, especially on what used to be referred to so regularly as the 'lush' holding turf of Wembley. With their trump card, the attack, therefore somewhat lopsided, West Bromwich earned great credit for making such a thrilling fight of it after also having to contend with the shock of falling behind as early as the second minute. From a clearance out of defence, Hooper pushed the ball across for Palethorpe to steer his shot past Harold ('Algy') Pearson, whose father, Hubert, had also kept goal for Albion. Hubert, nicknamed 'Joe,' would also have preceded his son as an England goalkeeper if he had not been forced to withdraw through injury after being selected to play against France. He was never given another opportunity.

The best goal of the game was the one with which West Bromwich equalised in the 21st minute. Ironically, the scorer was the only Sheffield-born player on the pitch – left-winger Wally Boyes, one of the two members of this Albion side who had not been in the club's winning team at Wembley four years earlier (the other was Jimmy Murphy, later Matt Busby's managerial assistant at Manchester United). Boyes, who had gone to the Hawthorns as a 16-year-old not long after scoring seventeen goals in one schools game, swooped onto a pass from Carter and hammered a fierce rising shot beyond the diving Brown's reach. The disappointment of finishing on the losing side in that final was to be tempered for Boyes the following month, when his selection for the first of his three caps made him, at 5ft 3in, one of the smallest players to represent England – and, surely, the first to have one leg slightly shorter than the other. Another honour came his way in the last pre-war season of 1938-39, as a League champion with Everton.

There were no further goals before half-time at Wembley in 1935, but the drama and excitement packed into the second half more than made up for that. Starling missed one good chance, and was foiled by a goal-line clearance, before Wednesday regained the lead after 67 minutes. Starling provided the pass from which Hooper eluded a couple of defenders and left Pearson helpless with a shot that entered the net off an upright. Within five minutes Albion were level again. Teddy Sandford, who had been one of the youngest Cup winners at the age of twenty in 1931, caught Brown wrong-footed when his powerful drive from the edge of the penalty area took a deflection off Millership.

At that point Albion looked the more likely winners, as they most probably would have been but for a mixture of bad luck and inaccurate finishing. Carter hit a post and put another shot wide. Then another excellent chance was wasted by W G Richardson, who was given the extra initial 'G', for 'Ginger', to distinguish him from the other, unrelated, Bill Richardson in the team. Boyes created a perfect opportunity for the Albion's ace marksman, whose eight goals in the lead-up to Wembley had included a hat-trick in a 7-1 crushing of Sheffield United, but he was inches out with his aim.

Encouraged though Wednesday were by those let-offs, extra time seemed inevitable when the scores were still level only three minutes from the end of the 90. That, however, was when Ellis Rimmer, hitherto untypically subdued, suddenly emerged as the match-winner. Superstitious folk have no doubt that his lucky horseshoe was responsible. Somebody had given it to him at the start of the Cup run, and he had taken it with him for each round – until, that is, the most important one of all, at Wembley. Not until the team arrived at their Bushey Wood headquarters two days before the final was it realised that the horseshoe had been left behind at Hillsborough. Fortunately for Rimmer's eventual peace of mind, Sam Powell, a former forward with the club who was the reserve trainer, spotted it lying there just before he left to join up with the main party, but he was unable to get it back to the winger before half-time.

If, in fact, the knowledge that Rimmer again had it on the premises did the trick, it certainly took quite a time to do so. But that only added to the drama of those last few minutes as this former tapper-out of tunes on the piano at the silent cinema came right on song with not just one goal, but two. According to Charlie Buchan, the former Sunderland, Arsenal and England forward who reported on the match for the *News Chronicle* (a newspaper, originally known as the *Daily News*, that has long been defunct), the first one was due not to the luck of the horseshoe but to 'one of the best referee's decisions ever made.' Ted Catlin was injured in a tackle, but Bert Fogg, the experienced referee from Bolton, realised that he was not seriously hurt and allowed play to proceed instead of beckoning the trainer onto the field to give the full-back attention. Rimmer raced in to meet a speculative lofted pass into the goalmouth, and, as the ball bounced, headed home a split second before Pearson could fist clear. Almost immediately afterwards, the goalkeeper failed to hold a shot from Hooper, and Rimmer nipped in to give the scoreline an even more flattering aspect. After for so long being well below his best, Wednesday's left-winger had joined the select band of those who have scored in every round of the Cup in which they have played in one season.

'Even now,' wrote Buchan many years later, 'I can picture the scene that followed. The disconsolate Pearson allowed the ball to rest in the back of the net. But, with only a couple of minutes left, Billy Richardson, Albion's dashing centre-forward, rushed back, retrieved the ball from the net, sprinted to the centre and restarted the game at once. He, and the Albion, were out to retrieve a forlorn hope. But Wednesday were on top and carried off the trophy for the first time in 28 years.' Ronnie Starling led his men up the famous 39 steps to receive it from the Prince of Wales, the heir to a throne from which he was to abdicate so sensationally late the following year.

One last, and most fitting, mention in this chapter is for the popular man who could be said, perhaps by even some of the sceptics, to have saved the day at Wembley by being so observant. Sam Powell, the bringer of the horseshoe, was promoted to first-team trainer in 1937 as successor to George Irwin, who had taken over that post following the sudden death of Chris Craig. After having had his playing career with the club ended by a broken leg, Powell was a valued member of the backroom staff, along with Tommy Walker, in service at Hillsborough that altogether lasted for more than 30 years.

CHAPTER SEVEN

A Close Escape from Relegation

When the 1935-36 season opened, Billy Walker's Wednesday were clearly top dogs on the Sheffield soccer scene. As FA Cup holders and the third best team in the First Division of only a few months earlier, they were widely regarded as one of the clubs with a realistic chance of becoming League champions. In sharp contrast, their United neighbours, bedevilled by dwindling gates and a lack of money with which to try to strength their side, seemed destined for another season of toil in the lower reaches of Division Two.

But what a reversal of fortunes there was so soon to come. After a misleading winning start away to Walker's old club Aston Villa, Wednesday plunged into a relegation battle they only just survived, and were taken to two replays before going out of the Cup. Meanwhile, United, under the astute direction of former Wednesday goalkeeper Teddy Davison, staged a grand revival that took them close to emulating West Bromwich's promotion and Cup-winning double of five years before. While Wednesday finished immediately above the two clubs that went down, United ended directly below the two that went up. And in providing Sheffield with Cup finalists for the second successive year, the Blades of Bramall Lane were one of Wembley's best losers. Their burly centre-forward 'Jock' Dodds, a Scottish international during the 1939-45 War, was only the width of the crossbar away from nullifying, with a header, the lone late Arsenal goal that beat them.

The pattern for Wednesday's dispiriting season was set from the opening weeks in which their narrow victory over Villa was the only one they gained in seven matches. At that point Jack Palethorpe had scored half of their ten goals, yet it was not long afterwards that he was allowed to leave one relegation fight for another – going from what might be termed the frying pan of Wednesday's narrow escape to the fire of Aston Villa's descent into the Second Division for the first time.

The danger bells really began clanging for Wednesday when the defence that had been their mainstay, considered by some to be the strongest in the League, suddenly started shipping goals at an alarming rate – seventeen of them in three consecutive games. A 1-5 defeat away to Sunderland's leaders and coming champions was followed by a 2-5 beating at home at the avenging hands of West Bromwich Albion and a 2-7 walloping at Leeds. Down the Owls fluttered to fifteenth place, their hitherto lethal wings disconcertingly clipped. The most impressive player in their less fluid forward line was now Neil Dewar, recalled at the head of it. He scored all but one of their five goals in those heavy setbacks, and was to end the season as their main marksman with twenty-one (two of them in a Cup 'run' that ended in a second meeting with Newcastle after a win at the second attempt against Crewe).

To lose so heavily to Sunderland, who were going so well that at one stage they romped eight points clear of their closest rivals, was no cause for particular alarm. The same, however, could not be said of those two other big reverses. Albion were fellow strugglers and Leeds, though higher up the table, had won only three of their previous thirteen games. It was the first time for more than three years that Wednesday had conceded five goals at home, and West Bromwich had then also been their visitors. In gaining some measure of revenge for their Cup final defeat, Albion were largely indebted to Sam ('Splinter') Wood, who had reclaimed their outside-left berth from Wally Boyes, Wednesday's most dangerous opponent at Wembley. Wood smartly wiped out the lead Dewar deceptively gained after only six minutes, then put West Bromwich ahead with a glorious left-foot drive, and made the next two goals for Teddy Sandford and Jack Mahon. W G Richardson, who was to be the League's leading scorer that season, netted Albion's fifth in a breakaway before Hooper obtained Wednesday's second in the closing seconds.

For Wednesday's next match after their demoralising trip to Leeds, Billy Walker reverted to his Cup-winning team except for having Dewar at centre-forward, and a welcome improvement was shown in a 3-0 home win against Grimsby. After having been at the foot of the table with Villa for several weeks, the Mariners had been convincing conquerors of Sunderland with a hat-trick from Welsh international 'Pat' Glover, and in their last two matches before meeting Wednesday they had won 6-2 at Villa Park (four more for Glover) and also defeated Wolves. At Hillsborough, however, they were second best from the 25th minute in which the impressive Dewar rounded off some skilful footwork with the opening goal. The normally reliable George Tweedy let a low drive from Surtees' pass through his hands for the second one, and Starling completed the scoring with a superb free kick, the ball entering the net just beneath the bar. Amazingly, those were the first goals scored by Wednesday inside-forwards in the first fifteen games of the season.

Hopes that Wednesday would now at last rediscover some consistency were promptly dashed. Defeat at Manchester City was followed by a home win against Chelsea, but then by four more failures culminating in the loss of both points at Everton on Boxing Day despite scoring three goals. But for goalkeeper Brown's agility, the losing margin at Maine Road would have been wider than 3-0 against a City side already without Fred Tilson, their England centre-forward, and down to ten fit men from the twentieth minute in which centre-half Donnelly pulled a thigh muscle that made him little more than a 'passenger' on the left wing. Matt Busby switched so successfully to fill the vacancy that Dewar did not have a scoring chance until the one he was unable to accept in the last minutes.

Chelsea were also depleted at Hillsborough, where 'Joe' Bambrick, the first scorer of a double hat-trick in a full international (for Northern Ireland against Wales in Belfast in 1930), was ordered off six minutes from time. The 18-year-old Jackie Robinson was a big success in his first home League game, but Wednesday were flattered by their 4-1 win after falling behind within five minutes to a spectacular drive by George Gibson, a skilful Scot who bore favourable comparison with Alex James. One of Wednesday's goals came from a hotly disputed penalty, two minutes before Bambrick's dismissal. Another was a gift for Hooper as Chelsea defenders stopped playing in expectation of a whistle for offside that never came.

On the day after that game, arguably unwisely in view of their subsequent disappointing form, Wednesday's players were sent across the English Channel and, looking tired, lost in Lille by the odd goal of five to a North of France XI. Dewar, who had been outstanding against Chelsea with his speed and brilliant ball control, twice equalised, but the outstanding player afield was his marker, Peter O'Dowd, a former England pivot who had fallen out with the Stamford Bridge club's management and gone off to play in France for bigger pay days.

The match with Everton at Goodison Park, after the Christmas Day meeting of the clubs at Sheffield had been postponed because of frost and snow, was another in which Wednesday's opponents were handicapped. In the 35th minute, goalkeeper Ted Sagar was injured in thwarting Ellis Rimmer, and he was on the left wing, with winger Albert Geldard in goal, when Wednesday went into a 3-2 lead two minutes after the interval. Five minutes later, after Geldard (the youngest League debutant at 15 years and 156 days for Bradford at Millwall in September 1929) had made two good saves, Sagar went back in goal but spent the rest of the match untroubled. Everton, whose left-winger, Torry Gillick, finished limping with a pulled muscle, rallied to score two more goals without further reply and also struck the framework of Wednesday's goal twice. It was quite a change for them to give their fans such a treat. They had not scored at home since the beginning of November.

Wednesday saw out the old year with a 5-2 home victory in which all their forwards scored against Aston Villa, who were then three points out of touch at the bottom of the table and had conceded 74 goals in 23 games. There was to be no escape from a first relegation for the club Billy Walker had served with such distinction, yet, fickle as football form so often is, only four days later, on the first one of the new year, Villa served up the most astonishing result of the season by beating Sunderland 3-1 at Roker Park. Sunderland went into the game seven points clear at the top of the First Division, and without having dropped a point on their own ground. But they were to have few further lapses and, with 25 wins to set against six defeats, crossed the finishing line eight points ahead of runners-up Derby County and third-placed Huddersfield Town.

In the meantime, the battle at the other end of the table became so intense that at one stage at least fifteen clubs were caught up in it. As late as early March only four points separated the bottom club, Blackburn, from Portsmouth, who were seventh. All this to the turbulent background of a 'war' between the Football League and the Pools promoters. The League decided that the Pools were a menace to the game, and, in their attempt to sabotage coupons by withholding fixture lists, names of opponents were filled in on posters outside grounds only a day or so before matches were played. *The Daily Telegraph*'s football correspondent, writing under the pseudonym The Pivot, declared: 'There is talk of revolution and heads in the basket. The central figure in the fight, Mr Charles Sutcliffe, has been credited with the astonishing statement that it is within his power to refuse to let the League have the fixtures next season unless his copyright is respected.'

A serious drop in attendances, an unavoidable consequence of the 'mystery' matches, ensured a quick end to the dispute. On Monday, 9 March the secret fixture plan was scrapped at a special meeting of representatives of League clubs, who were summoned by the Management Committee to Manchester, where the scheme had been launched less than three weeks before. Only clubs in the top two divisions were allowed to vote. So the Pools, which had been started soon after the First World War, continued to flourish, eventually reaching a peak where they became one of the country's top ten industries, employing more than 100,000 people, before their decline was speeded up by the competition introduced with the launch of the national lottery. Not until 1959 did the Football League establish the copyright of their fixtures and begin to receive payment from the Pools promoters.

Another hot topic during the 1930s was the recommendation of the Referees Committee that leagues and clubs should adopt the two-referee system. It stirred up much controversy when tried in an amateur international trial at Chester early in 1935, and in the professional trial at West Bromwich Albion's ground two months later. It failed to find favour at the Football League' annual meeting that year, and when further attempts were made before the war it was rejected by an increased margin.

Sheffield Wednesday did not have a match on New Year's Day. For them, 1936 began three days later with a narrow defeat at Wolves, but they then bucked up with victories by the odd goal at home to Arsenal and away to Preston before being held to a couple of 3-3 draws at Hillsborough – the first of them in the rearranged match with Everton in which Rimmer did the hat-trick. The win at Deepdale, gained with the fourteenth of the nineteen goals that made Dewar the club's top League scorer that season, came on a day, the first of February, when there were a record-equalling 209 goals in the 44 League games. That total had first been registered on the second day of January in 1932, when one fixture had been postponed.

Following a defeat by Portsmouth in their third successive home match, Wednesday had two newcomers in their line-up for a midweek visit to Derby. One was Tom Grosvenor, an elegant inside-right who had grown into a six-footer since being a pint-sized full-back in his schooldays; the other Charlie Luke, a former Durham miner, standing only 5ft 3in, who had developed into a speedy creative winger after being a prolific marksmen from inside-forward as an amateur with Bishop Auckland. In 1930-31 Luke had scored 61 goals for the 'Bishops' – nine of them, including two hat-tricks, on their way to the Amateur Cup semi-finals. Grosvenor, capped three times by England, arrived from Birmingham for a fee of £2,500, Luke from Huddersfield Town for not much less.

The new right wing formed by this pair got off to a promising start at the Baseball Ground, and from a corner Grosvenor gave Wednesday a lead they still held at half-time. Straight after the interval Dewar almost increased it with a splendid shot that hit the crossbar, but soon afterwards high-riding Derby not only equalised but also exploited defensive lapses to go in front. Near the end the outcome was put beyond doubt when Jack Bowers, scorer of the Rams' second goal, netted again from a free kick. Earlier in the 1930s, Bowers had been one of the few players to be the First Division's leading goal-getter in two successive seasons.

On the Saturday after their defeat at Derby, when the 'Pools war' was at its height as the air hummed with threats and counter threats, Sheffield Wednesday sank to 20th in the table, with only the ultimately relegated pair below them. The Owls had 25 points from 29 games, Blackburn 23 from 30 and Aston Villa 22, also from 30. But it was not another beating that intensified the plight of Billy Walker and his men. Their match at Birmingham that February afternoon was one of half-a-dozen abandoned or postponed because of snow that obliterated the pitch markings. Play at St Andrew's was stopped after 34 minutes, with the home side a goal to the good.

A week later there was more snow, and also sleet and rain, in the Midlands and North, but Wednesday were able to fulfil their fixture with Leeds at Hillsborough – and they won it by the healthy margin of 3-0 to zoom up to 16th. Their team that day included another new man. Harry Hanford, a Welsh international from Swansea, was at centre-half. Millership moved to the right flank of the middle line in place of Burrows, who switched back to the left. Wednesday were now one of four clubs in 27 points, below four others on 28, and three better off than Blackburn and Villa.

All three new signings did well in the next game, won by 2-1 away to Chelsea after Harry Burgess had opened the scoring against his old club from a free-kick in only the sixth minute. It was a regular problem for Wednesday that season to go behind early on. Starling headed an equaliser from a corner towards the end of the first half, and both teams seemed satisfied to play for a draw until Dewar suddenly broke away to set up Rimmer for the winner. Bambrick this time managed to see out the whole match, but was well held by Hanford. Chelsea were now in as serious trouble as any of the strugglers, six of whom were winners on that first Saturday of March – the bottom two among them. During the past two months Villa, putting up a belated but vain fight, had won almost as many points as Sunderland, who were thankful for their flying start in still looking virtual champions despite a dip in form.

Sunderland were Wednesday's next visitors, and they failed to win for the fifth consecutive match in being held to a scoreless draw that lifted the Sheffield club to the dizzy heights of 13th. A fortnight later, while Wednesday were beating Manchester City at Hillsborough with a Luke goal, the runaway leaders ran into deeper trouble in losing 1-6 at Middlesbrough – yet they still had a six-point cushion as their nearest challengers also failed to win. It was their biggest beating by Boro since the club's first met in 1902, and, to make matters even worse, their right-wing pair, Bert Davis and Raich Carter, were both sent off.

The temporary toils of the team at the top were as nothing, however, compared with the end-of-season slump that dumped Wednesday back towards the division's depths, immediately above the relegation trapdoor. The victory over Manchester City was one of only two the Owls gained in their last ten matches after the draw with Sunderland. In six of those games, three of them in succession, they again failed to score. On the day in March when Sheffield United reached an FA Cup final for the sixth time by defeating Fulham at Wolverhampton, Wednesday were again without a match – this time because their scheduled opponents, Grimsby Town, were in the other semi-final against Arsenal at Huddersfield. The game with Grimsby, at Blundell Park, was rearranged for the following Tuesday, when Wednesday conceded four goals without reply to a team that showed two changes, at left-half and outside-left, from the one that had failed to reach the final in being beaten by an only goal by the Gunners.

There were four draws, all at home, for Wednesday in those final ten matches, and three of them were goalless. The exception was in the return game with West Bromwich Albion, on the early April afternoon when England's encounter with Scotland at Wembley was also drawn. Wednesday were two up at half-time, but W G Richardson offset his disappointment at not being called up for his second cap by inspiring an Albion recovery in which Harry ('Popeye') Jones salvaged a point by scoring twice in ten minutes. The strong wind the visitors had to face before the interval was partly responsible for both Wednesday's goals. From a left-wing corner kick taken by outside-right Luke, the ball swerved violently to strike Dewar and was deflected across goal for Rimmer to net the first. The unmarked Dewar increased the lead when the ball was blown away from the man who was marking him, the other Bill Richardson.

So to Easter, from which Wednesday and West Bromwich emerged even deeper in trouble. On Good Friday, when Wednesday were without a game, the holiday period began for Albion with a 0-4 defeat away to Arsenal. Next day, they were beaten 3-5 at Everton while Wednesday played one of their scoreless draws at home to Blackburn. On Easter Monday, Jones, who was the holder of a Royal Humane Society medal for diving into a canal to save a child from drowning, gave Albion a lifeline by scoring the only goal of their return match with Arsenal, but Wednesday had only Blackburn below them in the table after producing no response to the five goals they let in at Middlesbrough. At that point Owls, with five games to go, and Throstles, who had only three more left, were both on 34 points. Directly above them were five clubs on 35 – Aston Villa, who had just two more matches to play, Chelsea, Grimsby, Wolves and Everton.

George Camsell bagged four of Boro's goals against Wednesday, but neither he nor his club led the way for scoring that day. Joe Payne obtained ten of Luton's dozen against Bristol Rovers, and Sunderland swamped Birmingham with seven in making sure of the First Division title. Camsell's first goal was an especially brilliant effort. In the 13th minute he dribbled through from the halfway line, baffling three men before beating Brown with a magnificent drive. Wednesday then had a fair share of the game up to half-time, but were overwhelmed afterwards.

Next day, although Camsell almost added to his tally at Hillsborough by hitting the bar, it took some good work by goalkeeper Gibson to deny Wednesday both points as another of their goalless games was sufficient to take them up three places. And at the end of the week a 3-0 win at Stoke lifted them to 16th with 37 points from 39 matches – on goal-average above Chelsea, who had a fixture in hand. Albion and Everton had 35 from 40 games, Wolves 35 from 39, Villa 35 from 41, and Blackburn 31 from 40. Blackburn were doomed despite a 3-1 home victory over Portsmouth, and on the following Saturday they dragged Villa down with them by winning 4-2 at Villa Park despite having to call upon a young inexperienced amateur to answer a goalkeeping emergency.

The success at Stoke was Wednesday's last of the season as they wound up with a 1-4 defeat at Birmingham, a 0-0 draw at home to Liverpool, and another loss, by a lone goal, at Huddersfield on the final day. So Billy Walker's current club finished three points clear of his old one, Villa, whose goals-against total of 110 made it obvious where they main weakness lay. After so many months with so many clubs involved in the relegation struggle, it was indeed remarkable that the issue was decided before the last day for the first time for several years. These were the final positions at the foot of a table that Sunderland headed with 56 points:

Season 1935-36	P	W	D	L	F	A	Pts
16 Everton	42	13	13	16	89	89	39
17 Grimsby	42	17	5	20	65	73	39
18 West Bromwich	42	16	6	20	89	88	38
19 Liverpool	42	13	12	17	60	64	38
20 Sheffield Wed	42	13	12	17	63	77	38
21 Aston Villa	42	13	9	20	81	110	35
22 Blackburn	42	12	9	21	55	96	33

For Wednesday it was to be just a drop deferred – and for only one more season.

CHAPTER EIGHT

Down to the Second Division

Halfway through the 1936-37 season there was no real indication that Sheffield Wednesday were heading for relegation. With 18 points from 21 games they were then better off than they had been at the corresponding stage of the previous year, and on the last Saturday before Christmas they inflicted, by 5-1, the heaviest defeat Manchester City suffered on their way to becoming First Division champions for the first time.

But what a contrast in the form of Wednesday and City there was so swiftly to be after that match between the clubs at Hillsborough. On Christmas Day, City again leaked five goals, losing 3-5 at Grimsby Town, and therefore stayed just two points ahead of the Owls in the middle of the table. That, however, was their last League defeat of the season. They won 15 of their remaining 22 games, with the seven others drawn. Wednesday, on the other hand, fell away to the extent of being beaten in 15 of their last 23 matches, winning only four and drawing four. City ended at the top with 57 points, Wednesday at the bottom with 30.

In looking back on the result in Sheffield that proved so perverse, Peter Doherty, the hugely gifted Irish forward whose transfer from Blackpool earlier in the year had cost City their then record fee of £10,000, conceded that it was 'as decisive as it was unexpected, a correct reflection of the game'. He added: 'Wednesday played a new right-half that day called Moss, who had evidently been instructed to stick to me like a shadow. He obeyed the order to the letter, and the only time I was able to shake him off was in the first half, when I scored City's solitary goal.'

That young man called Moss was Frank Moss, son of the wing-half of the same name who had been one of Billy Walker's team-mates with Aston Villa. Frank Junior had been taken on by Walker as an amateur only a few weeks earlier, after having had an unsuccessful trial with Wolves. The match with Manchester City was his fifth in Wednesday's senior side, but there were to be only just under two dozen all told before he was off-loaded to Aston Villa in the summer of 1938, some months after Walker had left Hillsborough. Moss's career did not really get going until he became a professional at Villa Park, and another famous international player, Tommy Lawton, was then also to pay high tribute to him by saying: 'I never got a kick when Frank was marking me – a great player, hard but fair.' Moss might well have made good with Wednesday if their fortunes had not been at such a low ebb during the two seasons he spent with them. He was an integral member of Villa's post-war team until injury forced him out of it in the mid-1950s.

Moss was one of about half-a-dozen players who failed to establish themselves after being introduced by Billy Walker into Wednesday's struggling side in the 1936-37 season. Among them was a former Northern Ireland centre-forward, Jimmy McCambridge, who had been an understudy to 'Dixie' Dean at Everton. McCambridge arrived as a top scorer with each of his last three clubs, Cardiff City, Bristol Rovers and Exeter City, but he was given only two League outings before being transferred to Hartlepools United. Having failed to find the net for Wednesday in a draw at Arsenal and defeat at Charlton, he promptly regained his scoring touch by doing for the 'Pool' what he had done for the Bristol club – get three goals on his debut.

Shortcomings in attack were a main reason for Wednesday's downfall. Whereas the club had exceeded 100 goals in three successive seasons in their not-so-far-off peak years (with the inclusion of Cup goals on the third of those occasions), they dropped out of the First Division with their output down to around half that number – 53. Injuries and inconsistencies in team selection were other contributory factors. Dewar was again the leading scorer, but with just ten goals, and in one of his frequent absences on the casualty list Walker even tried a full-back, Albert Ashley, as the attack's spearhead. Ashley, a former Mansfield Town defender who was eventually to be Joe Nibloe's successor at right-back, had first led the front line in the defeat at Huddersfield on the last day of the 1935-36 season. He was again called upon to play there early in February 1937, at Preston, for the first of six consecutive matches in which Jack Roy, another signing from Mansfield, was on the left wing as deputy for the injured Rimmer.

Wednesday's scorer in the 1-1 draw at Deepdale was Jackie Thompson, a youngster from Blyth Spartans who showed considerable promise, but was done no favours in being switched about to such an extent that in the remaining period up to the war he filled all five forward positions in the pyramid formation of those days. Although seen to better effect as a more settled inside-forward in averaging a goal for every two of the 115 games he played for the club during the war, he was transferred to Doncaster Rovers shortly before football got back to its normal peacetime pattern.

In the first post-war League season of 1946-47, Thompson was a member of the Doncaster side that set up several records in running away with the Third Division North title. Eighteen of their 33 wins were gained away from home as they amassed 72 points and suffered only three defeats.

The best unbeaten run Sheffield Wednesday were to enjoy during the 1936-37 season began with that visit to Preston – and it lasted for only three more matches, all at home. They drew with Arsenal and Chelsea, then gained a 3-1 win against Charlton Athletic, who, after two successive promotions, were to end their first Division One campaign as runners-up to Manchester City. The point gleaned in a goalless game with the Gunners was deserved, though Wednesday did not have to contend with the injured Drake and were fortunate when Alf Kitchen hit their cross-bar from a free kick. On a dull day, the gate of 35,813 was Hillsborough's biggest of the season in the League, but soon surpassed by the 48,960 who were packed in for the second replay of a fifth-round FA Cup-tie in which Sunderland took another big step towards carrying off the trophy for the first time by beating Wolves. Wednesday's own interest in that year's knock-out competition was ended in the previous round by Everton, to whom they also lost at Goodison Park during the first week of the season, but defeated 6-4 with the aid of a Dewar hat-trick in the return midweek game.

Heavy rain made the Hillsborough pitch a sea of mud for the match with Chelsea. George Mills, who that autumn scored three goals on his England debut against Northern Ireland, gave the Londoners the lead with a deflected shot in the 13th minute. Wednesday were out of luck when Roy cleverly lobbed goalkeeper Vic Woodley, only to see the ball rebound to safety off an upright, but Ashley equalised straight after half-time. Just over a month later Woodley was first capped, against Scotland in Glasgow – and in England's goal he stayed for their 18 other games up to the outbreak of war, the longest sequence of that kind until Ron Springett, of Sheffield Wednesday, had a run of 21 games guarding the England net in the early 1960s. Woodley was no longer first choice for either his club or country when peace returned, yet he had the fairy-tale experience of being a Cup winner when he made only his ninth appearance for Derby County in the first post-war final after being plucked out of non-League obscurity to answer the Rams' goalkeeping emergency.

Ashley also scored in Wednesday's defeat of Charlton, and again in a 1-5 trouncing by Grimsby that brought the 'purple patch' to an emphatic end, but he could be nothing more than a stop-gap front man as problems increased in an attack that had already been depleted by the departures of Jack Surtees to Nottingham Forest in October and Ronnie Starling to Aston Villa in January. With Tom Grosvenor and Charlie Luke joining Neil Dewar among the casualties, George Drury, later of Arsenal, was tried on the right wing, from where Mark Hooper was switched to spend most of the season at inside-left. In such difficult circumstances, as relegation came ever nearer, it was greatly to the credit of Ted Catlin and Jackie Robinson that they maintained a level of performance that kept them in the England reckoning. Catlin won the first three of his caps during the season, and both went on the summer tour of Scandinavia.

Wednesday had some hopes of another mini revival when they went from their sobering setback against Grimsby to four matches with fellow strugglers that took in the crucial Easter period. But they picked up only three points from the eight at stake, losing at Liverpool and Bolton, drawing at Leeds, and winning the return against Bolton on Easter Monday. Thompson was their only scorer in those games. A home defeat by mid-table Birmingham on the following Saturday had Wednesday in deep trouble, down to 20th place and above the bottom two only on goal-average. They were on 28 points with Leeds and Manchester United, who drew 0-0 at Old Trafford that afternoon, but, with six more games to play, they had one match in hand of Leeds and two of the Manchester club.

Two days later, on the first Monday of April, Wednesday's situation worsened as they also lost a rearranged fixture at Stoke, and at the end of that week a third defeat in a row, at Middlesbrough, deposited them at the foot of the table while Leeds won at home to Derby and Manchester United drew at Birmingham. Then back into the Wednesday's reckoning came West Bromwich, twice their opponents in the space of five days. Both games were decided by the odd goal of five, Wednesday failing in the first at home but winning the other at the Hawthorns.

Albion's victory at Hillsborough left the Owls looking doomed with 28 points from 39 games – two points behind Leeds, three adrift of Manchester United, and with their last three games all away from home. Leeds missed the chance to pull further clear in losing at Wolverhampton, but the Old Trafford club improved their chances of survival by narrowly defeating their Middlesbrough visitors. Millership, who frittered away one glorious opening, scored Wednesday's first goal in their home match with West Bromwich, but Dewar did not snatch their second one until five minutes from time. By then Albion were ahead through Welsh international Walter Robbins, who netted twice, and Jack Mahon, and, strongly as Wednesday pressed, an equaliser eluded them. Dewar was restored to the attack at inside-left that day, after having made only intermittent appearances since the end of November, but he switched back to centre-forward shortly before setting up that grandstand finish with his brilliant late goal.

At one stage after the turn of the year Albion had been below Wednesday in the table. Now they were six points above them, and, although the result of the return game between the clubs was exactly reversed, the Hawthorns victory came too late to give Sheffield's sliders any real hope of surviving. With each of the strugglers then having two games to play except Manchester United, who had only one, this was how they then stood at the bottom of the table: Albion 34 points, Liverpool 33, Bolton 33, Manchester United 32, Wednesday 30, Leeds 30 – in that order.

Unfortunately for Wednesday, the first of their remaining matches was at Maine Road against Manchester City, who went into it on the back of their long unbeaten run knowing that they needed just two more points to clinch the championship. And there was never any doubt they were going to get them from the 20th minute in which Eric Brook gave City the lead with a sizzling drive that Roy Smith, successor to Jack Brown in Wednesday's goal, could scarcely have seen. The England left-winger, noted for the power of his shooting, said afterwards that he had not hit a ball like that for years. Twelve minutes later, the game was as good as over, with City three goals ahead.

All three were down to the genius of Peter Doherty. Immediately after giving Brook a clear run for his bombshell, the Irish international created a simple chance for Fred Tilson with a dazzling run, then scored himself after a delightful interchange of passes with the centre-forward, another of the four players in the Manchester club's attack who represented their country. The other one was Alex Herd, though he was chosen for Scotland only during the war (it was his brother who was capped while with Hearts). Ernie Toseland, Herd's partner on the right wing, was unlucky not to play for England in the course of making more than 400 appearances for City before his transfer to Sheffield Wednesday as the war clouds were gathering.

Doherty's goal was described as 'one of the finest scored on any ground,' and he later said he believed he had 'never, in my whole career, taken part in such a perfect, goal-crowned movement.' This was how he described it:

'It all started from one of Frank Swift's lofty clearances. I gained possession just about the centre of the field, and Freddie and I went through the Wednesday defence with a rapid interchange of passes which carried us over 40 yards, and well into Wednesday's penalty area. It was a precision movement, a slick-passing shuttle which the Sheffield defenders were powerless to intercept. The ball finally came to rest in the corner of the net after Freddie had made the final pass and I had whipped it through. It was a fine goal, a product of splendid team work, and the crowd rose to us as we left the field at half-time.'

The crowd rose again at full time – and how! Rimmer gave doomed Wednesday a very small measure of consolation by scoring a quarter of an hour from the end after Swift had parried a point-blank drive from Luke, but Brook had the last word for City by completing a 4-1 win with his second goal in the last five minutes. As the final whistle blew, thousands streamed onto the pitch to acclaim the new champions, shouting and cheering. They packed in front of the main stand, and would not disperse until Bob Smith, the City chairman, and Sam Barkas, the captain, had appeared to acknowledge their greetings. What a poignant contrast it all was to the plight of Sheffield Wednesday, deposited back into last place by that afternoon's 3-0 home win for Leeds against Sunderland, and left contemplating life down in the Second Division. Sunderland, the deposed champions, were safely in the top half of the table, and preoccupied with their Cup final against Preston that was only a week away.

With Manchester United having completed their programme in defeat at West Bromwich, Wednesday still had the opportunity to hand over the wooden spoon to those relegation companions on goal-average, but even that glimmer of compensation was to be denied them. For the second season in succession the fixture list took them to Huddersfield for their final game, and again they lost it by an only goal. Huddersfield finished 15th with 39 points, and the clubs below them were:

Season 1936-37	P	W	D	L	F	A	Pts
16 West Bromwich	42	16	6	20	77	98	38
17 Everton	42	14	9	19	81	78	37
18 Liverpool	42	12	11	19	62	84	35
19 Leeds	42	15	4	23	60	80	34
20 Bolton	42	10	14	18	43	66	34
21 Manchester U	42	10	12	20	55	78	32
22 Sheffield Wed	42	9	12	21	53	69	30

If Wednesday thought the going might be at least a little easier in the Second Division, they were quickly disillusioned. They got off to a losing start at Chesterfield and went through their first eight games with only one victory – and that gained by only the odd goal of three against Fulham in their opening home match. Their unbeaten record at Hillsborough went by the board at its third defence, Tottenham scoring three times without reply in midweek, and two days later Aston Villa were also successful visitors. Following a draw at Bradford, West Ham were beaten by a lone goal from Rimmer, but the next five games resulted in four defeats and a draw – and, with Wednesday next to the bottom of the table, that was where Billy Walker's hold on the managership was broken.

The heaviest of those four defeats came at the beginning and end of that final bleak spell of his tenure. Wednesday lost 2-5 at Southampton, 1-4 at Barnsley. In between, they were beaten by an only goal by both Sheffield United and Manchester United, then equally shared six goals at home to Stockport County. The meeting of the two Sheffield clubs at Hillsborough brought them into opposition in the Second Division for the first time since they had both entered the League in 1892. The Blades, who also won the return game at Bramall Lane, went on to miss promotion by the whisker of goal-average, edged into third place as they and runners-up Manchester United finished four points behind champions Aston Villa. Wednesday showed little improvement that season after Walker's departure, and, although they were sixth from the foot of the final table, it took victories in their last two matches to leave them just two points above the relegation zone.

The pair that went down were Barnsley (most unluckily, as we shall be coming to in the next chapter) and Stockport, clubs from which Wednesday that season prised only the point gained from their home draw with the County. The defeat at Oakwell was Wednesday's eighth in 14 games, depositing them to next to the bottom of the table with only eight points, and this provoked some of their supporters into angry scenes at the annual meeting. One of them, a shareholder, was involved in an incident with Walker, and whether or not that had any influence on the manager's exit, the fact remains that he offered his resignation before the weekend was over, and chairman W G Turner accepted it. Walker claimed that the chairman was interfering in his control of team matters, but some of his dealings in the transfer market had not been popular. Dewar's return to Scotland had disappointed a great many, and another experienced player, Grosvenor, latterly used at wing-half, had been sold to Bolton Wanderers.

From early November in 1937, Wednesday were without an appointed manager until New Year's Day in 1938, when Jimmy McMullan took over on obtaining his release from Notts County. His reign began with a home win in the return match with Chesterfield, again with just one goal deciding the issue, and his signings of Douglas Hunt, from Barnsley, and Charlie Napier, from Derby County, helped Wednesday to average a point a game for the rest of the season.

Walker left describing his stay in Sheffield as 'bitter-sweet', though it was the sweetness that came first. Of the players who had taken part in his first game as Wednesday's manager, only two were in the side that lost in his last at Barnsley on 6 November 1937 – Millership and Rimmer. In those first 14 games of the 1937-38 season he had called upon 25 players in his frequent permutations. The only ever-present among them was Derek Goodfellow, who up to the war vied with Roy Smith for the goal-keeping position vacated by Jack Brown, but Albert Ashley missed just the opening match. Soon after the war Goodfellow moved to Middles-brough, Smith to Notts County.

Football had been such a paramount part of Billy Walker's life that it was impossible for him to keep out of it for long. That was why he did not need much persuading when he received an invitation to return, even though it came from outside the Football League. In January 1938 he became manager of Chelmsford City, the Essex club who were moving up from amateur status to turn semi-professional. A year later, he guided them to the third round of the FA Cup, in which they gained a 4-1 home win against Second Division Southampton. They were heavily beaten at Birmingham in the next round, but he had done enough to earn the League comeback he sought in resigning from the Chelmsford post soon afterwards, in February 1939.

Nottingham Forest appointed him as their manager the next month, and he was to remain with them until shortly before his death nearly 25 years later. After surviving a shaky start that included another relegation, he rose to the pinnacle of his managerial career in taking them to seasons that were the most successful in their history until the League championship and European Cup gained under Brian Clough.

CHAPTER NINE

Comeback at Nottingham

There was a real air of *déjà-vu* about Billy Walker's return to League football with Nottingham Forest. As at Sheffield Wednesday, he was only the second team manager to be appointed by the club, and he found the team struggling at the wrong end of the table.

Forest's form that season, 1938-39, had been showing little improvement on their plight of the previous one, and was to have only a slightly less fraught outcome. In the spring of 1938 they had escaped relegation to the Third Division in what Arthur Turner, who reported on their matches for the *Nottingham Evening News*, described as 'circumstances dramatic enough to be without parallel in football history'. And Arthur, a widely experienced sports journalist I later got to know on joining him in the press box at the City Ground, was not exaggerating. Forest stayed up by the two-thousandth part of a goal.

Through an outlandish coincidence of the fixture list, Forest had been called upon to play their final match against Barnsley, the very club whose fate was bound up with theirs. The result of that game was to decide which one of them would go down with Stockport County, who were already doomed in last place. And Barnsley had home advantage. Forest travelled to Oakwell level on points with the Yorkshire club, but above them on goal-average. They therefore required just one point from a draw to save themselves at Barnsley's expense – and it was the manner in which it was achieved that packed all the drama into the pulsating finale.

Of the game's four goals, only the first one was a genuinely commendable effort. It went to Forest, scored in style, after some smart approach work with Maynell Burgin, by Dave ('Boy') Martin, an Irish international centre-forward who acquired his nickname through having served as a boy drummer with the Royal Ulster Rifles. Martin had been finding goals harder to come by since breaking Forest's individual record for one season with 29 in the League (and two more in the Cup) straight after being signed from Wolves in the summer of 1936, but he was also to grab the controversial late equaliser that alone justified the fee paid for him, then the club's highest at near five figures.

A temperamental side to his character often had Martin in trouble with referees, but that was as nothing compared with what happened to Enoch West, the player from whom he took the Forest scoring record for one season that had been set at 26 goals as far back as 1907-08. West helped Manchester United to their second League title in four years after leaving Nottingham, but in 1915 he was among the players found guilty of 'fixing' a match with Liverpool. His suspension was the longest in League history, not lifted until November 1945. By that time he was in his early 60s.

The lead Martin gained in the vital match at Barnsley was wiped out by a 30-yard drive from Asquith, the ball bouncing over Forest's goalkeeper, Percy Ashton, as he dived. From looking disorganised, Barnsley were encouraged to take a grip that became even more ominous for Forest when Ashton, normally consistent but prone to the occasional mistake, made another, and more glaring, error of judgment. He did well to hold a fierce shot, only to turn back into goal and bounce the ball down over the line. What a gift for Barnsley, and what a demoralising blow for Forest. The forward who delivered that shot was Bert Barlow, later of Wolves, but transferred by them to Portsmouth in time for him to be one of the scorers in the shock defeat of Wolves in the last pre-war FA Cup final of 1939.

With Barnsley right on top after so fortunately getting in front, the Nottingham cause indeed appeared lost when, twenty minutes from time, half-back Bob Davies was injured and became little more than a 'passenger' on the wing before having to leave the field. Urged on by Tommy Graham, a centre-half of England standard, Forest's ten men battled back in an attempt to regain the initiative, but they would have fallen further behind if Ashton had not partially atoned by pulling off a brilliant save. That left Forest still in with the flickering chance that was so sensationally taken when play was into its last five minutes. This was Arthur Turner's description in his on-the-spot account:

'Trim [Reg Trim, the Forest right-back from Arsenal] planked the ball into Binns' arms, and Martin, no bustler of goalkeepers in the ordinary way, let loose a full-blooded charge that had Binns rocking and turning ... turning into goal with the ball in his hands. It was over the line all right, and, while Forest's players danced for joy, Barnsley's frantically appealed. The referee went over to a linesman and adhered to his original decision. A goal it was, the goal that saved Forest from relegation.'

Poor Clifford Binns. Turner also reported that 'the goalkeeper walked yards down the pitch, crying bitterly with his face in his hands.'

Even then there was still time for Barnsley to go desperately close to a winning goal that would have saved them from a return to the Third Division North (from which they would escape in the last full pre-war season). Ashton was left helpless by a shot from Logan, but Barnsley's last hopes were dashed as the ball rebounded from the crossbar and was safely cleared. Down they went by 0.002 of a goal. These were the final positions in the Second Division basement:

Season 1937-38	P	W	D	L	F	A	Pts
16 Blackburn	42	14	10	18	71	80	38
17 Sheffield Wed	42	14	10	18	49	56	38
18 Swansea	42	13	12	17	45	73	38
19 Newcastle	42	14	8	20	51	58	36
20 Nott'm For	42	14	8	20	47	60	36
21 Barnsley	42	11	14	17	50	64	36
22 Stockport	42	11	9	22	43	70	31

Newcastle, who had twice finished sixth, and once fourth, in the previous seasons since being relegated in 1934, were sucked into the mire by losing seven, and winning only one, of their last nine matches. In ending with a 1-4 defeat at Luton, they would have been just one-tenth of a goal away from tumbling into the Third Division for the first time if Forest had not gone even closer to going down with Stockport.

Forest's fortunes continued to be dismal in 1938-39. They began with three defeats, and although they went through the next five games unbeaten, winning three, that was to be their most successful spell of the season. They had lost a key player with the retirement of Billy McKinlay, and his replacement, Wally Alsford, a wing-half from Tottenham, who had been capped by England against Scotland, had suffered an injury at Bradford that had ended his career. Billy McKinlay, a strong tackler ever ready to join in the attack, played more than 350 League and Cup games in almost ten years with Forest. After the war his nephew Bobby, whom he recommended in his subsequent role as the club's scout in Scotland, raised Forest's record for League appearances to 614 (and 685 in all) on being converted from a right-winger into a commanding centre-half most unlucky never to be called upon by his country.

Besides no longer having Billy McKinlay available, Forest were further handicapped in 1938-39 by the injuries that several times put Tommy Graham on the sidelines. His absence was most keenly felt when seven goals were conceded at Chesterfield. But for making fewer appearances that season (26) than in all but one of his nine others as a first choice in peacetime, Graham would surely have exceeded 400 in League and Cup instead of falling just ten short. The last League game he played did not count because it was the first one of the 1939-40 season that had to be abandoned when war was declared. He played a few more times during the war, then became trainer, a post he held from 1944 until 1961, when he was forced to give up by ill health. Even then his long connection with the club was not severed. He was adviser to the youth teams and did some scouting.

With Forest failing to rise from the depths of the Second Division, they parted company with team manager Harold ('Harry') Wightman on 11 March 1939, a day on which a home draw with Fulham took them to 21 points from 32 games. They had gained only six wins to set against 17 defeats. Ten days later Billy Walker was named as the successor.

Wightman, who was born in Nottinghamshire at Sutton-in-Ashfield, had turned out more than 100 times for Forest as a guest player during the First World War after being signed by Chesterfield at the age of 17 in the 1913 close season. He was in the Forest team that won the Victory Shield in May 1919 by defeating Everton 1-0 at Goodison Park after a scoreless draw at the City Ground in which the Merseysiders missed a penalty, and there was much disappointment in Nottingham when, his registration with Chesterfield having lapsed, Derby nipped in to sign him a month later. For the Rams he played nearly 200 League and Cup games. He was an ever-present with them in the first post-war season of 1919-20, and after being a reliable centre-half he demonstrated his versatility at full-back when they won promotion back to the First Division in 1925-26. Although then losing his place to Tommy Cooper, a coming England defender and captain, he found another niche as assistant to manager George Jobey before rejoining Chesterfield in May 1929.

A year later, Wightman moved to newly relegated Notts County as coach and assistant to their manager, Horace Henshall, helping them to immediate promotion eight points clear at the top of the Third Division South. After just that one season at Meadow Lane he was appointed manager of Luton Town, for whom he formed the basis of the side that was to win the Third South title in 1937 before resigning because of differences with his directors. The biggest legacy he left behind for the Hatters was Joe Payne, the half-back signing who became a prolific-scoring forward capped by England. In October 1935, Wightman returned to Derby as chief scout, but three months later left again to manage Mansfield Town. Once more he soon had another change of scene. Mansfield offered him an increase in pay and a three-year contract when he told them he did not want to stay on beyond the end of that season, but he had his eyes on going back to another of his former clubs and in July 1936 he duly became the first team manager to be appointed by Nottingham Forest.

His seven predecessors had been secretary-managers, and the man from whom he took over the reins carried on with his administrative duties as secretary alone. This was Noel Watson, who in appearance always reminded me of Sidney Toler, one of the cinema's versions of the fictional Chinese detective Charlie Chan. Watson, a rather remote figure in the eyes of a very green young sports journalist such as myself, continued in his secretarial post in alliance with Billy Walker throughout the seasons of the 1950s in which I reported on Forest's home matches for the *Derby Evening Telegraph*.

Despite the experience he had acquired on the management side, Wightman was unable to make a success of the job after which he had hankered. Forest ended his first season as their manager, 1936-37, eighteenth in the Second Division, one place better of than where they had finished the previous campaign, but with one point fewer. Their total of 34 points put them four ahead of Bradford City, who went down with wooden spoonists Doncaster Rovers. Then came the close squeak to the detriment of Barnsley. And when Wightman left, Forest were in free fall towards another last-day escape against other opponents who were relegated instead of themselves. Forest had picked up a mere six points in winning only one of their last dozen matches. In successive games they had let in four goals to Tottenham and five to Coventry, and West Ham had also gone nap against them

On the first day Billy Walker was in charge, 18 March 1939, Forest were away to Blackburn Rovers, the division's champions-to-be, so it was not exactly surprising that the new broom could not sweep a path to victory. It was by only the odd goal of five that Forest failed, however, and Jack Surtees, reunited with his former manager, was one of their scorers. Surtees was also on target in each of the three wins gained in the next four games – an improvement interrupted by defeat away to Manchester City, who only two years before had been champions of the First Division. But there was only one more victory for Forest in the remaining five matches, and that, on the penultimate Saturday, was gained narrowly at home to Plymouth with the aid of an own-goal.

So it was that for their final match Forest again had to travel to meet 'rivals' for relegation. This time, though, there was a very important difference. Whereas they had required at least one point to secure safety at Barnsley's expense, they now knew that, because of their superior goal-average, they could afford to lose at Norwich as long as it was by fewer than four goals. Forest also held the advantage of having had the benefit of special training in the bracing air of Skegness while Norwich had been involved in a hard midweek game they had lost at Plymouth.

Against that, the absence of Tommy Graham, from whom Surtees took over the captaincy, was a big blow for Forest, especially as his usual deputy, Bob Davies, was also on the casualty list. Not until the morning of the match did it become clear that Graham had not fully recovered from the knee injury he suffered during the defeat of Argyle, and the switching of George Pritty, a former Aston Villa player, from right-half to take his place in the middle of the half-back line caused a hurried first-team recall for Billy Baxter from the Midland League side which met Scunthorpe that afternoon. Baxter, later of Notts County, had not played with the seniors for more than a year, but he did not let the side down in a typically wholehearted display. Another Forest change brought back Roy Brown, who had missed the match with Plymouth Argyle through injury, to the exclusion of Jim Dyson, but he was on the right wing instead of in his usual place on the left. That position was retained by Len Beaumont, who had also played at outside-right and inside-forward that season.

This was the full Forest line-up: Ashton; Trim, Munro; Baxter, Pritty, Clark; Brown, Fryer, McCall, Surtees, Beaumont. Only the goalkeeper, both full-backs and Baxter remained from the team fielded at Barnsley in that crucial game at the end of the previous season, but only Graham (indirectly replaced by Baxter) was missing from the side first put out by Billy Walker at Blackburn. Bob McCall, signed from his home club, Worksop Town, at the age of 19 in 1935, had followed Harold Crawshaw at centre-forward since 'Boy' Martin's move to Notts County, but he was to settle down at wing-half, then full-back, in becoming one of the few to play for the club before, during and after the 1939-45 War.

Having made his debut in a 4-1 win at Bradford on the first day of February in 1936, McCall did not play the last of his 162 League games for Forest until he was recalled in an emergency to lead the attack again in a 1-1 draw at Brentford on 22 September 1951. Since making what he had thought would be his last first-team appearance nearly 18 months before, he had become groundsman at the City Ground and also found time to captain and coach the 'A' team. He rejoined Worksop as player-manager in July 1952, and just over three years later, while also grounds-man at Firbeck Colliery, guided them to a third-round FA Cup-tie in which they lost by only one goal at Swindon.

Forest had to cope with early heavy pressure by Norwich in that rele-gation decider at Carrow Road on 6 May 1939. They had a big scare when Jack Munro, their former Hearts full-back, turned the ball against an upright, from where it went behind for a corner, in trying to cope with Harry Ware, a centre-forward who had helped Stoke City to the Second Division title six years earlier. Gradually, however, Forest came more into the game, and Jack Hall, in the home goal, had to make the best save of a scoreless first half when Jack Fryer, a forward from Hull City, packed plenty of power into his shot following a free-kick taken by ex-Bolton Wanderer Tom Clark. The leaping Hall just managed to turn the ball onto the underside of the bar, and he was mightily relieved to see Brown blast it over an open goal from the rebound.

After the interval it was Percy Ashton's turn to shine as Norwich dominated. He was powerless to prevent the goal Ware luckily scored in the 49th minute, but pulled off some brilliant saves to ensure there were no more. He continued at the top of his form even after being knocked out in making one of his spectacular interceptions to keep out a well-timed header from Coleman, the Norwich inside-right. Ware, who was to guest for Forest during the war, ran into the goalkeeper as he kicked clear, and although Ashton was soon able to carry on he looked decidedly shaky for a while. The goal came from a free-kick given away by Clark. Ware was standing in an offside position, but the ball was deflected to him off a defender and, unmarked, he was left with a simple task to place it in the net. Norwich had as many as eight men in attack at times, but their inability to increase that lead sent them down and kept Forest up. At the final whistle the band played *Auld Lang Syne*.

It was fitting that Forest owed their survival to their defence, for it was the fact that over the season they conceded nine goals fewer than Norwich which counted in their favour. They scored one fewer than the East Anglian club. This was how the bottom clubs finished:

Season 1938-39	P	W	D	L	F	A	Pts
17 Bradford PA	42	12	11	19	61	82	35
18 Southampton	42	13	9	20	56	82	35
19 Swansea	42	11	12	19	50	83	34
20 Nott'm For	42	10	11	21	49	82	31
21 Norwich	42	13	5	24	50	91	31
22 Tranmere	42	6	5	31	39	99	17

Forest's two away wins were gained in December, both by the odd goal – against Bradford (Park Avenue) and, a week after the 1-7 thrashing at Chesterfield, Sheffield United. This was the season in which the Blades, who had defeated Forest at the City Ground on the opening day, deprived their Wednesday neighbours of the second promotion place behind Blackburn. United edged a point ahead of Wednesday with a 6-1 trouncing of Tottenham at Bramall Lane in their final game, a week after the Owls had completed their programme by beating Spurs 1-0 at Hillsborough.

The enormity of the task facing Billy Walker in attempting to revitalise Forest was not confined to the depressing decline in form that had plummeted the club so desperately close to relegation in two successive seasons – having diced with the drop only a little less dangerously in the two before that. At the end of what was to be the last full pre-war season, 1938-39, Forest were faced with what Walker called 'a terrible financial burden up to the limit of the bank overdraft'. Not for the first time, members of the committee that then ran affairs instead of a board of directors had to dig deeply into their pockets to pay into the bank the money required to keep the club in existence. Walker disclosed that H R Cobbin, a member of the Forest committee since 1912 and its chairman since1920, handed over 'a very large cheque' without a word to his colleagues.

Despite being in such a parlous position from both the playing viewpoint and financially, Forest were able to give their fans some hope of better things to come by embarking upon their 1939-40 fixtures with a team augmented by two new signings. Billy Walker went back to Aston Villa to bring in wingers Colin Perry and Jack Maund, who were to share the 'phantom' experience of assisting Forest in the Second Division without featuring on the club's official list of League players. The three games in which they took part, Perry scoring two goals and Maund one, were expunged from the records when another world war intervened. Maund played quite a few times for Forest during the war (and for Notts County as a guest), but Perry made just one further appearance, in a home friendly with Grimsby. He was killed at Tobruk in November 1942 while serving in North Africa as a driver with the RASC.

Four other Forest players lost their lives during the war. Grenville Roberts, an inside-forward who had made half-a-dozen League appearances, died at Dunkirk in June 1940. He was a private in the West Yorkshire Regiment. The three others to perish were young reserves, Alf Moult, Joe Crofts and Frank Johnson. In peacetime, there was another tragic loss when Edwin Lindley, a 20-year-old inside-forward, died without regaining consciousness from head injuries suffered in a motor-cycle crash. At the time, in 1951, Lindley, the son of a Lincolnshire farmer, was on loan to Scunthorpe United, from whom Billy Walker had signed him two years before for £1,500.

For their first League match of the 1939-40 season Forest had to go back to Barnsley, where their air of some renewed optimism was promptly dampened by a comprehensive 4-0 defeat by the club that a few months before had stormed out of the Third North eleven points ahead of runners-up Doncaster Rovers. Spirits were revived by home wins against Newcastle United, in midweek, and the past season's Third South champions, Newport County, but by then war was inevitable. Germany invaded Poland the day before the second Saturday of the season, and on the Sunday morning Prime Minister Neville Chamberlain made his historic broadcast, announcing that Britain would keep its promise to the Poles by declaring war at the fateful hour of 11 o'clock. League football accordingly went into a void that was to last for seven years.

The abandoned Division Two table was headed by Luton and Birmingham, who both had five points from their three games. Forest were left in eighth place – the last, on goal-average, of six clubs on four points. They had scored five goals, as many as they had conceded.

The outbreak of war rang down the curtain on the League career Percy Ashton had begun as a 20-year-old newcomer in a home match with Stoke in September 1930. Having been signed from West Melton Excelsior as cover for Arthur Dexter after the transfer of Len Langford to Manchester City, he had to wait until halfway through the 1933-34 season for a regular place, but then remained first choice right up to the war. To his 185 League and Cup appearances he added the three games of the abandoned 1939-40 Second Division season, then eleven more in friendlies and the first wartime league. He last guarded Forest's first-team goal against Sheffield Wednesday at Hillsborough on 6 April 1940. Soon afterwards he joined Grantham Town, and it was not until the November of 1949, when he was in his 40th year, that he last played for them in the Reserves. From there he turned to running a Nottingham public house.

CHAPTER TEN

Forest in the War Years

All professional sport came to a halt with the outbreak of war on 3 September 1939. After first telling their clubs to keep players on stand-by, the Football League ordered that they all be released and paid up to the sixth day of the month.

The Government appreciated, however, that sport could have a beneficial effect on public morale, so within a few days they lifted the ban they had imposed on sporting activities outside highly populated areas. On 16 September the first friendly football matches to which spectators could be admitted were allowed, subject to local police sanction, except in areas barred under the defence regulations. To begin with, games could be played only between clubs no more than 50 miles apart but this restriction was soon widened, with the proviso that visiting teams must complete their return journeys within the day.

A limit still remained on the size of crowds, which were to be no more than half the capacity of the stadiums. During the 'phoney war', when there were none of the anticipated air raids, curbs on attendances in that first wartime season were also imposed by the icy grip of one of the worst winters, and by shift work in factories on Saturday afternoons. At the end of the season, extended to early June, there was a crowd of less than half Wembley's capacity – officially given as 42,399 – for the War Cup final in which West Ham defeated Blackburn Rovers, but two seasons later, by which time restrictions had been relaxed, gates at some matches compared favourably with many of the inter-war years. From the revenue raised throughout the war, football made the substantial contribution of nearly £120,000 to various good causes, notably the Red Cross and St John.

Several clubs did not immediately start up again after the short hiatus following the outbreak of war, and Nottingham Forest were very nearly among them. Only after what Billy Walker called 'a crisis meeting' did they decide to carry on. As he put it: 'Although things looked very black, the committee decided that they owed it to the boys who were going to war, and as a means of keeping up the morale of the people.'

Forest played five friendlies, beating Lincoln City and Notts County but losing at Peterborough and at home to Grimsby Town and Sheffield Wednesday, before taking part in one of the eight regional league competitions that were organised by a war emergency committee jointly formed by the FA and Football League. Six goals were scored without reply from Lincoln at Sincil Bank, but the first wartime meeting of the two Nottingham clubs was won by only the odd goal of three at the City Ground, a Coventry City guest named Ellis Lager scoring Forest's decider. It attracted a crowd of only 4,000. Seven members of the Notts team were guest players from Derby County, who did not arrange any fixtures until Christmas Day 1941, after a crowd of fewer than 2,000 turned up for their first friendly match, at home to Leeds, following the abandonment of the League programme.

'Once things began to be organised nationally,' wrote Walker in his recollections of the war years, 'we were involved in football for good or ill, in duty bound to accept all the commitments consequent upon playing in a league competition. It does not sound much, but the League, at their annual meeting with the Football Association, fixed a match fee of 30 shillings, and in the circumstances that was in itself a problem as gates were not big enough to cover expenses. Thus it was that all the members of the Forest committee had to dig into their pockets again and find the money to keep going. I can assure you this happened on many occasions in the first couple of seasons.'

From 1943-44 players received £2 a match, and that payment was increased for 1945-46 after there had been a very real threat of a players' strike. The main bone of contention arose from the Football League's original proposal that there should be a maximum of £8 a match for players returning to their clubs after demobilisation, and £4 for professionals who were either still in the Services or on munitions or other work connected with the war (which was still going on in the Far East at the start of that transitional season). It was a differential that had to be abandoned to avert a strike, just as the pre-war idea of paying star players £20 a match, and others £10 although on the same side, had also been turned down because, as Sammy Crooks, then chairman of the Players' Union, explained, 'the players themselves did not want it.' The view that every man in any side should be paid the same rate makes very strange reading these days, considering the huge and varied extent to which wages have soared since the abolition of the maximum.

A strike was averted in November 1945 when the Football League capitulated three weeks after sweeping aside all claims for wage improvements. The maximum was increased immediately from £8 to £9 a week, pre-war bonuses of £1 for a draw and £2 for a win were restored, and the match payment for guest players and Servicemen was raised from £4 to £5. On the resumption of League football in 1946, when another strike was averted, the maximum wage was agreed 'under protest' by the

Players' Union at £10 a week in the winter and £7 10s in the close season, compared with the pre-war figures of £8 and £6. Bonuses were unchanged, but benefits were increased from £650 to £750 maximum. Referees and linesmen also had a pay rise after the war, to four guineas and two guineas per match, respectively.

The wartime regional competitions, interspersed with a few more friendlies and a cup contest in which Forest lost to Fulham after knocking out Charlton and Southend, got under way on 21 October in 1939. Forest began their East Midlands Section with a 0-3 defeat by Sheffield United at Bramall Lane, but soon afterwards they won 6-2 against Mansfield Town, another guest, former Wednesdayite George Drury, doing the hat-trick. Six goals were also scored against Notts County (two more for Drury), but that was the last of only five wins Forest gained in their twenty league matches. They finished tenth of the eleven clubs in the group, and below them, on goal-average, were their neighbours from the other side of the River Trent, who at least had the pleasure of beating them, if by only 4-3, at Meadow Lane. Drury netted another brace in that game, and the 26 goals he altogether scored for Forest that season also included a hat-trick against Rotherham United. Forest and Notts both totalled 14 points in a table headed with 30 by Chesterfield, to whom Forest again lost heavily, by 1-6, at Saltergate.

With another of Billy Walker's former players, Ronnie Starling, and two of those who had been Villa team-mates, Billy Kirton and Eric Houghton, also among the guests, Forest altogether called upon almost 50 players during that first wartime season. And one of the others was a certain W H Walker. At the age of 42, manager Billy Walker first returned to playing action with Forest, six years after his last League game, at outside-left in a 4-1 friendly win back at Chelmsford on 4 November 1939. He did not score that day (Drury claimed another couple), but a fortnight afterwards, again on the left wing, he got one of the goals in a 9-3 away victory over Bristol City. And in his third friendly match near Christmas he scored another, from centre-forward, as visitors Stockport County were beaten 6-0.

Drury was again on the mark in both those big wins, but the main scoring honours were shared by Tom Hinchcliffe and Len Beaumont. Hinchcliffe did the hat-trick in Bristol, Beaumont against Stockport. Hinchcliffe, a former Grimsby and Huddersfield forward who had then not long left Derby County for Blackpool, was one of Forest's own players by the time League football resumed in 1946. He played in their first Second Division game after the war, but, as one consequence of defeat, was not called upon at that level again.

The 1939-40 season stretched into the first week of June because of bad weather, and on its last day Billy Walker was back at inside-left as Forest wound up their East Midlands programme with a 3-4 defeat away to Grimsby Town. It would be fitting to say that Walker finished things off with another goal, as one source states that he did, but that is not confirmed by Forest's official statistical record compiled by Ken Smales. A former secretary of the club, Smales' chief claim to sporting fame is as the cricketer who took all ten wickets for Yorkshire with his off-spinners in a Gloucestershire innings at Stroud in 1957.

Billy Walker also played for Forest in the first two full wartime seasons. In 1940-41 he kept goal in a home friendly with an RAF XI and a Midlands Cup-tie at Lincoln, and was at outside-left in a South Regional League match at Stoke. In 1941-42, he again filled what had been his emergency position of goalkeeper in a League Cup qualifier at Chesterfield.

Forest beat the airmen 4-1, and although they lost 1-2 away to Lincoln, they had defeated them by 4-2 at home the previous Saturday and therefore progressed on aggregate. Out they went, however, in the next round, which was decided over just the one match. The knock-out blow was decisively delivered, 6-2, by Leicester City, who later also dispatched Forest from the War League Cup. Three of Leicester's six goals came in as many minutes, two of them penalties by full-back Bert Howe. The game at Stoke resulted in another comprehensive defeat. Forest could find no response to the four goals they conceded and finished 28th out of 34 in a league table decided on goal-average alone. They won only seven of their 25 matches and lost 15, with goals figures of 50-77 that gave them an average of 0.649. The top team, Crystal Palace, averaged 1.954.

Chesterfield was again an unhappy hunting ground for Forest in the cup qualifier of 17 January 1942 in which Billy Walker finally bowed out as a player, but this time the Derbyshire club were limited to just the one goal. In the knock-out stages Forest repeated their aggregate victory against Lincoln, after an eventful away leg they lost by the odd goal of eleven, but Grimsby then swept them out with wins by 3-1 and 5-1. Exceptional though eleven goals in one match were, even in the unusual conditions of wartime when teams were weakened and much changed, there was another game during those years which Forest won 7-6 at Walsall. Four of their goals that April afternoon in 1941 were scored by another of their Aston Villa guests. Frank Broome filled four of the five forward positions of the contemporary 2-3-5 formation in winning seven England caps at the end of the 1930s (and an emergency goalkeeper while later with Derby). Double-figure scores by other teams alone were not uncommon – most notably a 15-2 win by Arsenal against Clapton Orient in which Leslie Compton himself scored ten times.

In May 1941, shortly after the City Ground had staged an international match in which Don Welsh, of Charlton Athletic, scored all England's goals in a 4-1 defeat of Wales, Forest had to spend all of £75 for the repair of bomb damage to their pitch. Only a short distance away, Notts County were much harder hit the following month. A bomb destroyed the north wing of their main stand, as well as leaving a crater on the pitch to be filled in. They had to sit out the 1941-42 season, the one in which Forest fielded their record number of no fewer than 94 players in fulfilling 34 fixtures.

Billy Walker was not in favour of over-doing the guest system that was an inevitable outcome of wartime's selection problems, but Forest supporters wanted to see some of the leading players of other clubs in their team at the City Ground, so he duly obliged – up to Christmas in particular. 'As I am always willing to try anything once,' he said, 'I followed the trend and introduced guests into the Forest teams. Yet, as I feared, it was not a success. Forest's record in that season showed very plainly that a team of one's own, performing consistently together, is a far better proposition than one of imported stars. It is impossible to get a real blend. A collection of individual stars may look brilliant on paper, but on the field a very different story is told.'

For a League South game Forest lost in September, despite scoring three goals at Northampton, goalkeeper Riley and outside-left Jack Ward were the only players Walker could call his own in this team: Riley; Challinor, Kirton (both Stoke City); Iverson (Aston Villa), Mason (Coventry City), Jones (Arsenal); Broome (Aston Villa), Smith (Fulham), Hullett (Manchester United), Meek (Bradford), Ward.

Bill Hullett, who guested for several other clubs while in the RAF, was a prolific scorer for Merthyr Tydfil after leaving Manchester United in 1945, so much so that their fans raised quite an outcry when he was transferred to Cardiff City early in 1948. Late that year he was signed by Forest, having found it a tough job to follow Welsh international Stan Richards at Ninian Park, but he was soon on the move again – back to Merthyr as player-manager. Under his leadership, they equalled a 52-year-old record set by Southampton in winning the Southern League title for three successive seasons. Hullett's first game as a Forest player, in the Second Division at Tottenham, was into only its 18th minute when it had to be abandoned because of fog. His last was a Midland League match in which he scored three goals.

The number of Forest's guests was reduced after the turn of the year into 1942, but there was still a fair quantity. Walker said he 'went back to my own ideas and persevered with my own players' during the second half of the season, but it was slightly stretching a point for him to claim that his team at times contained as few as two guest players during that period. For instance, the side that lost to Sheffield Wednesday when he returned to Hillsborough on the final day did largely comprise Foresters, but it also borrowed Bill Corkhill from Notts County and had a left-wing pairing of Ronnie Starling, the forward Walker had transferred to Aston Villa after resurrecting his career at Sheffield, and Colin Lyman, then of Spurs but signed by Walker after the war from Port Vale.

For several matches after Christmas two of Derby County's internationals, Sammy Crooks and 'Dally' Duncan, were on the wings. Other capped players called on that season included full-backs Andy Beattie (Preston), who was to be Walker's first successor as Forest's manager, and George Cummings (Aston Villa), and centre-forwards Freddie Steele (Stoke) and Jack Bowers (Leicester, ex-Derby). George Hardwick, the Middlesbrough full-back who was England's captain in the early post-war years, also appeared.

Thirteen of Forest's games in 1941-42 were played up to Christmas in the first part of the League South, in which they finished twelfth, next to last, with only two wins against ten defeats. After Christmas, most of their matches were in the League Cup's qualifying and knock-out stages, which counted in the second half of the League South, but Forest did not rate a place in that table because they were two games short of the required 18. They won only six of the 29 games they played overall in the league, losing 21. With the two other matches drawn, they garnered just 14 points.

The five other fixtures Forest fulfilled that season were friendlies, of which they won three and lost two. They should have played 14 games in the first half of the league, but lost their way to Norwich. On arrival at Peterborough, where they had to change trains, they were misdirected onto a train going North, to Louth in Lincolnshire, instead of one travelling East to Norwich. By the time they reached Louth they had no way of getting to Norwich in time, so some 3,000 of the City's fans had to be satisfied with a seven-a-side exhibition match in which Harry Goslin, the Bolton Wanderers captain, took part. Just over two years later, in December 1943, Goslin was killed while serving with the 53rd Field Regiment, Royal Artillery, in the Apennine Mountains. His unit was under a fierce German attack when a shell exploded in a tree directly above his head.

By comparison with such a tragedy, Forest's misfortune at Peterborough was of little consequence, but it was not the first time they had gone astray in that town during the war. It was there that they played their first match, a friendly, following the abandonment of the Football League season – and they faded to a 3-4 defeat after being three goals up at half-time. On that occasion, however, the journey had some profit, quite apart from the very modest financial one of £40 9s 7d, in the currency of the time, which represented the 50 per cent of the gate Forest had been guaranteed (the players were each paid 12s 6d – a big drop from the £8 a week maximum of peacetime). As Billy Walker later explained: 'It was in this game that I was impressed by the young inside-left of 17 years who was on a month's trial with Peterborough. In fact, I was so impressed that I determined to keep in touch with him before the war swallowed him up. His name was Tom Johnston.'

Thomas Deans Johnston was duly signed by Walker as an amateur in 1942, and he turned professional after being Forest's joint second highest scorer with a dozen goals, chiefly as a left-winger, in the 1943-44 season. Johnston, who hailed from Chirnside, a village near Duns in the Borders, topped the half-century for goals in just over 100 games for Forest before League football was resumed. He also featured in one of the oddities of the guest system. In 1945 he played for Derby against a Leicester City side that included his Forest clubmate Billy Baxter, and less than two months later, again at the Baseball Ground, he was on Leicester's left wing when Baxter was at left-half for the Rams. In the transitional League South season of 1945-46, Johnston was Forest's leading scorer with 28 goals in 44 appearances, and he demonstrated his versatility not only at outside-right and inside-left but also as goalkeeper in a friendly match with Notts County that Forest won 3-2.

It was to Notts County that Johnston, once a reserve for Scotland, was transferred a few days before the 1948-49 season, after adding two dozen goals to his Forest tally in 64 Second Division games. With the Magpies he scored 92 more in 285 League and Cup matches, helping them to promotion as Third South champions in 1949-50 as the regular outside-left in a high-scoring attack led by Tommy Lawton. After coaching in Finland and at Birmingham City, Johnston entered management with Rotherham United, taking the Millers to the verge of the First Division in 1954-55 and to the first League Cup final of 1961 (they lost to Aston Villa only after extra-time over two legs).

Johnston also managed Grimsby Town and, in three spells, Huddersfield Town, but he enjoyed most of his other success in that role with York City, transforming them from re-election candidates of 1969 into promotion winners from the Fourth Division in 1971, and three years later guiding them up to the Second Division for the first time in their history. That was quite some achievement on a shoestring budget, especially considering that early in 1973 some of his players revolted against his authority, preparing a list of grievances in the belief that their case was strong enough to force his resignation or dismissal. It was not, but in 1975, within 24 hours of York's producing one of the shocks of the FA Cup's third round by holding Arsenal to a draw at Highbury, Johnston sprang another big surprise by announcing that he would return to Huddersfield as general manager after the replay at Bootham Crescent (which the Gunners won 3-1).

The quietly spoken, pipe-smoking Johnston had traits in management that were the hallmark of Billy Walker's most fruitful years in that role. He was a shrewd strategist, a stickler of discipline, a good motivator, and an excellent judge of players' ability and character. The strong line he took, however, led to his first departure from Huddersfield after the upheaval of eight players being transfer-listed, and in 1978 he left that club for a third time, complaining that 'the trouble with Huddersfield is that they expect you to win every match'.

Other talent Billy Walker unearthed during the war came from the Colts teams he started to run in September 1939. He recalled: 'It was at this early period that I decided I had a wonderful opportunity of finding young talent on our own doorstep. I am proud to claim that I was the first manager in wartime to embark on such a venture. During the war years I tried out more than one thousand young local players. A great number, of course, did not make the grade, and only about 50 made good.' For help in running the Colts while the war was on, Walker acknowledged his indebtedness to Jimmy Bagshaw, Walter Bee, Len Hillyard, George Boaden, Cyril Jackson and Harry Fletcher. Bagshaw, who was capped by England in 1919, during the last of his ten peacetime seasons as a Derby wing-half, assisted as trainer and scout, despite often being far from well. After the war, Bee switched from being in charge of the Colts to taking on the same duties with the reserve side.

More than a dozen of the wartime colts featured in Forest teams of the Football League's early post-war seasons. Three of them, full-back Geoff Thomas, wing-half Bill Morley and Ron ('Tot') Leverton, were prominent members of the team that won the Third South championship in 1950-51. Moreover, Thomas and Morley were also regulars in the side promoted from the Second Division in 1957. Thomas was on the small side for a full-back at 5ft 9in, but he was speedy and had a good sense of anticipation. Morley, formerly of Nottingham Boys, was spotted in action against Forest Colts for Grove Celtic, a local junior club with which his team-mates included Dicky Dulson, who played for Forest during the war, and Geoff Brunt, later of Notts County. Quick in recovery, Morley worked hard to improve the constructive aspect of his play. The firmer the going, the better he performed.

There were particularly high expectations of another colt, Jack Hutchinson, a forward turned defender from Heanor, in Derbyshire, who, like Derby-born Thomas and Leverton, who came from the Derbyshire mining village of Whitwell, was pinched from under Derby County's nose. The Rams, however, profited from Forest's release of a former Derby Boys player after he had been given trials as an inside-forward. Bert Mozley was spotted by a Derby scout in his first game as a full-back on his return to his local club, Shelton United, and it was in that position that this clean-kicking defender played for England as well as in more than 300 games for Derby. And he would have had a longer international career but for an injury that cost him a fourth cap. When fit again he found a fellow named Alf Ramsey too firmly installed to dislodge.

Billy Walker was convinced that Jack Hutchinson would become England's left-back, but that was one of the few occasions when he was not spot-on with an assessment. Hutchinson, a resourceful and intelligent footballer who had a natural aptitude for positional play, was among the Forest players coveted by other clubs during his most successful post-war season of 1947-48, but he not only failed to win an international cap but also had to contend with strong competition for a Forest first-team place from, initially, Bob McCall, then from Thomas and Bill Whare, a Channel Islander whose grip on the right-back position became so strong that Thomas had to switch over to the left to stay in the side himself. Hutchinson still managed, just, to exceed 250 League and Cup appearances, but it took him a dozen post-war seasons to do so.

Hutchison, along with Thomas, was first brought into Forest's team during the 1943-44 season, the second of three in succession in which the club competed in the League North. In each of those seasons the championship was again in two parts. As in South League of 1941-42, the first one, up to Christmas, was straightforward enough, but the other one afterwards included cup-ties in those peculiar circumstances of wartime. Forest's constantly changing team finished below or around halfway during the war seasons with only one exception – in the second half of 1944-45, when they were 16th in a mammoth table of 56 clubs.

The wartime North Cup, with a qualifying competition preceding the knock-out stages, did precious little to brighten Forest's fortunes. In

1942-43, when they squeezed through as last but one of the 32 qualifiers, they defeated Leicester City on aggregate over two legs before going out to Sheffield Wednesday. In both the next two seasons they failed to qualify, but were most unlucky in 1944-45 when they headed the list of those ineligible and were eliminated only on goal-average. The home leg of the tie with Wednesday, which Forest won by a lone goal, produced the City Ground's wartime record receipts of £974 from an attendance of 13,404. Wednesday coasted through the return game 5-1, and Billy Walker's former club went on to reach the final, in which they drew with Blackpool at Bloomfield Road but lost to them by the odd goal of three at home. The Seasiders then upheld the honour of the North by beating Arsenal, winners of the Southern War Cup, in a challenge match at Stamford Bridge.

The Midland Cup was the trophy Forest went closest to collecting during the war. After equally sharing four goals in the first leg of the final against West Bromwich at the Hawthorns, they seemed certain to be the winners on aggregate when they went into a 3-2 lead late in extra time in the return game at the City Ground on 6 May 1944. So certain, in fact, that many of their supporters, thinking it was all over, invaded the pitch and began carrying the home players towards the main stand for the presentation by the Lord Mayor of Nottingham. But there were still two minutes left for play, and after police had restored order Albion equalised straight from the resumption. With the teams still deadlocked at the end of the extra period, the match continued until another goal was scored, and after a further nine minutes of this 'sudden death' that goal was put past Forest's guest goalkeeper from Chesterfield, Ray Middleton, to give the visitors an overall 6-5 victory.

Almost exactly a year later, on 9 May 1945, Forest met Derby County at the Baseball Ground in one of the matches clubs arranged to celebrate VE (Victory in Europe) Day. A crowd of just below 7,000 on that Wednesday afternoon saw the Rams struggle to force a 2-2 draw with a second goal from Peter Doherty after 'Tot' Leverton had equalised the Irishman's first one before half-time and then given Forest the lead fifteen minutes from the end.

For the transitional season of 1945-46 Forest were back in the League South, which was run on the peacetime pattern of 22 clubs, but with most of the fixtures between them arranged home and away on consecutive weekends. Forest were 15th with 37 points from 12 wins and 13 draws in a table Birmingham headed on goal-average from Aston Villa, both on 61 points. By then the guest system was being phased out, its end hastened by the need to get back to a normal footing with peace in sight,

and by the criticism of the poor standard of the 1945 South Cup Final
that Chelsea won with only three of their own players to Millwall's seven.
No guests, of course, were allowed in the FA Cup that was revived in
1945-46, and most clubs did not resort to as many as the six to which
they were now restricted for other games. Two of the few used by Forest
were Raich Carter and Frank O'Donnell, who had both scored when on
opposite sides in the 1937 Cup final (O'Donnell netted in every round his
club played that year). Carter captained Sunderland to victory against
Preston at Wembley, and, with Derby County, he was soon to be the only
player to gain a winner's medal either side of the Second World War.

Almost 50 games were played by Forest in 1945-46, with the inclusion
of friendlies. For one of them the team travelled into war-torn Germany
to meet a Rhine Army XI. The soldiers were 4-1 winners, but Forest were
to gain one of their most famous victories in the same Mungersdorfer
stadium 34 years later. On 25 April 1979, after being held to a draw at
home, they won the second leg of a European Cup semi-final against FC
Cologne and progressed by 4-3 on aggregate to a final in which they lifted the trophy for the first of two successive years.

CHAPTER ELEVEN

Giant-Killing in Manchester

Nottingham Forest resumed League life at Barnsley on the last day of August 1946 with a team that included just two players who had taken part in the corresponding, but invalid, opening Second Division game at Oakwell in September 1939. They were full-back Bob McCall and centre-half Bob Davies, who, with George Pritty and Bill Baxter, formed the select band to figure in Forest's senior side before, during and after the war.

McCall, although, like Davies, by then into his 30s, was to play more than 100 post-war League and Cup games for Forest, a good number of them as captain, before finally bowing out with his one-off recall as an emergency centre-forward in 1951. With the inclusion of some 200 wartime appearances, that took him to a total of nearly 400 overall. Davies, a wartime Welsh international, lasted for only half-a-dozen post-war games, for an aggregate beyond 150, but it was a wonder he was there are all. Both his legs had to be encased in plaster after an unduly heavy landing in the last of the many parachute jumps he made while in the RAF during the war. Despite having only a fleeting taste of post-war League football, Davies surpassed even the evergreen McCall for his length of service with Forest. It was spread across almost 40 years, as player, trainer, coach and physiotherapist. He was also the physio at Walsall, where a testimonial match was played for him the week before his death at the age of 64 in May 1978.

Billy Walker had to continue operating under severe financial con-straints when he got back to the serious business of running a profes-sional football club in peacetime, but he pulled off an astute deal in tak-ing Bert Brown, known as 'Sailor' because of his rolling gait, from Charlton Athletic. Astute in light of this gifted ball player's ability as both scorer and schemer, though there was one big snag. Walker got his man with the knowledge that he was unlikely to keep him for much more than a year. Brown had become unsettled at the Valley because he and his wife had been unable to regain possession of their house at Blackheath that had been requisitioned during the war, but the main reason for his eager-ness to leave was that he had fallen out with Jimmy Seed. On asking for a transfer, he had been told by Charlton's manager that he would not be allowed to join another London club or any of the others in the First Division – in particular Aston Villa, the player's preferred choice.

Consequently, Brown agreed to join Forest only when his contract with them included the stipulation that he could leave for Villa after that first post-war season if he then still wished to do so and Villa still wanted him. And he, and they, did do. Even so, the arrangement still benefited Forest from both the playing and financial viewpoints. Brown, though not far off his 31st birthday, missed only one match in finishing as the club's top scorer with sixteen goals, and the £10,000 fee Villa paid for him showed a nice little profit on the £6,750 Forest had handed over to Charlton. Welcome as the money was, however, Walker would rather have obtained a player in exchange, but his old club rejected the approaches he made for any one of three forwards, George Edwards, Jackie Martin and Dickie Dorsett.

The prematurely balding Brown, wartime captain of the RAF team, arrived at the City Ground in May 1946, shortly after scoring in England's defeat of Switzerland at Stamford Bridge in one of the two Victory internationals he added to the four appearances he had made for his country the year before. He was never on the losing side in those six matches, for which caps were not awarded, and he was seen at his best on the afternoon he netted one of England's six goals in their record win at Hampden Park in April 1945. One critic praised him for his 'delightful footcraft', another for being 'ever a forager and a worrier'. One of the last of nearly 200 games he played for Charlton (most of them during the war) was staged at Britain's other major stadium, Wembley, in the first post-war FA Cup Final that Derby won after extra time.

There were two other new signings in the Forest team that was again required to open the season at Barnsley in 1946 because the fixture lists were the same as those that had been arranged for the abandoned one of 1939-40. Both had been wartime guests – goalkeeper Reg Savage and centre-forward Frank O'Donnell. Savage, who had also guested for Derby County and Blackpool, came from Queen of the South, O'Donnell from Aston Villa. Savage had been in the Blackpool side that in 1943 had won both the Northern War Cup and the challenge match with Arsenal's Southern winners.

Barnsley repeated the win they had gained against Forest on the eve of war, and it looked like being just as emphatic when their Chilean centre-forward George Robledo, six years later scorer of the goal that retained the FA Cup for Newcastle, completed a hat-trick in the second half. That, however, was when Forest at last began to assert themselves, spurred into a two-goal revival by the industrious Brown. The Charlton cast-off cut the lead by rounding off a move he had started, and six minutes from the end he again did the spadework for the centre from

Johnston from which O'Donnell headed home. By then Forest had built up a good head of steam, but an equaliser would have been a real injustice to Barnsley.

Neither Savage nor O'Donnell saw out the season as Forest regulars. Savage, who moved to Accrington Stanley in August 1947, did not finally drop out of the side until early April that year, but O'Donnell played fewer than a dozen games before going back home to Scotland. Full-back Frank Shufflebotham was given even shorter shrift. He made only a couple of League appearances before being sold to Bradford City for £1,000. He had been on Forest's books for seven years, but because of the war, during which he guested for Dundee and Kilmarnock, Billy Walker had seen him play only five times (the three others in the Midland League).

Reg Savage, who was born at Eccles, joined his first League club, Leeds United, from Stalybridge Celtic as far back as February 1931, but in just over eight years before leaving for Queen of the South he had to face such strong competition – notably from internationals Albert McInroy and Jim Twomey – that his first-team opportunities fell short, if only a little, of three figures. Frank O'Donnell entered senior soccer with Glasgow Celtic, one of eight teams (three at junior level) in which he and his brother Hugh played together. Their eldest brother, Jim, was with East Fife before moving, as a reserve, to Tottenham, another of the clubs for which Frank guested during the war. Early in 1949 Frank returned to England as the first player-manager employed by Buxton, Derbyshire members of the Cheshire County League. After giving up playing, he guided them to the third round of the FA Cup as their part-time manager, but he had to resign through ill health in the summer of 1952 and died two months later at the early age of 40. I had the pleasure of meeting him at Silverlands on the day, 15 December 1951, when Buxton dramatically surged into a four-goal lead in the first sixteen minutes of their second-round tie with Aldershot and then just held out for a 4-3 victory. Further progress was denied them at Doncaster, though they did not let themselves down in going out to two first-half goals.

Nottingham Forest fielded another newcomer when they were also beaten in their second match of the first post-war Second Division season, conceding two goals without reply at home to Newcastle in mid-week. It was a League debut for Jack Edwards, a Salford-born product of Manchester junior football, but he had played once for the club during the war after being recommended to Billy Walker by a commanding officer he had impressed in a Royal Navy XI. The team into which Edwards was introduced against Newcastle included two other players who first turned out for Forest while the war was on. They were Eddie Barks at right-half, and George Mee on the right wing. Mee made only a few more appearances, but Barks stayed in for most of that season and also the next. Quite often Barks showed his versatility as leader of the attack. He had started out in that position with Mansfield Town, the club he rejoined in 1949, ten years after his move from there to Forest. He and Jack Hutchinson learned their football together at a Heanor school.

At the third attempt in the 1946-47 season Forest got off the mark in some style, thrashing Newport County 6-1 at the City Ground. And again there was a new face. Billy Walker's fine judgment of a player was soon vindicated by Freddie Scott, a diminutive former England Boys right-winger for whom he paid York City their then record fee of £4,500 in plucking him out of the Third Division's Northern Section.

Scott, a North-Easterner who had been with Bradford and Bolton before the war, and partnered 'Sailor' Brown as a Charlton guest during it, was then only a month from his 30th birthday, but not until 15 September 1956 did he make his 322nd and final appearance for Forest. He became the oldest to play in the club's first team when, only twenty days short of turning 40, he was recalled at inside-right at Rotherham. What was more, he scored the first of Forest's two goals. There was, however, no happy ending. Rotherham obtained three. Neither was there a happy ending to Scott's long stay with Forest. He had been their chief scout for a year, after being player-coach, when he was given a month's notice in July 1958 – a decision that it was believed Billy Walker opposed. Scott afterwards also scouted for Sunderland, Sheffield Wednesday, Southampton and Blackpool.

Two of the Forest manager's other dealings in the transfer market during the first season after the war provided only temporary solutions to his team problems. Colin Lyman, given little chance to settle through his constant changes of position in the forward line, left for Notts County less than a year after being signed from Port Vale. Harry Brigham, a full-back from Stoke City, moved on to York City, also after only the one sea-son as a first choice. Lyman, who had played for Southend and Northampton, as well as Tottenham, before the war, and then guested for Derby besides Forest during it, had one purple patch of five goals in two successive League games – three in a 5-2 win in the return game at Newport, two of six, with none conceded, at home to Southampton.

Eleven goals in the two meetings with Newport might be considered some going, but not so exceptional against a defence that conceded thir-teen in one afternoon on Tyneside – six of them to Len Shackleton, the self-styled Clown Prince of Soccer making his first appearance for Newcastle after being barracked out of Bradford. Newport altogether

leaked 133 goals that season in plunging straight back to the Third South
from which they had emerged as convincing champions in 1939.

Although Forest finished in a comfortable mid-table position, after
spending most of the campaign in the lower half, they did have something in common with the Welsh club's strugglers. Both had their pitch
flooded as normal football was welcomed back by freak weather that varied from storms to a heat wave, and then to fog and a Big Freeze culminating in the worst peacetime hold-ups since the League's formation in
1888 (during the war only two important games had been possible on 3
February 1940). Thirty-one of 58 English and Scottish matches could not
be played on 15 February 1947; 23 of 44 Football League games were off
on 22 February. And postponements rose into three figures over a six-
week period with the calling-off of 27 games out of 44 on the second
Saturday of March in 1947, leading to the extension of the season into
mid-June for the clearing of the back-log.

Many of Forest's records were damaged when flooding of the City
Ground towards the end of November compelled them to switch their
match with Manchester City to Meadow Lane as the home of their Notts
County neighbours remained playable despite being only just across the
other side of the River Trent. On the same day Newport were saved from
being flooded out at Somerton Park for the second time that season as
the local fire brigade pumped water off the pitch just in time for the
game with Millwall, another of the Second Division strugglers, to go
ahead. Newport were rare winners, but Forest, who the weekend before
had gained their first away victory with a Johnston goal at Bradford's Park
Avenue, lost by the same narrow margin to Manchester City, who were
heading for promotion as champions.

Fog foiled Forest a few weeks later when their game at Fulham had to
be abandoned midway through the second half when they were a goal up.
Defeat at Newcastle in front of 57,000, the biggest crowd of New Year's
Day, left Forest only four points above the relegation zone, but the triumph at Newport then heralded their most successful spell of an often-
disappointing season.

Larry Platts, a goalkeeper who had been among Billy Walker's wartime
colts, and who was to be one of Frank O'Donnell's successors as
Buxton's manager, made a rare League appearance in Savage's absence as
Forest swept to the 6-0 home win over Southampton that was their
biggest in the League since a 9-2 demolition of Port Vale in November
1935. Southampton were newly deprived of sharpshooter Doug
McGibbon, who the same January afternoon of 1947 repaid some of the
£8,000 Fulham had forked out for him by doing the hat-trick against

Plymouth. McGibbon had scored twice in the Saints' 5-2 defeat of Forest at The Dell the previous September, when George Ephgrave, their 6ft 4in goalkeeper, had crowned a superb display by saving a Brown penalty in the last minute. Brown was usually reliable from the spot, but only a few weeks later, after converting one penalty in a drawn home match with West Bromwich, he failed to score from a second – no doubt distracted by the pitch invasion by Albion fans that its award provoked.

A week after hitting Southampton for six in their revenge win at the City Ground, Forest pulled off an FA Cup giant-killing act in front of not far short of 60,000 at Maine Road, where the victims, Manchester United, were temporary tenants of their City neighbours because of the bomb damage done at Old Trafford during the war. Forest earned that demanding visit to the third-placed team in the First Division by clinging onto a first-half lead to knock out Third Division Lincoln City at Sincil Bank. The only goal of that third-round tie was scored by Colin Rawson, who failed to establish himself with Forest but went on to help Rotherham United out of the Third North before being with Sheffield United and Millwall. Forest had another Rawson around that time who was a dependable reserve centre-half after being another of the club's wartime colts. Ken Rawson served in India during the war with his fellow colt Frank Knight, who made some appearances in the team that played out there under the captaincy of Tommy Walker, the Hearts and Scotland forward Chelsea signed after the war.

Knight, Forest's regular left-half for most of the first post-war season, became assistant trainer at the City Ground after captaining the reserves to the Midland League title. He was on the club's staff for 33 years in all before, at the age of 51, he fell victim to the changes behind the scenes Dave Mackay made on taking over as manager near the end of 1972. Out with Knight went trainer-coach Bob McKinlay (after 23 years with the club) and the youth team coach Alan Hill, whose goalkeeping career with Forest had been ended by a compound fracture of his right forearm. Hill was later associated with Mackay at Derby. McKinlay became a prison officer at a detention centre near Nottingham. Knight, whose uncontested redundancy claim brought him just over £800, had a hotel in the city to run with his wife.

By the time of Forest's fourth-round Cup trip to Manchester in January 1947, Colin Rawson had been replaced by fit-again Jack Edwards. This was the full Forest line-up: Platts; Brigham, McCall; Pritty, Blagg, Knight; Scott, Brown, Barks, Edwards, Lyman. Worksop-born Ted Blagg, signed on his demobilisation from the Army, followed Davies as the first-choice centre-half until he broke his nose midway through the following

season. Unable to regain his place, he left for Southport. His first FA Cup
experiences were in sharp contrast to the one he so enjoyed against
Manchester United. In the 1945-46 season, when the competition was
resumed after the war with two-leg ties up to the semi-finals, he conceded the own goal that enabled Watford to draw in the third round at the
City Ground. Then, after the return game had produced the same 1-1
result, he again put the ball into his own net, in extra time, for the only
goal of the replay at White Hart Lane – a match that started 40 minutes
late because Forest were delayed on their train journey.

Manchester United went into their Cup-tie with Forest in the first
post-war season fresh from a four-goal flourish at Middlesbrough. They
were to finish runners-up to Liverpool in the First Division, only one
point behind, and were also to be second for three more seasons before
carrying off the title in 1952. Form therefore clearly favoured them, even
though Forest had been raised to the highest position they were to occupy in the Second Division all season, tenth, by their eclipse of Southampton. Bert Brown was the architect of the shock outcome at Maine Road,
the brains behind the attack as United's star-studded team could find no
response to goals scored by Barks and Lyman, one in each half.

Larry Platts played the game of his life in again keeping a clean sheet,
but on the following Wednesday, when Forest were away to Luton in the
League, he missed his train from Brighton, where he was stationed in the
Forces, and winger Tommy Johnston was the emergency choice as his
replacement in a narrow defeat. Platts did not get another first-team
chance until midway through the next season. Before he left for
Chesterfield in the 1951 close season, the door to a regular place was
firmly slammed shut on him, and on other deputies over the next seven
seasons, by another signing that ranks high among the best Billy Walker
ever made.

The manager's namesake Harry Walker arrived from Portsmouth,
whom he had helped to their shock victory over Wolves in the last pre-
war Cup final, in time to play in the Forest's last four games of the 1946-
47 season. Although this efficient Yorkshireman reached the age of 31
during that period, he was to guard Forest's goal in exactly 300 more
matches before, in 1955, injury finally forced him out of a League career
he had entered with Darlington in the 1930s. Uncanny anticipation and a
very safe pair of hands made him fully deserving of his 'Mr Consistency'
nickname. He was only three months from his 39th birthday when he
finally bowed out.

In being drawn at home in the fifth round of the Cup after their
defeat of a Manchester United team captained by Johnny Carey, who was

to be one of Billy Walker's successors as manager at the City Ground, Forest again faced the team third in the First Division. Middlesbrough had briefly risen there with a win at Preston whereas Manchester United had been heavily beaten at Arsenal. Forest had faltered in the meantime, gleaning only one point from games at Luton and Coventry, but again they rose to the occasion. And once more Brown was their inspiration. On a pitch cleared of snow and liberally sanded, Wilf Mannion, Boro's masterly England forward, opened the scoring within six minutes of the kick-off. Scott crowned good work by Pritty and Brown to equalise on the half-hour, but soon after the interval Johnny Spuhler, Mannion's right-wing partner, regained the lead from a corner kick taken by George Dews, who in the summer played cricket for Worcestershire.

And that was how it still stood midway through the second half, at which point Mannion scored again – but this time for Forest. Dropping back to assist his harassed defenders in a goalmouth melee, he turned the ball past Scottish international Dave Cumming for the goal that forced a replay. Another upset seemed in store when Forest led 2-1 at half-time at Ayresome Park through Barks and Edwards, but Mannion was to have the last word after all. He completed a hat-trick as Boro stormed back for a 6-2 victory that swept them to a quarter-final they lost after another replay to Burnley, losing finalists at Wembley.

On getting back to League fare, Forest had some difficulty shaking off relegation fears, though thankful that they had only one position in the drop zone to worry about because Newport had become so far detached at the bottom of the table. Postponements during the six weeks or so when the weather was at its worst did not help, and even the welcome rise in temperatures did not bring immediate relief. In late March, with the terraces again bathed in sunshine, Forest's home match with Bradford was the only one off in Division Two.

Defeat by 0-2 at Tottenham on Good Friday sank Walker's men to 19th place, with only his old club Wednesday and Swansea and Newport below them. Due to the hold-ups at the City Ground, that game at White Hart Lane was Forest's sixth in succession away from home in the League – and there would have been a seventh if a visit to West Bromwich had not also been called off. The worried frowns deepened when, in their next matches on their travels, Forest also conceded two goals without reply at Hillsborough and then gave away five at both Bury and in their rearranged game at West Bromwich.

Fortunately, their home form was their saviour. After losing to Manchester City in the match that had to be switched to Meadow Lane, they went through their remaining thirteen League games at the City

Ground without defeat, winning nine and drawing four. All but nine of the 40 points with which they finished were gained at home, and all but three of their seventeen defeats were suffered on opponents' grounds.

Through the rearrangement of postponed fixtures, Forest's last three matches were all at home – and they won each of them to zoom up to a final eleventh place, edging West Ham into the top of the bottom half by a fraction of goal-average: 69-74 to 70-76. Tommy Johnston scored the goal that beat Chesterfield, netted twice in a 5-1 victory over Plymouth, and rounded things off with a hat-trick on being moved from the left wing to inside-right in a 4-0 defeat of Bradford.

It was an encouraging end to the first post-war season, but a deceptive one. The next two were to be traumatic ones for Billy Walker and his players, leading to the club's fall into the Third Division for the first time.

CHAPTER TWELVE

First Descent to the Third South

Billy Walker concentrated on the development of high-speed moves in training, and a week before the 1947-48 season began he gave that aspect of Forest's play a big boost by signing George Lee, one of the fastest wingers then in the game.

Lee had been the British Army of the Rhine's champion over 100, 220 and 440 yards while serving with the Black Watch during the war, averaging 10.2 seconds for the 100 in those days. He had also been a star turn at outside-left in the BAOR football team, attracting so much attention that Walker had to beat competition from several other clubs to sign him from York City for a fee of £7,500.

York was Lee's birthplace, but it was for Scarborough that he first played after leaving school, appearing in their Midland League side at the age of fifteen. He joined York City in 1939. The Bootham Crescent club's secretary was so keen to land him as a professional that he visited Lee at his home on the eve of the player's 17th birthday and kept him talking until a few seconds after midnight. He then produced the forms to which Lee put his name. Before being called up into the Army, Lee played a few times for York during the war in partnership with 'Sailor' Brown, one of the City's guests.

In the BAOR team Lee's partners included Billy Steel, a coming Scotland forward for whom Derby County paid Morton the then record transfer fee of £15,500 shortly before Lee's move to Nottingham. That Army side also included a couple of future England internationals: full-back Stan Rickaby, with whom Lee again teamed up after leaving Forest for West Bromwich, and Eddie Baily, the Cockney forward who eventually found his way to the City Ground while Billy Walker was still manager there.

Lee, strongly built and with a powerful shot in his left foot, scored on his debut for Forest, and he missed only one match in the first of the two seasons he spent with them. In the other he was absent seven times, through injury, but still finished as their top scorer – if with a modest total of ten goals that equalled his 1947-48 tally. For both those seasons, however, he had the misfortune to be involved in a constant battle against relegation, and his departure to a higher grade of football became inevitable when Forest dropped out of the Second Division in 1949, a year after only just managing to stay in it.

The first of nearly 80 games Lee played for the club resulted in a home victory over Bury, but only narrowly, and that was promptly exposed as a false dawn by six successive defeats. Another scoring debut was made during that bleak spell by Wilson Jones, a former Welsh international centre-forward from Birmingham City who converted a penalty for Forest's only goal in reply to Chesterfield's three at the City Ground. Two of the four other goals Jones scored in just seven League appearances also came from the spot – one in the last minute of a beating at Brentford, the other in defeat at home to Cardiff – but he then dropped out of the side injured and was unable to get back before leaving for Kidderminster Harriers.

Billy Walker's next transfer expenditure brought in George Wilkins, an experienced former Brentford forward, from Bradford on the evening of Boxing Day in 1947, and on the following afternoon he, too, got off to a scoring start. This time Forest had a victory to celebrate, their first in eight games. It was gained by 4-2 in the return game with Doncaster Rovers, fellow strugglers who the previous day had sent Forest to the bottom of the table with a 2-0 win at Belle Vue. Those positions were reversed by the result at the City Ground. The £7,000 paid for Wilkins increased Walker's outlay on new players since the war to £24,000, a sum from which all but £4,000 had been recouped in outgoing transfers.

Wilkins, a Londoner whose sons Ray, Graham and Dean followed him into League football (Ray, known as 'Butch', played for England), had helped Brentford to beat Portsmouth in a London Cup Final at Wembley in 1942, and had also played for them in a drawn challenge match with Wolves, winners of that year's northern trophy, at Stamford Bridge. By the time he joined Forest, however, he was into his 30s, and, injury prone, his appearances became increasingly spasmodic as their relegation worries multiplied. He had made only two dozen for them in the League when their descent into the Third South was confirmed, and in the autumn of 1949 he had a month's trial at Leeds before going into the Midland League with Boston United. Soon after that he was engaged as coach by Hayes, the club from which he had moved to Brentford before the war.

It was another Londoner who proved the most enduring of Billy Walker's signings during the 1947-48 season. Blond-haired Horace Gager turned 31 the month before costing Forest their then highest fee of £8,000 from Luton Town towards the end of February, but he was the pillar of their defence for 268 League and Cup games until he retired at the age of 38 in 1955. Gager, who stood nearly 6ft, began as an inside-forward with Vauxhall Motors, a Spartan League side based at Luton, to where he had moved with his family as a schoolboy. Luton Town signed him in the 1937-38 season, and after establishing himself in their Second Division team he continued in their attack during the war before a sudden emergency found him to be a natural centre-half. As a guest, he also played in Northern Ireland in the same Glentoran team as the former Forest favourite 'Boy' Martin, then resumed his League career as Luton's captain.

Gager might never have left Luton for Forest but for an injury that caused him to miss a third-round FA Cup-tie at Plymouth in January 1948. His replacement, Leslie Hall, did so well that Gager was unable to regain his place when fit again, and that was why he made the request for a transfer that put Billy Walker on his trail. For the rest of that season and the ensuing six he was an automatic choice, successor to Bob McCall as club captain, and an ever-present when promotion was gained back to the Second Division in 1950-51. He was a dominant figure on the field, but an unobtrusive one off it. On long journeys to away games he sat in a quiet corner doing crossword puzzles. He was also a lover of classical music besides being a keen cricketer and golfer. And after he had settled down to married life at West Bridgford he became a keen gardener.

The other newcomers to Forest's League side in the 1947-48 season included three more of the colts who had played in the first team during the war: Bernard Elliott, Gordon Kaile and Roland Wheatley. Elliott was released to Boston United, and Wheatley to Southampton, after having few post-war opportunities, but the slightly-built Kaile was George Lee's regular successor at outside-left for the 1949-50 season before his transfer to Preston. Kaile, who hailed from Pimperne, near Blandford in Dorset, was discovered while playing for the Royal Engineers Postal Section in the Notts Amateur League and signed as a professional before his posting to India. On 21 January 1950, he was married in the morning and delayed his honeymoon to play for Forest in their home match with Torquay United (who won 2-1) that afternoon.

Wheatley was one of the first paratroopers to land in France on D Day. He took the first two prisoners of the invasion, but was later wounded by fragments of a German mortar bomb. Several months after his departure to Southampton he was diagnosed with arthritis and heart trouble by medical specialists who advised him to give up playing. His heart problem was due to a bout of rheumatic fever contracted when young, but he regained a sufficient measure of fitness to turn out a few more times for Grimsby and Workington.

Another Forest debutant in the second post-war season was a 21-year part-time professional who went to the City Ground only as a spectator for the match with Luton Town (and Gager) on 13 December 1947. Harry Walker was in the dressing room lacing his boots when he was suddenly struck by lumbago. So Dennis Ward, an ex-Artilleryman who had been recommended to the club while with the Army in India, was called in from the crowd to deputise in goal, and it was through no fault of his that he finished on the losing side. Luton won by the odd goal of three with the aid of a penalty converted by Frank Soo, a former Stoke, Leicester and England wartime wing-half who was the son of a Chinese laundry proprietor but born at Buxton. On the Monday morning Ward went back to his job at an engineering works, and, with Platts taking over in Walker's other rare absences, he did get another look-in before moving to Stockport County. He was afterwards with Bradford.

Luton completed the double over Forest, by the same score, in the return match on the last day of the season, just a fortnight after the relegation trapdoor over which the Nottingham club had been hovering for so many weeks had slammed shut with Doncaster and Millwall the unhappy pair below it. Only the year before Doncaster had stormed out of the Third North with eight points to spare over runners-up Rotherham. They were to be promoted again just two seasons later. Millwall sank into the new Fourth Division in 1958 and did not get back to the Second until 1975.

For all their failings, Forest at times played more like champions than candidates for the drop. This was especially so when, two days after winning at home, against West Bromwich, for the first time in eight weeks, they pulled off the victory that made them almost certain to stay up on the Monday evening of April 12. With Gager and the newly recalled 'Tot' Leverton, livewire scorer of two of their goals, outstanding, they gained only their second away win of the season, by 3-0 at Tottenham. The other one dated back to November, when Noel Simpson, a diminutive former Notts County amateur Billy Walker had converted from a forward to a half-back, netted twice at Newcastle. That was also a meritorious Forest performance, but Newcastle, who subsequently recovered to go up with Birmingham, were unsettled at the time by rumours of unrest, dissension and transfer requests by star players. The display at White Hart Lane was more impressive, although there were again some mitigating circumstances. Spurs had been on a wretched run since losing to Blackpool in a Cup semi-final. Defeat by Forest was their fourth in their last five home games, each without scoring and three of them on successive Mondays.

Jack Edwards was the schemer of that triumph at Tottenham which left Forest needing only one more point from their last three matches to make sure of safety. They picked it up at the next opportunity, coming from behind to force a draw at Barnsley through second-half goals from Bill Morley, who had been switched from wing-half to partner Scott on the right flank of in attack, and Gager. With another draw, at home to lowly Plymouth, then preceding the defeat at Luton, Forest ended in 19th place, one point above Bury and six clear of both Doncaster and Millwall. These were the final placings in the basement:

Season 1947-48	P	W	D	L	F	A	Pts
18 Leeds	42	14	8	20	62	72	36
19 Nott'm For	42	12	11	19	54	60	35
20 Bury	42	9	16	17	58	68	34
21 Doncaster	42	9	11	22	40	66	29
22 Millwall	42	9	11	22	44	74	29

The big topic at the start of the following season of 1948-49 in which Forest did drop into Division Three was the refusal of Wilf Mannion and Albert Stubbins to re-sign for Middlesbrough and Liverpool. Both did so eventually, and Stubbins, who had earlier been the subject of a swap unsuccessfully suggested by Billy Walker when Liverpool had made an approach for one of his players, scored one of the goals that knocked Forest out of the FA Cup's third round. Forest had lost at Anfield at the same stage of the competition the previous year, but this time they took the League's first post-war champions to a replay after going within a minute of repeating the shock they had sprung on Manchester United in 1947.

Stubbins was not risked for the original meeting at the City Ground despite reporting recovered from a leg injury, and Forest were without skipper Bob McCall, for whom Jim Clarke, another of the wartime colts, deputised at short notice. Clarke, a studious type of player who worked part-time as a dental mechanic, came from the same Staffordshire town of Wednesbury as Billy Walker, and had attended the same school there. His other first-team outings were rare, but he was a reliable member of the reserve side in the Midland League before moving on to Boston.

Forest, who had done their training indoors, because of snow, in preparation for the home tie with Liverpool, surged into a two-goal lead by half-time, through Scott and an own goal, and they still held that advantage when they lost goalkeeper Walker with a facial injury with twenty minutes to go. Tom ('Tucker') Johnson, a forward signed from Gateshead in the opening weeks of the season on the recommendation of Fred Scott, pulled on the jersey, but his lack of inches was shown up when Willie Fagan, who played for Scotland during the war, headed

Liverpool's first goal eight minutes later. And he was again beaten by a header as Cyril Done, Stubbins's deputy, equalised from a corner kick in that fateful last minute.

Bill Hullett, who had a slightly pulled muscle, went in goal for the extra period, during which Forest's ten men had the better of the exchanges and almost regained the lead when Lee had a shot cleared off the line. The second meeting, however, was a very different story. One down at the interval on Merseyside a week later, Forest conceded three more goals without reply. On the same afternoon, Lincoln City, the only team below them in the Second Division table, drew level on points, but still behind on goal-average and with two games more played, by winning at home against Brentford.

Forest had once more been struggling in the League since losing at home on a very wet opening day of the 1948-49 season to a 55th-minute goal scored for West Bromwich by Irish international Dave Walsh. Billy Walker had spent the preceding week prospecting in Lancashire and Scotland, but the only new player fielded against Albion was the adaptable Syd Ottewelll, who hailed from next-door Derbyshire. Ottewell, briefly a Wolves amateur in 1936, after captaining Belper and the county side in schools soccer and taking part in an England boys' trial, entered the Second Division with Chesterfield when only sixteen. During the war he was an Army physical training instructor in India, where he played in the team gathered by Scottish international Tommy Walker to entertain the troops.

After that he developed a real wanderlust. In the summer of 1947, eleven years after first joining Chesterfield as a 15-year-old amateur, he moved to Birmingham City for £3,500. Within six months, his value risen to £5,000, he was with Luton Town, the Hatters' interest in him aroused when he scored five goals against their reserve team. Just over six months after that Forest paid £7,000 for him, and early in 1950 he turned down Bristol City before making Mansfield Town his fifth club in a little more than two and a half years. From there, two years later, he was transferred to Scunthorpe United, then became player-manager of Spalding United in the United Counties League.

Regrettably, Ottewell left Forest in acrimonious circumstances. After filling five positions in attack and midfield before his appearances dwindled towards the end of the relegation season, he got into a dispute with the club that resulted in his suspension – originally *sine die*, but reduced to a fortnight – and then granting his request for a transfer. Following an appeals committee hearing at which Forest were represented by chairman Jack Brentnall and secretary Noel Watson (Billy Walker could not attend because of illness), Forest agreed to pay Ottewell until he was no longer with them, to allow him to continue in his job outside football, and to meet all expenses incurred in connection with a house.

Shortly before Ottewell dropped out of the Forest team, one of Billy Walker's excursions into Scotland paid off with the arrival of Johnny Love, a six-footer of an inside-forward from Albion Rovers who had rejected previous offers from England, one of them by Newcastle, because he was then intent on building a business life for himself and was learning the furniture trade. When Forest made their approach Albion Rovers were also in danger of relegation – they did go down as a very poor last – and welcomed their major share of the £7,500 fee to alleviate a desperate financial situation. At least £1,000 of it went to Leith Athletic, in accordance with an agreement reached when they parted with Love to Albion two seasons before. During the war Love first served in Bomber Command, but it was as a gilder pilot that he was awarded the DFC. Although seriously wounded by shrapnel, and in intense pain, he insisted on staying at the controls at the airborne crossing of the Rhine in 1944, and he landed safely despite damage from anti-aircraft fire that rendered both flaps and brakes useless.

Love was also an accomplished golfer, and in each of his three years with Forest he entered the professional footballers' championship in company with Geoff Thomas, Horace Gager and Bill Morley. Thomas, who at one time toyed with the idea of taking up golf professionally, was runner-up for that title at Liverpool in 1950, but he had to curb his activities in that direction after accepting a job outside football as a commercial traveller.

Forest were languishing next to the foot of the Second Division when Love made his debut as Leverton's replacement at inside-right for a visit to Luton on the last Saturday of February in 1949. And after a 3-4 defeat they stayed there only on goal-average as Lincoln City pulled level with them on points, but with a game more played, in winning at home against Sheffield Wednesday. Love did not score that afternoon, but he ended the season with the very fair return of seven goals from his thirteen games. That left him only three goals behind George Lee, the club's leading marksman after almost three times as many appearances.

Love was on the winning side for the first time in his fifth match, won 3-0 at home to Coventry City, but a week later Forest briefly sank to last place by losing at Leeds while Lincoln edged a point ahead of them by beating Blackburn. Then came the vital Easter programme, at the end of which Forest still looked favourites to go down with Lincoln in spite of completing the double over lowly Bradford and then holding high-flying

Tottenham to a draw. Lincoln, meanwhile, had their fate sealed by three consecutive defeats, the last of them a six-goal walloping at Luton. These were the positions at the bottom of the table as Forest travelled to meet West Ham on the last day of April:

	P	W	D	L	F	A	Pts
18 Plymouth	39	12	10	17	46	56	34
19 Brentford	39	11	12	16	38	48	34
20 Leicester	39	9	15	15	59	74	33
21 Nott'm For	40	12	7	21	44	54	31
22 Lincoln	41	7	12	22	50	91	26

Leicester had been dragged into the maelstrom under the distraction of reaching the F A Cup final, giving them the unique mixed prospect of becoming the first club to win the trophy and be relegated to the Third Division in the same season. The first of those possibilities went by the board as they lost to Wolverhampton Wanderers at Wembley on the afternoon when Nottingham Forest renewed a lingering, if fragile, hope of beating the drop by suddenly surging into a five-goal spree against the Hammers. That put them above Leicester on goal-average, but with only one more game to play as against the City's three. West Ham ended the season as high as seventh, but were also on the receiving end of Forest's previous biggest winning margin of the campaign. Early in December, they conceded three goals, also without reply, as Forest won at home for the first time in two months – and there would have been at least three more but for the brilliance of goalkeeper Gregory. One of the men who did beat him that day was Bill Hullett, another of Forest's scoring newcomers.

Two of the goals that earned both points at Upton Park were scored by the recalled 'Tucker' Johnson, who had been out of the League side since mid-January, troubled by nose, groin and weight problems. He had excelled for the Reserves on the Thursday, and he carried on from where he had left off by crowning a neat body swerve with a scorching shot that opened the scoring just after the half-hour. His other goal was one of the three that came in as many minutes during the second half. Leverton scored the two others, and Love applied the finishing touch as West Ham were denied even one reply.

Leicester were left with the intimidating task of fulfilling their remaining three fixtures on the following Wednesday, Thursday and Saturday. They began by again pulling two points clear of Forest with a hard-earned win at Bury, where they owed much to their goalkeeper, Leslie

Major, after big Dave Massart had halved the two-goal lead they had gained in the first half-hour. Next evening, however, they were at home to a West Bromwich team that had just as big an incentive to win, but for a very different reason, and the Throstles underlined the gulf between them by comfortably clinching their return to the First Division they had left eleven years before. Behind gates that were closed on a crowd of 34,585 before the kick-off, there was never any doubt about the outcome from the twelfth minute in which the visitors went in front. Leicester fell further behind before the interval, and the scoring was completed by Albion's third goal ten minutes into the second half.

That left Forest still two points behind Leicester, but with their superior goal-average, and only one game remaining for both of them. And Forest had to finish at home, against Bury, who were tenth in the table, whereas City were away to fourth-placed Cardiff. So yet again Forest went into a final day with their fate hanging in the balance, and it once more looked likely to tip in their favour when they and Cardiff both went ahead after a scoreless first half. George Lee's goal was sufficient to give Forest both points, but thirteen minutes from the end at Ninian Park Jack Lee, soon fleetingly to be an England centre-forward, grabbed the equaliser that saved Leicester and made Billy Walker the manager of a relegated club for the second time. Forest had good reason to rue the fact that only a few weeks earlier Leicester had picked up a point at Plymouth after the referee had awarded Argyle a goal but then reversed his decision on being persuaded to consult a linesman.

This was how they finished at the foot of a table in which Fulham nicked the title from their promotion companions West Bromwich by beating West Ham in their final match, while Albion ended with a defeat by Grimsby:

Season 1948-49	P	W	D	L	F	A	Pts
18 Brentford	42	11	14	17	42	53	36
19 Leicester	42	10	16	16	62	79	36
20 Plymouth	42	12	12	18	49	64	36
21 Nott'm For	42	14	7	21	50	54	35
22 Lincoln	42	8	12	22	53	91	28

In totalling the same number of points with which they had survived by six the previous year, Forest won two more matches, and conceded six fewer goals, compared with their statistics of 1947-48. Their scoring rate dropped, however, from 54 to 50, and they suffered 21 defeats as against nineteen, with drawn games reduced from eleven to seven. The crucial spine of the team had been rebuilt efficiently in two respects, Harry Walker and Horace Gager having become unassailable in goal and at centre-half. The third one, at centre-forward, was about to be found with the signing of one of the most prolific post-war scorers.

Aston Villa with 1919-20 FA Cup. Back: G B Ramsay (secretary), T Smart, P Bate (director),
Sam Hardy, F Miles (trainer), Frank Moss, H Spencer (director). Middle: J Devey (director),
W J Kirton, Andy Ducat, F Rinder (chairman) with Cup, Billy Walker, Clem Stephenson,
A E Jones (vice-chairman). Front: C Wallace, Frank Barson, Tom Weston, A Dorrell

Sheffield Wednesday with 1934-35 FA Cup. Back: Nibloe, Brown, Catlin, Millership,
G Urwin (trainer), Burrows. Front: Sharp, Hooper, Surtees, Billy Walker (manager) with Cup,
Palethorpe, Starling, Rimmer

Billy Walker (Forest manager) drinks from the trophy following the defeat of
Luton Town in the 1959 FA Cup final at Wembley

Nottingham Forest with 1958-59 FA Cup. Back: G N Watson (secretary), W Whare,
J McDonald, R McKinlay, R Dwight, C Thomson, J Whitefoot, T Graham (trainer).
Front: J Quigley, W Gray, J Burkitt, Billy Walker (manager with trophy), T Wilson, S Imlach

Aston Villa players take a bath after training during the 1923-24 season.
Front bath: Tom Jackson and Tom Mort. Rear bath: George Blackburn and Billy Walker.
Tom Smart (left) Dicky York (centre) and Joe 'Toby' Corbett (right) stand at the back

The England team which played Belgium at The Hawthorns in December 1924.
Back: Tom Magee, Bill Ashurst, Henry Hardy, Alfred G Bower, Fred H Ewer.
Front: Frank Osborne, Frank Roberts, Joe Bradford, Billy Walker, Arthur Dorrell, John Butler

The 1959 FA Cup final at Wembley. Thomas Hodgson (Luton chairman, left) and
Billy Walker (Nottingham Forest manager) lead out the two teams

Billy Walker, right, in action for Aston Villa during the 1924-25 season

Billy Walker stoops as Villa team-mate
Billy Kirton leap-frogs over him

Billy Gray in his Chelsea days. He was
inside-left for Forest in the 1959 Cup final

Billy Walker working at his old-fashioned desk as manager of Nottingham Forest

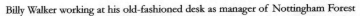

Peter Small, the Forest winger signed
at Billy Walker's bedside

Tommy Capel, who enjoyed his best
season in Forest's 1950-51 team

Left:
Wally Ardron in
typical Forest pose,
shooting for goal in
the early 1950s

Right:
Horace Gager, the
Forest centre-half
and captain who
made the last of his
268 League and Cup
appearances for the
club at the age of 38
in 1955

Billy Walker, right, shakes hands with the Duke of Edinburgh before the 1959 FA Cup final. Forest skipper Jack Burkitt and goalkeeper Charlie Thomson also in the picture

Billy Walker, arms spread, keeping his eyes on the ball in his Aston Villa days

CHAPTER THIRTEEN

Enter Ardron the Record Breaker

Great credit was due to Nottingham Forest's committeemen for keeping faith with Billy Walker in 1949 despite the club's first descent into the Southern Section of the Third Division, then the joint lowest sphere of the Football League with its Northern counterpart. By the game's current standards he would have been unlikely to have survived the narrow escape from relegation that immediately preceded the dreaded drop.

That faith was amply rewarded as manager and club remained loyal to each other for eleven more years, with Walker then staying on as a member of the committee until the breakdown of his health. And it was because Forest were looking for the sort of commitment he gave them that Brian Clough, the controversial figure who was to surpass even Walker's exceptional achievements, settled into the City Ground hot seat just over a year later than he might otherwise have done. At the time of Clough's resignation at Derby in October 1973, Forest were deterred from appointing him to fill the vacancy caused by Dave Mackay's departure to follow him at the Baseball Ground because of the unpleasant circumstances that had arisen there. Paradoxically, they decided he was just the man they were looking for, reckoning that he had become more mature and experienced, after he had also quit Brighton and been sacked in short order at Leeds.

For their return to the Second Division, Forest were also kept waiting a year as their Lawton-led Notts County neighbours carried off the Third South championship of 1949-50, seven points clear of runners-up Northampton and nine ahead of fourth-placed Forest. That season had still to start when Billy Walker lost two of his best players. Jack Edwards went to Southampton for £10,000, George Lee to West Bromwich for £11,500. They, along with Jack Hutchinson, were the players for whose transfers a total of £30,000 had been turned down even while they had been in a struggling team more than a year before. Liverpool had made a big offer for Edwards after he had done well against them in the first of those cup-ties at Anfield, and Forest had also rejected bids for him, each said to be in the region of £15,000, from three other League clubs. Relegation, however, forced Walker's hand. Edwards, like Lee, asked for a transfer.

In leaving one club newly demoted, Edwards joined another that had also just experienced bitter disappointment, for Southampton had missed promotion to the First Division by one point after having topped the table by eight before an injury to their ace marksman, Charlie Wayman. The Saints registered an even closer near-miss in the first season Edwards spent with them. They would have gone up with Tottenham's champions if they had beaten West Ham 6-2 instead of 3-2 on the final day. As it was, they shared Sheffield United's fate of finishing with the same number of points as runners-up Sheffield Wednesday, but behind them on goal-average. Southampton did get out of the Second Division in 1952-53, the first season after Edwards left them for Kidderminster Harriers – but at the opposite end. Lee, meanwhile, was heading for higher things. In 1954 he laid on West Bromwich's first goal in their defeat of Preston in the FA Cup final.

Billy Walker more than offset the departure of his left-wing pair by handing over a five-figure fee to Rotherham United for Walter Ardron, a sturdy centre-forward who had added 98 League and Cup goals in the first three post-war seasons to the near-100 he had netted for the Millmoor club during the war. In each of those three seasons Rotherham had the frustrating experience of missing promotion as runners-up in the Third Division North, but they eventually made it up to Division Two in 1951 in the company of Nottingham Forest's Southern Section champions. And in 1955 Rotherham very nearly did what Forest were to do two years later – climb into Division One. They finished with the same number of points as the promoted pair, Birmingham City and Luton Town, but were pushed into third place on goal-average.

Statistics emphasise that Billy Walker pulled off one of his biggest bargains in securing Ardron. In his first season with Forest, this former railway fireman stoked up an attack that had been faltering by scoring 25 goals. In his next, when promotion was won, he increased the club's individual record to 36, being particularly appreciative of the accuracy of Freddie Scott's centres. And by the time he left for Selby Town in 1955 he had 124 to his name in 191 Forest appearances. That gave him a most impressive total of 217 in 305 games for his two League clubs, plus five goals in the FA Cup but discounting matches played in wartime. He was the first to reach the double-century for post-war League goals. Not bad going for somebody who was 28 within three weeks of scoring the first of them in Rotherham's 4-1 away win against Tranmere on the opening day of the first post-war season.

Yet Rotherham very nearly let this natural goal-getter slip through their hands. He was a teenage stripling when they rejected him after he had turned out just the once in their Third Division side in 1939 following his signing from Swinton Victoria. But, having built up his physique with a course of physical culture, he looked a far different proposition when Rotherham officials spotted him doing well with Denaby United in the Midland League two years later. The invitation to return to Millmoor (the transfer fee all of £100) was readily accepted, and after warming up with his wartime goals he set a Rotherham record that still stands by scoring 38 times in 40 Third North games in 1946-47. His overall total of 40, with the inclusion of cup-ties, was exceeded by his successor, Jack Shaw, in 1950-51, but nine of Shaw's 46 goals during that promotion season came in the FA Cup. That left him one behind Ardron's total in the League.

Rotherham's failure to recognise Ardron's potential at the outset was not the first setback to his footballing aspirations. That came while he was still a schoolboy at Swinton-on-Dearne, his birthplace. The master responsible for the team supplied the players with boots at six shillings (30p) a pair, and that sum had to be repaid at sixpence a week. Ardron found those payments a problem after raising one shilling (5p), and therefore decided to return his boots. The master told him he could keep them if he scored three goals in the next match. He kept them. More of a boot-trick than a hat-trick.

Ardron passed on a tip to his son Barry that encapsulated the secret of his success. After 11-year-old Barry, also a centre-forward, had scored eleven goals in a schools game, he said: 'Dad tells me that when you get into the penalty area shoot hard. And that's what I do.'

Forest shared the points with Brighton at Hove when Wally Ardron opened his account for them on the first day of the 1949-50 season, but they had some excuse for yielding a 2-0 interval lead because an injury to 'Tucker' Johnson threw their attack out of gear. Johnson had to go off on the half-hour, just after Ardron had increased a lead gained with an early own goal, and he hobbled on the left wing throughout the second half. It was a wonder he was able to do that, for an x-ray subsequently revealed that he had broken a bone in his lower leg. He made a scoring return on Christmas Eve in a win at Walsall that was made out of the ordinary because the final whistle was blown ten minutes too soon. The players had to turn back on their way to their dressing rooms when a linesman pointed out the error to the referee, who had forgotten to allow for the interval time.

Only a few weeks later, Johnson was also a scorer in a 5-0 victory at Swindon that equalled the biggest win of the season Forest had gained at home to Exeter City (Ardron scored twice in both). But Johnson cracked the same bone during that visit to Wiltshire, and he did not figure in the first team again until the opening match of the following season, when he was once more on the mark as both points were claimed at Newport. He made a notable contribution to the winning of promotion in that 1950-51 campaign, scoring some vital goals among his 15 in 32 League appearances besides doing the hat-trick in a Cup trouncing of Torquay, but not long afterwards this most unlucky footballer had to undergo a cartilage operation that was only partially successful. His right leg would no longer stand the strain of playing because of a loose knee joint, so, with his career at a premature end, he stayed on with the club for a while as coach to the third team in the Notts Central Alliance.

The need for strengthening at inside-forward became even more urgent in the third month of the 1949-50 season when 'Tot' Leverton also broke a leg, and Billy Walker parted with what was then Forest's highest fee of £14,000 to bring in the long-striding Tommy Capel from Birmingham City. Leverton suffered his serious injury, from which he was slow to recover, in a collision with the Orient goalkeeper during a game at Leyton in which Johnny Anderson, a new wing-half from Manchester United, obtained the goal that earned a point. Anderson had been a spectacular scorer for United in their recovery to Cup victory over Blackpool at Wembley in 1948, but he soon lost his hold on a regular place, and that was to be his only goal for Forest before he left for Peterborough United, then members of the Midland League.

Tommy Capel played a few times in Manchester City's promotion-winning side of the first post-war season, then gained a little First Division experience before moving to Chesterfield. With him from Maine Road to Saltergate went wing-half Peter Robinson, a friend from schooldays who was later with Notts County. They played together for Manchester Boys and signed amateur forms for Manchester City on the same day. Two years later, shortly after turning professional, they enlisted on the same day – Capel in the Royal Marines, Robinson in the Army. And in 1946 they were demobilised on the same day. Capel guested for Plymouth Argyle during the war before serving in Ceylon, where he helped a Combined Services side to defeat Tommy Walker's XI and was in a Marines team that also included Eddie Quigley, a forward (originally a full-back) who cost Preston the then record fee of £26,500 when transferred from Sheffield Wednesday in December 1949 – the month after Capel's switch to Forest.

Capel and Robinson left Manchester City in exchange, plus some cash, for Billy Linacre, a slimly-built winger whose 'Legs' nickname was given a cruelly ironic meaning when he broke a leg for a third time in a career that also took him to Middlesbrough. Capel's brother Fred, a full-back, was among Linacre's team-mates at Chesterfield, for whom Tommy was signed by the manager, former Burnley forward Bob Brocklebank, who, as later manager of Birmingham, also negotiated his transfer from Saltergate to St Andrew's.

Forest's acquisition of Capel, who packed a powerful shot into his left boot (but, unfortunately, not into his right), spelled the end of hopes of a regular first-team place for Alan Ashman, a Yorkshireman who was another of the club's wartime colts. For £5,000, Ashman went to Carlisle, with whom his hat-trick on debut was a fitting reflection of the form that had helped Forest's reserve team to two consecutive Midland League championships. Knee problems forced Ashman's retirement as a player after he had scored nearly 100 League goals for Carlisle, but he then turned to management with considerable success. Between two spells in charge of the Cumbrian club, during which he took them to one season in the First Division through three promotions, he guided West Bromwich to victory in an FA Cup final and to the quarter-finals of the European Cup-winners' Cup.

In signing for Forest, Capel, then 26, joined the small band who had played at all three levels of the Football League since the war. He just failed to equal Alec Blakeman's record of having done so in one season (with Brentford, Sheffield United and Bournemouth). When Capel arrived on the second day of November in 1949, Forest were down to ninth place in the Third South table, the lowest position they were to occupy all season. They ended that month up to second after a home victory over Bristol Rovers gained with the two second-half goals that opened Capel's account, but they were never in with a real chance of reclaiming the leadership they had held as early pacemakers after their defeat of the other Bristol club at Ashton Gate on a Tuesday evening in late August. The usually reliable Ardron failed with a penalty in both those games. He missed a hat-trick in shooting wide from the spot before scoring the goals that beat City; against Rovers he had his shot saved by Jack Weare, a goalkeeper then in his 38th year.

Southend, Northampton and Reading also had turns at the top before Notts County's hold on that one promotion spot became unbreakable – even though it was reduced to a single point at one stage. Forest's neighbours were five points ahead of them, with a game in hand, after being held to a scoreless draw at Torquay while Bristol Rovers were losing at the City Ground, and a fortnight later, after the intervention of the Cup's first round, they pulled further away by winning the first League match between the Nottingham clubs in nearly fifteen years. That match, also at Forest's home, was memorable for a goal that was hailed as 'the header of the century.' It was certainly the greatest scored with the head I have seen, or ever expect to see. Tommy Lawton, as one of soccer's most accomplished headers of a ball, was the inevitable scorer. 'I never hit a ball as hard before,' he said afterwards. 'Everything went exactly right. I just got clear and my jump was carrying me forward as I met the ball full on my forehead.'

Jackie Sewell, soon to become the costliest player in the game with his £35,000 transfer to Sheffield Wednesday, forced the corner from which Notts went ahead in such spectacular fashion around the half-hour. From the flag kick, Frank Broome, who had made his way from Aston Villa via Derby, pulled the ball back towards where Lawton was hovering on the edge of the penalty area, and Harry Walker had not the ghost of a chance as it zoomed past him, bullet-like, into the top right-hand corner of his net. No wonder *The Official History of Notts County* states: 'People still talk about it in Nottingham, even those of us that weren't there!' Nine minutes from time, Lawton returned the compliment by breaking away down the right and slinging across the centre from which Broome doubled the lead. Only three minutes remained when Capel replied in the gathering gloom – too late for it to be anything more than slight compensation for Forest fans in the all-ticket crowd of nearly 38,000.

The big attraction Lawton was in Nottingham had been underlined the week before, when the 28,584 gate at Meadow Lane for the Cup-tie in which non-League Tilbury were brushed aside had not only been the biggest of the first round but also more than 13,000 above that at the City Ground, where Forest knocked out Bristol City. Forest were beaten by Stockport in the next round despite again having home advantage, but Notts were successful in front of Rochdale's record crowd of 24,231 before 44,000 saw them eliminated by their First Division visitors from Burnley. The biggest attendance for a Notts County home match was then 45,019, dating back to a Cup-tie with Aston Villa in 1921. On 22 April 1950, it was exceeded at the return League game against Forest. Lawton was again a scorer, this time with Sewell, as Notts completed a double to the delight of the majority in a crowd of 46,000. Five years later, the existing record of 47,310 was set up for an FA Cup quarter-final in which Notts suffered a shock defeat by York, only the third Division Three club (after Millwall and Port Vale) to reach the last four.

Forest regained second place, but six points behind Notts, who had two games in hand, with a 3-0 home victory against Newport County on Easter Monday, 10 April 1950, a day of high winds, heavy rain, and snow in some parts. The referee at the City Ground had to hold the ball down for Newport's goalkeeper to take goal kicks after the Welsh club's captain had chosen to face the 60mph gale. Two goals down at the interval,

Newport were too tired to harness the wind when it was in their favour, and Forest's revenge for their 1-4 defeat at Somerton Park on Good Friday was assured by the time the visitors were further handicapped by the shoulder injury their goalkeeper suffered when heavily charged by Capel.

On the following Saturday, Notts County's lead was cut to five points – but not by Forest. While Notts, looking anything but a promotion side, were losing at relegation-threatened Aldershot, Forest were beaten at home by Southend United, who consequently replaced them as the County's closest challengers. The Essex club were outplayed for three-quarters of the game at the City Ground, but they transformed it after falling behind to a Capel goal by switching 19-year-old Reg Davies from outside-right to inside-left. Davies headed the equaliser, then provided the pass from which the winning goal was scored by Albert Wakefield, a former Leeds centre-forward who might have made his name in Italian football if he had not turned down several offers he received after serving in that country during the war.

A week later, Notts County's 2-0 victory at home against Forest after a scoreless first half made them sure of going up, and they rounded off their Meadow Lane fixtures in style the next Thursday by beating Northampton Town, who had become the new runners-up after defeating Southend United. Lawton scored the two goals Northampton Town conceded without reply, taking him to a total for the season of 31, plus two more in the Cup. Wally Ardron finished as the second highest scorer in the Third South, six behind the Notts captain, with the goal he scored as Forest defeated Port Vale in their final match, but Wakefield totalled 28 with the addition of his Cup goals to the 23 he netted in the League.

Victory over the Vale enabled Forest to reclaim third place on goal-average from Southend, who were held goalless at Norwich the same day, but those positions were again reversed as the Shrimpers drew their remaining two matches. Notts, without Lawton, came a 5-1 cropper in their prompt return game with Northampton, then ended with a 2-2 draw at Exeter that took them to 58 points – the smallest number to achieve promotion from that division since Newport's 55 in 1939. Jackie Sewell, who also missed those last two matches, was Notts' second-highest scorer with 19 League goals and one in the Cup, followed by ex-Forest forward Tommy Johnston, whose respective figures were 15 and two. These were the final leading positions in the last Third South table of 42 matches before the expansion to two dozen clubs with the election of Colchester United and Gillingham for the 1950-51 season:

Season 1949-50	P	W	D	L	F	A	Pts
1 Notts County	42	25	8	9	95	50	58
2 Northampton	42	20	11	11	72	50	51
3 Southend	42	19	13	10	66	48	51
4 Nott'm For	42	20	9	13	67	39	49
5 Torquay	42	19	10	13	66	63	48

Division Three North was now extended to include Scunthorpe & Lindsey United (as they were known until 1958) and Shrewsbury Town.

Of the two dozen players Forest called upon in 1949-50, Ardron and Freddie Scott made most appearances, both missing only one match. Harry Walker and Gordon Kaile were absent twice. Of the team that played in the first game, Ardron and Scott were in the line-up for the last, along with Geoff Thomas, Bob McCall, Bill Morley, Horace Gager and John Love. Thomas only just made that list, for he was recalled on the final day, having dropped out through injury following the home defeat by Notts County in early December. With McCall joining Morley in having a lengthy spell out of action, the vacancies that opened up at full-back were beneficial for Jack Hutchinson and Bill Whare.

Jack Burkitt, a wing-half who had become a regular member of the side the previous season, would almost certainly also have played in Forest's last match of 1949-50 as well as the first but for a knee injury he suffered in mid-February. Both internal and external cartilages had to be removed, yet he recovered in time to be an integral part of the team that immediately followed Notts County up to the Second Division. And there he stayed throughout the 1950s, rising to the captaincy and setting a Forest appearances record of 503 since overtaken only by Bobby McKinlay. Consistent and constructive, Burkitt might well have played for England had he been with a more 'fashionable' club.

Like his manager, Burkitt hailed from Wednesbury. He served as an apprentice engineer's draughtsman after leaving school, and at weekends played for West Bromwich Colts and various junior sides before joining Darlaston while in his teens. Darlaston were runners-up in the Birmingham Combination in his first season with them, and they won the title the next year. Burkitt was a centre-half, aged 21, when Billy Walker first spotted him in a game at Nuneaton which the Forest manager attended in his search for a centre-forward, and after being signed he captained the 'A' team from that position to a league and cup double in 1947-48. With Gager and McKinlay the firmly installed pivots during his fifteen seasons at the City Ground, it was indeed just as well for both player and club that Walker then decided wing-half was Burkitt's best position.

CHAPTER FOURTEEN

Flying Start to Promotion

Nottingham Forest got away to a flying start in their Third Division South promotion season of 1950-51, winning each of their opening four matches and losing only one of the first nineteen up to the beginning of December.

That pacesetting run of fourteen victories and four draws against the one defeat was built on the combination of a settled rearguard and a free-scoring forward line in which there was a new driving force on the left wing. In defence, Bill Whare and Geoff Thomas were the full-backs in front of the ever-present Harry Walker, and Horace Gager, who also did not miss a match, was flanked in the half-back line by Bill Morley and Jack Burkitt. In attack, the Tommies Johnson and Capel were the most-used inside-forwards (with 'Tot' Leverton fitting in when needed or fit), and spearhead Wally Ardron was just one appearance from joining the two others who played in all 46 League games and two FA Cup-ties – wingers Freddie Scott and the newcomer, Colin Collindridge.

Forest could have had Collindridge for nothing more than the £10 signing-on fee instead of the £12,000 required to secure his transfer from Sheffield United on 11 August 1950, but they were in good company in failing to appreciate their first sight of him. He was released by Rotherham within weeks of joining them on his 17th birthday in September 1937, and Wolverhampton Wanderers also soon let him go after he had declined the offer of only part-time terms Forest made because they had doubts about his ability to stand up to League football. He was fourth-time lucky with Sheffield United, who signed him in 1939 from a Barnsley junior club, on the recommendation of their left-half Alf Settle, after he had been with Wombwell Main at intermediate level. Then came the war, during which he served in the RAF and guested for Notts County and Lincoln City before helping the Blades to win the League North title in the transitional 1945-46 season with 16 goals in 19 of their 42 games.

When Collindridge's Football League career at last got under way, his extreme pace and fierce shooting made him the Bramall Lane club's top scorer in each of the first three post-war seasons, jointly on one occasion. To his personal-best 18 First Division goals in 1946-47 he added a memorable hat-trick from centre-forward against Neil Franklin, England's reigning centre-half, in an FA Cup-tie with Stoke City. Stoke went to

Sheffield already two goals to the good from the first leg, and they doubled that lead after a remarkable opening quarter of an hour in which both sides had two goals disallowed. Collindridge, one of the players denied during that period, then wrested a 3-2 second-leg lead in a dramatic comeback, and in the closing seconds he almost forced extra time with a header that goalkeeper Denis Herod only just managed to scramble away. Stoke therefore progressed 4-3 on aggregate, but, after also knocking out the other Sheffield club, they were unable to overturn a two-goal deficit from the first leg of their sixth-round tie with Bolton on the afternoon of the disaster at Burnden Park in which 33 people perished, and some 500 were injured, in the crush when crowd barriers broke.

Collindridge played for Sheffield United at inside-left in addition to centre-forward and the left wing, and his versatility also even stretched to keeping goal for all but the first seven minutes of a First Division match with Manchester United at Bramall Lane. He took over there when Jack Smith, who resumed on the wing after the interval, was carried off injured, and was beaten only once as his team ended their fellow United's undefeated run of sixteen League and Cup games. The winning margin would have been wider than 2-1 but for a penalty save by the visitors' stand-in goalkeeper, Bobby Brown, a youngster serving in the RAF who was making his League debut at short notice in the absence of Jack Crompton with laryngitis.

Effective though he could be at centre-forward, as he so clearly proved against Stoke, Collindridge much preferred playing at outside-left. It was because he was again called upon to play at the head of the attack, at a time when England selectors had been eyeing him as a prospective left-winger, that he asked for a transfer during the 1948-49 season in which Sheffield United were relegated. He did stay on for a season in the Second Division on reverting to the wing, taking his goals tally for the club to 52 in 142 League appearances, but then had an interview with Preston North End. Billy Walker was alerted when news reached the City Ground that Collindridge was not keen on a move to Lancashire. Determined not to let such an obvious talent elude Forest again, Walker realised he might be able to play a trump card because it was recalled that the player had married a Nottingham girl while in the RAF. He therefore rang through to Bramall Lane and suggested that Collindridge might be interested in living in Nottingham. On being given permission to approach him, he learned that that was indeed the case, and a week after signing for Forest Collindridge made a scoring debut in the 18th minute of a 2-1 win at Newport on 18 August 1950.

The arrival of this cheery character, an excellent club man who had an important influence on morale in the dressing room as well as on the field, would have kept Gordon Kaile out of the left-wing running in any case, but Kaile was also sidelined by a cartilage operation from which he was slow to recover before he made the move to Preston that Collindridge had refused. Kaile, who had a tendency to over-elaborate, was unable to establish himself in a North End team freshly restored to the First Division, and he was teaching in Bristol when Exeter City came in for him three years later.

A regular first-team place with Forest on their path to promotion in 1950-51 was also lost to John Love. After having had to wait for a recall until just before Christmas, when one of Johnson's absences ended a sequence of eleven games with an unchanged team, Love was also badly injured, and he had few other opportunities before moving into the Southern League as Llanelli's player-manager. Three years later, early in 1955, he went to Walsall, where he was put in charge of the youth training scheme before succeeding the veteran Major Frank Buckley as manager. Not much more than a year after that, however, he resigned (soon to manage Wrexham) because he objected to the newly appointed coach, Andy Beattie, being given widespread powers over the playing staff. Beattie, a former Preston and Scotland full-back, also quit within the hour. Three years on, in September 1960, Beattie became Forest's choice as their first new manager since March 1939, filling the vacancy caused by Billy Walker's move 'upstairs' to join the club's committee.

The match in which, on 23 December 1950, John Love made what was to be his only appearance of Forest's promotion season until its final week resulted in a defeat at Norwich. It was only the second time Forest had lost in twenty games (the other at Torquay in September), yet it enabled the East Anglian club to pull level with them on 32 points at the top of the table, if with an inferior goal-average. Until then Forest, whose defence was breached twice, had only once failed to score in a match that season (in a home draw with Ipswich), having totalled 58 goals as the League's leading marksmen with high spots of seven against Aldershot and nine against Gillingham. But for some brilliant saves by Gillingham's goalkeeper, former paratrooper Larry Gage, who was applauded off the field at the finish, Forest might well have at least equalled the club's record of the dozen goals put into Leicester Fosse's net in a First Division game in 1909.

Ardron did the hat-trick in both those big wins of late 1950, and he could have taken only nine minutes to complete the one against Aldershot, whose goalkeeper, George Warnes, had been with him at

Rotherham, if he had not driven a penalty kick onto the crossbar. Capel was the scorer of four goals in the rout of Gillingham, the first three of them inside the opening half-hour. The romp at Aldershot's expense came straight after the defeat by the odd goal of five at Torquay, where they conceded both points for the third successive season in losing their unbeaten record in their tenth match, and immediately before they yielded the leadership they had held since the first tables were compiled in being held at the City Ground by Ipswich. Defeat might have been avoided at Torquay if Ardron had been fouled a few inches nearer goal. As it was, Capel's free-kick from just outside the penalty area was saved.

Forest held onto first place from Millwall on goal-average, with a game in hand, after that setback at Plainmoor, but they were overtaken by the Lions of London after being thwarted by Ipswich manager Scott Duncan's tactical plan. First-time tackling threw Forest's attack completely out of gear. Victory at Newport lifted Millwall a point ahead, but for only a week. Millwall were then held at home by third-placed Norwich while Forest further improved their superior goal figures with a comfortable win away to Leyton Orient (two more for both Ardron and Capel) in a match that marked Horace Gager's 100th League appearance for the club.

By the end of October, Millwall were still level on points with Forest, though still with one more match played, so the meeting of the top two on the first Saturday of November was a natural crowd-puller, attracting a crowd of 33,384 that was the City Ground's biggest of the season. And Forest were not found wanting, scoring through Ardron and Scott without reply. Gager knew too much for Millwall's twin centre-forwards, Jimmy Constantine and Frank Neary, who were unable to unsettle him with their constant switching, but he was fallible when entrusted with a penalty kick. He put the ball too close to goalkeeper Ted Hinton, an Irish international. Harry Walker had a more difficult save to make on the only occasion Neary broke free of Gager's clutches.

In the FA Cup at the end of that month, Forest avenged their defeat at Torquay by sweeping the Devon club out of the first round at the City Ground. Johnson's hat-trick was supplemented by two goals from Collindridge, and one from Scott, for a 6-1 win. 'We want to get through the next round and then be drawn against Tottenham,' said Billy Walker. 'Not that I think we would beat them, but the match would tell me whether the stuff my lads are playing is as good as the other Third Division sides make it look.' But that wish could not be put to the test – not against any of the leading First Division lights, let alone Spurs. Forest did not get through the next round. Drawn away to Rotherham United, they gave their worst display of the season in the battle between the Third Division's North and South leaders, and were undone by a hat-trick from Jack Shaw, the Yorkshire club's replacement for Wally Ardron. With Ardron blotted out by quick tackling, Capel was the scorer of Forest's lone reply.

Forest's return to League action after that defeat was delayed by the postponement of their home match with Newport on a December day of icy conditions in which Sunderland slithered to a remarkable defeat by the odd goal of eleven over at neighbouring Derby. The other clubs forced out of action that afternoon included Norwich, who by then had come through as Forest's closest challengers, and Millwall, who had faltered with further reverses on their travels at Aldershot and Colchester. Norwich, indeed, had not been beaten for eighteen matches at that stage – not since their visit to Forest on 26 August, when Tommy Capel had rounded off a 4-2 home win with a spectacular shot from some 35 yards. After being caught by Norwich in losing the return game at Carrow Road on the last Saturday before Christmas, Forest dropped another point in a scoreless draw with Colchester at the City Ground on Christmas Day, when Norwich were without a match, but they then pulled two points clear by winning at Colchester with two Ardron goals on Boxing Day while Norwich could do no better than draw away to lowly Brighton.

Forest's lead was halved as Norwich again shared the points at home to Brighton in the only League match of the next day, a Wednesday, and on the Saturday the calling-off of Forest's home match with Northampton because of the frost and snow enabled Norwich to end the year in first place with a 5-1 win at Torquay. How desperately close, however, Norwich went to having their undefeated run ended in that second meeting with Brighton. A minute from time Bill Lewis, the City left-back, made a faulty back-pass, and Ken Bennett nipped in to open the scoring for the Sussex club. Straight from the restart, Norwich tore into the attack, and winger John Gavin headed a dramatic equaliser as the referee was preparing to blow the final whistle. There was no time to kick off again, and many in the crowd did not know if that goal counted until the result was announced over the loudspeakers.

Norwich's continued involvement in the FA Cup on the first Saturday of the New Year enabled Forest immediately to reclaim the top position. But it was by only one goal, scored by Capel in the opening half, that Forest overcame the bottom club, Crystal Palace, at the City Ground, whereas Norwich emphasised what a big threat they were to them in the League by winning their third-round home tie against Liverpool, finalists of the previous season. With Everton beaten at Hull, it was the first time both Merseyside clubs had fallen at their first fence in the same year since 1904.

Fickle, however, as football form can be, just a few days later Norwich lost for the first time in two dozen outings in their rearranged away game with Leyton Orient, who were fourth from the foot of the table and had won none of their last nine matches. On a pitch made ankle deep in mud by continuous rain, Norwich were unable to reproduce the flair and poise that had eliminated First Division opposition, and they went on to lose further ground in dropping a home point to Aldershot and losing at Swindon. They were soon to renew their strong challenge, but in the meantime second place was taken over by Bristol Rovers, who were also enjoying a good Cup run (it was to take them to the sixth round for the first time before ending in a replay defeat by Newcastle, the eventual winners of the trophy).

Forest kept a couple of points ahead of the Eastville club despite successive 1-1 draws at Port Vale and at home to Reading. They felt particularly aggrieved about the result against Reading, who were in fourth place, because they held a deserved lead through a great goal by Leverton until conceding a debatable penalty from which the visitors equalised. The referee ruled that Geoff Thomas had handled, but the full-back afterwards complained that 'the ball was going wide, and it hit me before I knew what was happening'. There could be no excuses, however, when later in the season, with the promotion race hotting up to its climax, he gave away a penalty from which Southend United scored their winning goal in the last minute. Forest's wiping-out of a two-goal deficit by a three-minute burst of scoring towards the end of that match in Essex was nullified when Thomas punched the ball over the bar from a corner kick. 'Sorry, boss,' he apologised to Billy Walker. 'I was too enthusiastic.'

Two months before that, on the last Saturday of January, Forest tightened their grip on the leadership in taking advantage of the Cup calls on Bristol Rovers and Norwich. A 6-1 away victory over Crystal Palace, in which all five of their forwards scored, took Forest four points clear of both those rivals, and each had then fulfilled the same number of fixtures (26) because Forest's postponements due to the weather had offset the absences of the two others on Cup duty. After sending Palace packing, Forest again defeated Torquay so decisively that the manager of those visitors, Alex Massie, said they were 'out of their class in Division Three,' yet they promptly failed to exploit their challengers' commitment to another Cup round by losing at Bournemouth.

It also looked ominous for Forest's prospects when Norwich were left to concentrate on the League by a fifth-round exit at Sunderland that one of their officials quixotically blamed on the thick fog of the preceding Friday night ('the players were staying at a sea-front hotel, and they are not accustomed to ships' sirens and fog horns at minute intervals.') In midweek, however, Norwich missed the chance to get within a point of Forest by losing at Reading, who three days later dislodged them from second place —on goal-average, but with two games more played – by also defeating Exeter while Norwich's match at Eastville was controversially abandoned at half-time, with Bristol Rovers leading 2-1, because of the muddy conditions. Forest lost that same Saturday afternoon to a lone goal at Aldershot, where George Warnes put behind him memories of that seven-goal thrashing with a brilliantly defiant display despite limping throughout the second half after having to be carried off with a twisted right knee.

A week later, a young man named Purdie had the misfortune to be Warnes' deputy when seven more goals were put into Aldershot's net at Reading. Forest kept three points ahead of the Berkshire club, with two games in hand, by winning at Ipswich, but next time out they shared Norwich's discomfiture in losing to Leyton Orient. Alec Stock, the Orient manager, was quite right in believing that the good conditions at the City Ground would 'help my boys to play football', though it was a masterly defensive performance that prevented Forest from cancelling out the decisive first-half goal.

Forest bounced back from what was to be their only home defeat of the season with victories at Walsall and at home to Watford, but they were fortunate not to be at least two goals behind at Fellows Park before themselves scoring twice after the interval. Walsall's centre-forward hit a post with the best shot of the game, then failed to score when it seemed impossible to miss. The defeat of Watford took Forest into the Easter programme two points above Norwich, who had returned to second place while Reading had slipped to fourth behind Bristol Rovers after losing heavily to them at Eastville. On Good Friday, Reading were restored to the runners-up spot with the help of a hat-trick against Bristol City by Ronnie Blackman, a centre-forward who was to join Forest just over three years later – and also with the aid of the weather. Forest's game with Bristol Rovers was postponed because of the waterlogged state of the notorious Eastville pitch, and Norwich's match at Newport was abandoned in such acrimonious circumstances that referee Arthur Blythe had to be smuggled out of the ground disguised as a St John ambulance man. The anger of Newport fans who most emphatically disagreed with the decision that the pitch had become unfit for further play was hardly surprising. Their team led 5-1 when the halt was called twenty minutes from time. And when the match was replayed a month later, with Norwich still very much in the hunt for promotion, those Welsh supporters had more reason to feel aggrieved as the again-outplayed visitors salvaged a lucky draw against a team that had only nine fit men for the last quarter of an hour. At the request of Newport, who only the week before had had let in nine goals away to Brighton, there was a different referee on that April evening when Forest also dropped a point – at home to Northampton after leading.

In their home match with mid-table Newport on a very wet Easter Monday, Norwich fell behind during the last ten minutes of the first half to a goal scored on his wedding day by Cliff Birch, one of their former players, while Reg Foulkes, the City's centre-half and captain, was off the field concussed. Foulkes, who had been carried off unconscious after heading the heavy ball immediately before the abandonment of the Good Friday game, resumed after the interval at outside-left in the Easter Monday match, and within ten minutes defied his injury to head an excellent equaliser. A minute later there was more frustration for Newport and their fans when Noel Kinsey, newly capped by Wales, scored the Norwich winner. The hard-earned victory kept Norwich two points behind Forest, who won at home that day against Bristol Rovers by the same score. Ray Warren, the Rovers' captain, had a penalty saved by Harry Walker in the first minute.

At the end of that week, however, the lead was down to one point as Bristol's other club held Forest to a goalless draw in the heavy going of the City Ground while Norwich comfortably disposed of Exeter. Ardron let slip the best chance of that match with Bristol City, shooting straight at the goalkeeper when clean through, but another week later, on the first Saturday of April, he was back to his best with a first-half hat-trick in a 4-1 win at Gillingham that pulled him level with 'Boy' Martin's club record of 31 goals in a season. Norwich won that afternoon at Southend, where on the following Tuesday Forest's last-minute defeat by the penalty Geoff Thomas so controversially conceded led to their loss of the leadership the next day as Norwich snatched both points at Ipswich to reach 56 from 39 games. Forest, who were to go through their remaining eight games unbeaten, then had 55 from 38.

Foulkes excelled in the Norwich defence as Ipswich dominated the first half, then scored the only goal of the match four minutes from the end of the second. 'It was all or nothing if we were going to get that promotion rise,' he said, 'so I shouted to Pickwick [City's right-half] that I was going up into the attack. When I saw the ball coming over I could see a nice vacant spot and I only had to turn my head.'

That record-breaking goal was proving elusive for Ardron. At Southend he hit an upright and missed a gift. In his next match, at home to Bournemouth, he twice hit the bar. The framework of those visitors' goal was altogether struck four times, but a second-half goal from Scott kept Forest just one point behind Norwich, who narrowly defeated third-placed Reading. Forest were at home to Swindon the next Wednesday, April 18, and it was then that Ardron made the record his own – after again twice hitting the framework (and having two other efforts well saved). His second-half goal was the winning odd one of three, but Norwich made the most of their visit the same evening to a Crystal Palace side rooted to last place, enjoying a 5-0 romp. This was how the top of the table looked after those matches:

		P	W	D	L	F	A	Pts
1	Norwich	41	24	12	5	73	35	60
2	Nott'm For	40	25	9	5	93	35	59
3	Reading	42	20	13	9	85	51	53
4	Southend	43	20	9	14	86	64	49
5	Bristol Rov	39	18	12	9	55	34	48

Three days later Forest were back on top – and there to stay. Billy Walker, faced with the decision of whether to have Leverton or Johnson at inside-right for the trip to Exeter, made a good choice. Johnson opened the scoring, and completed a hat-trick after two more goals from Ardron as Forest also forged to a 5-0 away win. Norwich, meanwhile, lost at Plymouth, a Foulkes penalty being all they could manage after being two down at half-time. And at the end of another week, on the Saturday when Newcastle lifted the Cup at Wembley, Norwich lost their unbeaten home record to Ipswich as Forest increased their lead to three points by winning their return game with Southend. Bill Morley, told by his manager to mark Southend danger man, Eire international Jimmy McAlinden ('never leave him and we are on the way to two points'), did such an efficient job that the Essex club's attack was never a real threat. There was no reply to goals scored by Ardron, Johnson and Collindridge. The former Sheffield United winger was entrusted with a penalty after the failures from the spot by Ardron and Gager.

On the following Monday evening, Norwich went to Eastville for their penultimate match knowing that they had to end Bristol Rovers' unbeaten home record to keep in the promotion race. Twice ahead, they were leading 3-2 with eight minutes left for play when Vic Lambden, the Rovers' centre-forward, was brought down in the penalty area. Ray

Warren, the home captain, was a noted spot-kick king, and he duly converted to force the draw that made Forest sure of going up. Two days later, Forest had a struggle to win at home against Newport, Capel grabbing the second-half winner after Collindridge had wiped out the visitors' deserved lead with another penalty, but they were given a great reception as the new champions of the Third Division South.

The very next day, Thursday, Forest had to beard Bristol Rovers in their Eastville stronghold, and they deservedly became the first visitors to succeed there for fourteen months, extending their lead to six points with goals headed by Love (recalled in Capel's absence) and Johnson after 12 and 44 minutes.

So to the final Saturday, 5 May 1951, on which Forest gained a fourth successive victory, and their fourteenth away from home – though it was not until the closing minutes that Collindridge edged them 3-2 in front at Swindon, this time without recourse to a spot kick. That goal took the left-winger to 18 in League and Cup in his first season with the club, and the extent to which he had repaid the confidence placed in him was shown soon afterwards when he was voted one of the most popular men in Nottingham sport.

Forest's other scorers at Swindon were Johnson, who tied in total with Collindridge, and Ardron, whose new Forest record of 36 for one season put him at the top of the Third South's individual scoring list. Ardron finished one ahead of Ronnie Blackman in the League, but four behind him when the Reading centre-forward's Cup goals were taken into account. With Capel contributing 23 goals (and another in the Cup), despite missing a few matches early on through loss of form, Forest were the highest scorers in the whole League with 110 goals against 40 conceded. Only Rotherham's Third North champions also got into three figures, totalling 103. And only Rotherham exceeded, by just one, Forest's number of away wins. These were the final positions at the top of the Southern Section:

Season 1950-51	P	W	D	L	F	A	Pts
1 Nott'm For	46	30	10	6	110	40	70
2 Norwich	46	25	14	7	82	45	64
3 Reading	46	21	15	10	88	53	57
4 Plymouth	46	24	9	13	85	55	57
5 Millwall	46	23	10	13	80	57	56
6 Bristol Rov	46	20	15	11	64	42	55

While Forest celebrated, the club Billy Walker had formerly managed was cast in gloom. The year before, Sheffield Wednesday had pipped their

United neighbours for promotion to the First Division by 0.008 of a goal. Now they were banished back to the Second by 0.044 of a goal – despite breaking the transfer record to sign £35,000 Jackie Sewell from Notts County and crushing Everton, their relegation companions, by 6-0 in their final match. Chelsea pulled off one of the biggest of escape acts by winning each of their last four games after a run of fourteen without a victory had left them six points adrift.

CHAPTER FIFTEEN

On the Fringe of Another Rise

Promotion back to the First Division they had left in 1925 was almost achieved by Nottingham Forest straight after their rise from the Southern Section of the Third. On their return to Division Two, they ended the 1951-52 season in fourth place after being in the lead for several weeks until mid-March, and then still in line to go up again as runners-up with just half-a-dozen games to play. Five more years, during which they again finished fourth but also sagged to as low as fifteenth, were to go by before the big jump to join the elite was accomplished.

That Forest did so well as Second Division new boys in 1951-52 was all the more praiseworthy because they lost key players through injury at critical times. At the end of September, Bill Whare and skipper Horace Gager were casualties during a home game against Doncaster from which Forest were thankful to salvage a point after those visitors had controversially been denied a goal for offside. Whare dislocated his right elbow in the first minute and was out of the team until Boxing Day; Gager damaged a knee a quarter of an hour from the end and was absent for a month. On the day Gager returned, the luckless 'Tucker' Johnson played what was to be his last first-team game for Forest as another home point was fortuitously gleaned from West Ham, who hit both bar and upright and had a penalty disallowed when there was more than a suspicion that a defender had handled as the ball trickled along the goal-line off an upright.

In the eyes of many, however, the injury that did most harm to Forest's promotion prospects was suffered by Colin Collindridge. The popular left-winger's sequence of 72 League appearances since his signing was broken after a defeat by Birmingham City, again at the City Ground, at the end of December. It was Good Friday, when another home point was dropped to Leeds, before he resumed his regular place in the side for the last five games of the season, and even then he was below his best.

The victory with which Birmingham avenged a home defeat inflicted by Forest on the first day of September was gained despite the loss of their captain, Len Boyd, who broke his left leg just before half-time in challenging for possession when the ball, struck with terrific force by his centre-forward, Tommy Briggs, rebounded into play off the crossbar. Briggs, also a prolific marksman with Grimsby and Blackburn, again hit the bar before scoring the only goal of the game in the last ten minutes. Danny Canning was the goalkeeper who had to fish the ball out of the net. He had helped Cardiff out of the Third South, but was only a short-term stand-in for Harry Walker with Forest, whom he joined from Swansea, before going into the Eastern Counties League with Great Yarmouth.

Birmingham's win at the City Ground on the last Saturday of 1951 lifted them to second place in the table on goal-average behind Sheffield Wednesday, whose win at Southampton that afternoon regained the leadership they had lost in taking just one point from their two games with Forest over Christmas. The biggest crowd of the holiday, 61,187, saw Forest force a 1-1 draw in Sheffield on Christmas Day, and 24 hours later thousands were locked out of the return match, with 39,380 inside, as Wednesday could come up with only one reply, from their new scoring sensation, Derek Dooley, to first-half goals by Ardron and Leverton. Forest's scorer at Hillsborough was Noel Kelly, a former Shamrock Rovers, Glentoran and Arsenal forward signed by Billy Walker from Crystal Palace. Kelly, who had made his debut for Forest, along with Canning, in the win at Birmingham, was a delightful ball player, but inclined to be inconsistent. In his four seasons at the City Ground, he fell just short of a half-century of League appearances, scoring fewer than a dozen goals, but one of his rich spells of form, in March 1954, earned him his lone Republic of Ireland cap for a World Cup qualifier against Luxembourg. At the end of the following season he became, at 32, currently the youngest manager of a Football League club with Tranmere Rovers. After two years in that post he was Ellesmere Port's player-manager.

Forest's temporary toppling of Sheffield Wednesday on Boxing Day in 1951 was the third occasion that season on which they defeated Second Division leaders. Under the considerable impetus of Dooley's 46 League goals, Wednesday continued their up-and-down existence of the 1950s by going on to win promotion as champions the year after being relegated, but up to mid-November it was their neighbours over at Bramall Lane who set the pace. And Forest first overcame the team at the top by ending Sheffield United's run of eight home wins by the emphatic margin of 4-1. Tommy Capel celebrated his recall from the Reserves, to which a falling-off in form had consigned him since early September, by equally sharing their goals with Wally Ardron – and Colin Collindridge enjoyed himself against his old club by making three of them.

That defeat did not dislodge United from the leadership, but another one by the same score at Brentford did do so on the following Saturday.

While Rotherham were taking over from the Blades by beating Notts County, Forest went down one place to seventh in being held at home by Barnsley in the most dramatic finish to a game at the City Ground all season. A minute from time the teams were level at 2-2, Capel having again netted twice. As spectators started to drift home a shot from Collindridge was turned into his own goal by 'Skinner' Normanton. Both points for Forest surely? But no. Straight from the restart Barnsley tore back into the attack, and as the referee got ready to blow the final whistle little Cecil McCormack burst through to equalise with his second goal. More drama came at four o'clock the next morning, when David Lindsay, who had played on at right-back for Barnsley despite stomach pains, was rushed to hospital, where he underwent an operation for appendicitis.

Just as Forest were to make something of a habit of halting leaders, neither was it new for them to be involved in such an eventful climax. A couple of months earlier, they outplayed their Notts neighbours for most of the match at Meadow Lane, even though Ardron was handicapped by a muscle injury, and they looked comfortably on the way to victory with goals scored by Collindridge and Love after ten and 48 minutes. Yet they had to settle for a draw. With only five minutes left, Frank Broome was allowed to run through to score when he looked well offside, and in the next minute winger Bob Crookes, a part-timer who taught at a school at nearby Retford, was on the spot to equalise when Harry Walker could only parry a powerful shot from Tommy Lawton. Leon Leuty, a Cup winner with Derby in the first post-war final, was a notable absentee from the Notts defence that afternoon, suffering from gastric influenza. Four years later he died at the tragically early age of 35, the victim of constant buffetings around the area of his kidneys.

Forest's second success of the 1951-52 season against leaders came a month after their emphatic defeat of one Sheffield club (United), and just under a fortnight before they got the better of the other. Their 4-2 home win against Rotherham enabled Sheffield United to have another week at the top, on goal-average, by sharing the points with the team then at the bottom, Blackburn Rovers. Billy Walker was not given to extravagant praise, but after Rotherham had been sent packing he felt moved to say: 'You did well, lads. It's a fine double.' Ardron, captain for the day against his former club, scored twice – as Tom Johnson had done in the 2-0 victory at Millmoor on the opening day that had avenged the Cup defeat there of the previous season.

Ironically, the victories over Rotherham and Sheffield Wednesday were the only ones Forest gained in nine matches around the turn of the year. The last two of those nine were in the Cup against Blackburn, who

by then were off the foot of the Second Division table and heading for
a semi-final with a Newcastle side set for a successful defence of the trophy. That lean sequence for Forest, after seven games unbeaten, began on
a December day of high winds and driving rain. A penalty tipped the
scales against them on their visit to Queen's Park Rangers, whose win by
the odd goal of seven was their first in more than two months. There
were three penalty kicks in the return game in late April, when a 3-1 victory for Forest confirmed QPR's relegation – and each of them was
missed. After Collindridge had failed from the spot, Harry Walker saved
a penalty taken by Conway Smith, but the referee ruled that the goalkeeper had moved too soon and ordered a retake. This time Ernie
Shepherd, a winger from Hull, had a go – and his shot hit an upright.
Smith, who had been signed from Huddersfield just before the March
transfer deadline, preferred to be called Conway, but he had been named
William (Billy) after his famous father, the former Huddersfield and
England outside-left. Dave Mangnall, then the QPR manager, had also
played for Huddersfield.

In their next away match after losing to QPR in London, Forest also
conceded four goals to Cardiff, then began the New Year by letting in
three more in treacherous conditions at Leicester, where the ground staff
worked well into the night to make the flooded pitch fit for play. That
game was the first of nearly a dozen without Collindridge, for whom
Capel and Love deputised in the League between recalls to the left wing
for Leverton. For the home third-round Cup-tie with Blackburn, the
week after the defeat at Leicester, Billy Walker decided to give a first run
in that position to 18-year-old Brian Burton, a boys' clubs international
who had been showing good form in the Midland League. There were to
be only two further first-team chances for this young man – and those
not until 1954, when he was on National Service – but it was not down
to him that Forest failed to progress. Defensive errors enabled Rovers to
earn a replay they won with two first-half goals.

Burton was an apprentice draughtsman at an engineering works when
he became the seventh Forest newcomer that season. The others, in addition to Canning and Kelly, were Alan Orr, Tommy Wilson, Bob McKinlay
and Alan Moore. Orr, a £10,000 buy from Third Lanark, was a clever and
constructive wing-half who had once been a reserve for Scotland, but he
was unable to adjust to the pace of English football. This drawback was
especially evident when he was tried at centre-half during Gager's
absence, and he lost his regular place after the defeat at Cardiff. Not until
after that match did Jack Burkitt re-establish himself, with Bill Morley in
the other wing-half position. Some doubts had arisen about the con-

structive side of Burkitt's game, but on his return he swept them aside so
decisively that at the end of the season he was regarded as Forest's most
improved player. He was back to stay at left-half, occasional injuries apart,
for the rest of the decade.

Bob McKinlay made his debut, replacing Orr as Gager's deputy, in a
3-3 draw at Coventry on 27 October 1951, only just over a fortnight past
his 19th birthday. Bill Bradbury, aged eighteen, was at left-half for the
first time in the home side. All Coventry's goals, in reply to two by Kelly
and one from Johnson, were scored by centre-forward Ted Roberts, who
insisted on playing despite having broken his nose at Leicester the previous weekend. With Gager fit to resume for Forest's next match, that
opportunity at Highfield Road – for which he had waited two years since
being signed – was the only one McKinlay was allowed that season. There
were to be just four more during the following two seasons, but after that
he was such a natural successor when Gager retired that he was unchal-
lenged for the centre-half position from 1954 until late in1968. Eight
times he was an ever-present in the League – six of them in succession
while he made 265 consecutive appearances.

Tommy Wilson also proved an excellent signing, if not on such a
spectacular scale, after being forced to wait patiently for a regular place.
He came to Forest's attention as an outside-right with Cinderhill Colliery,
and it was in that position that he had a couple of games when Fred Scott
was switched to inside-forward in October 1951. Earlier, when Scott had
been out injured, the right-wing position had been entrusted to John
Linaker, a direct type of player with a hard shot who had been signed
from Southport, his home club, after being spotted by G S Oscroft, a
member of the Forest committee. Linaker had to face keen competition
for a first-team place, however, and was soon released to York.

Wilson was 21 only a few weeks before his League debut in a home
win against Luton, and he had then been on the books for just under six
months. He was to make only twice as many first-team appearances as
McKinlay over the next two seasons, but eventually found his most effective niche at centre-forward before his £4,000 transfer to Walsall towards
the end of 1960.

Alan Moore was also a right-winger who had his moments at the head
of the attack. At one stage, indeed, Billy Walker had great hopes of him
as a centre-forward, but it was at outside-right (with his fellow North-
Easterner Scott often showing his versatility in either of the inside berths
before losing a regular place) that he made most of just over 100 appearances, scoring nearly 40 goals, before he left for Coventry shortly before
Christmas in 1954. Moore, who hailed from Hepburn in County

Durham, was one of ten brothers, eight of whom played football. He first came to the fore in his school team at the age of seven, and would later have played for England Boys if the outbreak of war had not cancelled the match for which he was selected. On leaving school he became an apprentice electrician and played for his works team at inside-left. Chosen to play for a Tyneside Youth XI, he scored twice in a drawn game, then netted seven of the nine goals with which his side won the replay in front of his home crowd at Hepburn.

Sunderland were his first Football League club – but only as a part-timer because his father insisted he should first finish his apprenticeship. Soon afterwards he joined Spennymoor United, and it was then that he started to play on the right wing – so successfully that Chesterfield had to shell out the then record fee for a North-Eastern League player to take him to Saltergate, where Tommy Capel was one of his team-mates. After recovering from twice breaking an ankle while with Chesterfield, Moore moved to Hull City, with whom Raich Carter and Don Revie were among his inside partners. Even in a team well beaten by Forest on Humberside, he did enough to convince Billy Walker that he was worth a few thousand pounds of Forest's money, and on 19 January 1952 he almost got off to a dream start in the return home game against Notts County. He put the ball into the net with his first kick, only to have the goal disallowed for some reason not satisfactorily explained. Ardron (2) and Morley got the ones that did count as Forest came from being behind at half-time to win 3-2.

The leadership of the Second Division changed hands yet again that afternoon. Cardiff City, who had taken over from Sheffield Wednesday earlier in the month by beating Doncaster while the Owls were losing at home to Sheffield United, were themselves displaced by a team who were winners against Doncaster. Birmingham City scored five goals with no reply from Rovers at Belle Vue; Cardiff let in three at Everton. A week later, Birmingham were also beaten by Everton, and the Welsh club went back on top with a narrow home victory over Southampton. Forest, meanwhile, defeated their visitors from Brentford, and this time Moore not only scored a valid goal but also provided the centre from which Ardron headed the second.

Moore took on the look of a lucky talisman as Forest extended their unbeaten run since his arrival to seven games. On 9 February, when a minute's silence was observed at all grounds in memory of the late King George VI, a Capel header two minutes from time gave them both points at Doncaster and lifted them to third place, behind Wednesday and Cardiff only on goal-average. All three were on 35 points after Jackie

Sewell had 'done a Dooley' by scoring four goals as Wednesday rallied from being two down at half-time to defeat Cardiff at Hillsborough and reclaim the lead, but the Welsh club had a game in hand. So close was the battle for promotion that Birmingham and Leeds were both on 34 points, Leicester 33, Rotherham, Brentford and Everton all on 32, and Sheffield United, down in tenth place, on 31. Leeds, Leicester, Rotherham and Brentford each also had a game in hand. Just a dozen points separated the top three from the bottom two, Hull and Coventry.

One week on, Forest became the sixth club to nudge in front as they battled back from a half-time deficit to draw 3-3 at Luton. Wingers scored four of the goals – Moore and Leverton (2) for Forest, Bert Mitchell for Luton. The two others, on his debut for the Hatters, were notched by Hugh McJarrow, a former Chesterfield and Wednesday centre-forward. Defeats for Wednesday and Cardiff let in Leicester to second place with a win at Bury, all three a point below Forest. Cardiff lost at Coventry. Wednesday were edged out in a nine-goal thriller at Barnsley, where centre-half Matt McNeil, who resumed limping after being carried off with an ankle injury early in the second half, headed the home side's decider in the last five minutes.

Forest again equally shared six goals after trailing at the interval another week later, this time in a home friendly with First Division Bolton Wanderers on FA Cup fifth-round day. On getting back to League business, they stayed in the lead with home victories over Bury and Coventry either side of a win at Swansea, but then dropped to second behind Birmingham with successive defeats at West Ham and at home to Sheffield United. They looked little like promotion material in winning at Bury with a 70th-minute goal Morley scored past an unsighted goalkeeper, and almost conceded a late equaliser when Harold Bodle, a former Birmingham forward, shot into the side net. Ardron was held in a firm grip by Bert Head, who was making his debut for Bury after his transfer from Torquay, and, with Leverton switched to lead the line, the normally ace marksman was rested from the visit to Swansea.

It was only the fourth time Ardron had been out of the side since his arrival from Rotherham, but he was back with a goal in the 3-1 defeat of Coventry. He was also Forest's only scorer at West Ham as Birmingham took over the lead on goal-average by winning at Barnsley under the handicap of losing winger Jackie Stewart with a fractured cheek bone. On the same day, Derek Dooley equalled Jimmy Trotter's Wednesday record of 37 League goals in a season by scoring twice in a draw at Notts County. Two more in his next game, in a midweek home win against Luton, gave him the record outright and helped Wednesday back to the

top. Ardron was to end the season with a creditable total of 29 goals, but
he was outscored in the Second Division by both Dooley, who finished
with 46 (plus one in the Cup) despite not getting into the Wednesday
team until October, and Leicester's Arthur Rowley, who that season took
his club's record from Arthur Chandler (then their assistant trainer) with
38 League goals and two in the Cup – a total he exceeded with 44 in 1956-
57 on his way to becoming the League's most prolific scorer of all with a
career aggregate of 434.

Forest faltered on the 1951-52 run-in by gaining only one victory in
seven matches before their last-day defeat of Queen's Park Rangers. And
that success was achieved by the flattering margin of 4-0 against the only
club then above QPR in the table – Hull City, who had Viggo Jensen,
their Danish international, ordered off, and had to put wing-half Bill
Harris in goal when Billy Bly, one of their most long-serving players,
withdrew from the action with an injured back. Hull managed to pull
clear of relegation (Coventry went down with QPR), but their misery was
completed that Easter afternoon when Neil Franklin, their former
England centre-half, missed a penalty in the last minute.

Forest's attack was below par in the 0-2 home defeat by Sheffield
United, though Capel was out of luck when he headed the ball down-
wards towards the corner of the net, only to see it bounce over the bar
with the goalkeeper powerless to intervene. They were also beaten at
Blackburn, but a draw at Barnsley, and two more with Leeds on Good
Friday and Easter Monday, kept them in third place until Cardiff pushed
them down to their final position of fourth, on goal-average, by winning
3-1 at home to Blackburn as the finishing line loomed.

Sheffield Wednesday, having regained the lead they had again temporarily lost to Birmingham, had by then made sure of the championship.
With one game to play they had 52 points. Birmingham, who also had
one match remaining, were second, three points behind, but had left
themselves wide open to being beaten to the other promotion place by
Cardiff after losing to the Welsh club in their return Easter Monday
match at Ninian Park and then being thrashed away to Notts County, four
of whose five goals were scored by Ron Wylie. Forest and Cardiff were
on 47 points, but whereas Billy Walker's men had only the fixture with
QPR to fulfil, Cardiff had two more games left. And both those were at
home – against Bury, who were not far above the relegation zone, and
sixth-placed Leeds, whose star man, John Charles, had just had a cartilage
operation after injuring his left knee while playing for his Army unit.

On April 26, Birmingham completed their programme with a home
win over Luton that put them two points behind Wednesday in what they

hoped would be the final reckoning. Sewell missed a penalty for the Sheffield club, who had to come from two goals down to draw with West Ham at Hillsborough. But Cardiff disposed of Bury while Forest, though out of the hunt, ended on a winning note. This meant Birmingham faced an anxious wait to know their fate. Cardiff were not to play their final match until the following Saturday. Consequently, on 3 May much attention was diverted from Wembley, where Newcastle defeated injury-hit Arsenal to keep the Cup, to what was going on at Ninian Park. And it was as good as over by half-time. Cardiff were then two goals up against Leeds, and went on to gain a 3-1 victory that took them above Birmingham on goal-average. They were back in the First Division after a lapse of 23 years during which they had sunk as low as having to seek re-election to the League. These were the final leading positions:

Season 1951-52	P	W	D	L	F	A	Pts
1 Sheffield Wed	42	21	11	10	100	66	53
2 Cardiff	42	20	11	11	72	54	51
3 Birmingham	42	21	9	12	67	56	51
4 Nott'm For	42	18	13	11	77	62	49
5 Leicester	42	19	9	14	78	64	47
6 Leeds	42	18	11	13	59	57	47

Home form clearly counted for Cardiff, whose number of away wins was exceeded even by bottom-of-the-table QPR. The only winners at Ninian Park in the League that season were Rotherham United, who finished ninth. They were successful there by 4-2 on the evening of Monday, 20 August. Five days later, Cardiff gained the first of their two away victories – against Nottingham Forest. All the goals in their 3-2 win came in the first half. Blackburn, who came fourteenth, were the only other club Cardiff defeated away from home, by 1-0 in November. Cardiff also failed to beat Third Division Swindon Town in the Cup, losing a replay in Wiltshire by an only goal in extra time.

CHAPTER SIXTEEN

A Poison-Pen Letter

Billy Walker made a double splash in the transfer market in an attempt to arrest a run of five defeats in seven games that caused Forest to slip just below halfway in the Second Division towards the end of October in 1952. He paid out £15,000 to bring in Tommy Martin, an inside-forward, from Doncaster Rovers. Next day, the last one of the month, he signed wing-half Jack French from Southend United for £10,000.

The beneficial effect was immediate, though not to be sustained sufficiently for another promotion bid to succeed. Forest won each of their next five matches – one of them at St Andrew's, where they inflicted Birmingham's biggest defeat since the war. Wally Ardron, who had been a doubtful starter because of an ankle injury, scored three of the five goals to which there was no reply from a side deprived that week of their ace marksman by the transfer of Tommy Briggs to Blackburn.

Ardron was himself missing, rested, when Forest's unbeaten run since the double signing ended at Blackburn on the last Saturday before Christmas, but on Boxing Day he was back with a four-goal broadside at home against Hull. He had twice scored four times in a match for Rotherham – curiously enough on the same date, 13 September, in successive years, 1947 and 1948, against Carlisle and Hartlepool.

Forest conceded a penalty for the third successive game when Viggo Jensen popped in Hull's only goal in the second half of that match at the City Ground. At Blackburn there were two spot kicks, both forcefully converted by Bill Eckersley, the Ewood Park club's England full-back. In the match before that, the successful taker was another capped defender, Peter Sillett, who helped Southampton to a draw at The Dell. Two seasons later Sillett, whose brother John accompanied him from the Saints to Chelsea, hammered home the winning penalty past Wolves' England goalkeeper Bert Williams that as good as clinched a first Division One title for the Stamford Bridge club.

Forest's attack was led by Alan Moore in the absence at Blackburn of Ardron, whose 22 goals that season made him Forest's top scorer for the fourth consecutive year despite his also missing several matches with back trouble. This was at the time when Billy Walker had particularly high hopes of Moore as a centre-forward. The former Hull player had scored thirteen goals from that position for the Reserves in seven Midland League games, six of them in the last two, but he was soon back in his usual right-wing groove. Ironically, he was at inside-left when he achieved his biggest haul of five goals in one game for the club, but that was only in a friendly at Bexhill-on-Sea, where Forest were 12-1 winners.

The scorer of Forest's reply to Eckersley's first-half penalties at Blackburn was 'Tot' Leverton, who had forced his way back into the first team at inside-right after refusing to join Southend in part exchange for French. His preference for staying in the Nottingham area was satisfied with a change of club early the following season, when he threw in his lot with Notts County on the same October day that the Magpies also signed winger Billy Coole from Mansfield Town – both for a fee just under five figures. Just over a week later, Leverton revisited the City Ground as one of five former Forest players in a Notts team well beaten by 5-0. The others were Aubrey Southwell, Bill Baxter, Jack Edwards and Tom Johnston (who was debited with an own-goal).

Leverton, whose slight build (hence his nickname) was strengthened by the weight-lifting he took up as a hobby with advice from Ardron, occupied all five positions in the forward-line formation of the time in making 105 League and Cup appearances for Forest following his return from wartime Army service in Palestine. To the 36 goals he scored in those games he added just five in 50 first-team outings for Notts County before dropping back into the Third Division South with Walsall. In his one season there he took his career totals to 44 goals and 172 games, then joined another former Notts player, Jesse Pye, who made the move from Derby County, in signing for Wisbech Town during the 1957 close season.

Walsall might also have been a destination for Noel Kelly. Forest agreed terms for his transfer to that club on the day Tommy Martin was brought in, but he refused to go even though his first-team opportunities would obviously become further restricted. Martin had himself just declined a move – to Leicester City, whose offer had been accepted by Doncaster. With Preston among the other clubs interested, Billy Walker and chairman Jack Brentnall hurriedly made the 45-mile car journey to Doncaster to complete a deal to which Martin was more amenable because Alan Orr, one of his new clubmates, was an old friend. Orr, however, lost his place at right-half to Jack French on the day, the first of November, when Martin made his Forest debut in a win at Rotherham at the expense (more irony) of the club's previous costliest capture – Tommy Capel.

The tall and fair-haired Martin played for Tollcross YMCA and Shettleston Juniors before joining Hearts as a teenager in 1942. After seven years at Tynecastle he had been with Stirling Albion for only a few months when he was transferred to Doncaster in the summer of 1950. At £6,000, he proved a real bargain for the Yorkshire club under the astute direction of player-manager Peter Doherty, to whom he bore a strong, and often confusing, on-field resemblance. It was said that the likeness first prompted Doherty to operate his switching of positions in the forward line that so baffled opponents during games.

Like Orr, however, Martin was unable to hold a regular first-team place with Forest for long – at either inside-forward or wing-half. Even so, he attracted the attention of Derby County while the Rams were unsuccessfully struggling to avoid falling into the Third Division for the first time, and he would have gone to the Baseball Ground if they had been prepared to pay the £8,000 fee Forest were asking. The move Martin eventually made, in the 1955 close season, took him to Hull City for £1,000 less. He was at his most influential for Forest in the club's Midland League title-winning team of 1953-54, when he and Bill Morley, who was out of first-team favour for the whole of that season, injected valuable experience into the middle line. That was also the season in which Orr enjoyed his last short spell in the League side. He and Martin both just failed to complete a half-century of senior appearances for Billy Walker.

The downturn in fortune Martin experienced at the City Ground also spread to his golf game during his stay with Forest. In the professional footballers' golf championship at Little Aston, Birmingham, on 12 October 1953, he putted beautifully on the 18th green. The ball went straight to the hole, hit the back of the tin, and came out. That cost him the title. His round of 78 left him tied for first place with Ronnie Simpson, the Newcastle goalkeeper, and he lost the play-off.

Forest also had to face keen competition to sign Jack French, a strong-tackling attacking type of wing-half who quickly became one of the out-standing members of the team. His appetite for a higher grade of foot-ball had been whetted a few months before he left Southend by his selec-tion for an England 'B' trial team that defeated the British Olympic XI at Highbury. For just short of 60 consecutive games he formed an impres-sive middle line with Gager and Burkitt before damaging an ankle back where he had started out with Forest, at Rotherham. The injury was slow to mend, and he had been out of action for nearly three months when he began his comeback in the Midland League.

Not for just over a year did French get back into the Second Division side – and then, on 12 February 1955, it was at inside-right, from where he scored the goal that appeared to have earned Forest a point at Meadow Lane until Notts County scored three times in the last ten minutes to

complete a season's double over their neighbours. It was a most inappropriate occasion for Wally Ardron to play his final, isolated, League game
for Forest. After the short spell that Ardron, a qualified masseur, spent
with Selby Town the following season, he was manager-coach of
Rawmarsh Welfare, the Yorkshire League club for which his younger
brother Charlie had been a regular scorer in the Sheffield Association
League.

By the time of French's return to Forest's team in the forward line, the
right-half position was firmly back in the possession of Bill Morley after
this wholehearted Nottingham-born player, originally a forward, had
been out of the first-team reckoning for the remarkable span of two
years. Morley missed only six games in two seasons, four of them
through injury during the 1950-51 promotion campaign, before loss of
form and a slipped disc made him something of a forgotten man. After
his belated return he was a first choice for four more seasons – an ever-
present when promotion was again won, to the First Division in 1956-57.
His final appearance for the club, on the last day of the 1958-59 season,
was his 301st in League and Cup. Tees-sider Jack French got close to a
century of Forest games before returning to Southend, who had first
signed him from Middlesbrough. In July 1958, after two seasons back in
Essex, he moved to Folkestone.

There were two other Forest newcomers besides French and Martin
in 1952-53. Sid Thompson, a youngster from Durham, had just a couple
of games early on as Morley's deputy at right-half, but over the next two
seasons he showed more promise, if with limited chances, at inside-forward before leaving for Scunthorpe. Difficult to shake off the ball, he
possessed a strong shot in either foot that brought him eight goals in
twenty-two appearances. The other debutant, Arthur Lemon, was primarily regarded as a centre-forward when he joined Forest on a supporter's
recommendation in February 1951, while serving in the Army, but it was
at inside-left that he was introduced to Second Division action at
Leicester two years later. Moore led the attack in one of Ardron's
absences that day, and scored the goal that earned a draw. Lemon was also
in an unbeaten side as he kept his place for the next two games – drawn
goalless at home to West Ham and won with an own goal at Fulham –
but, with Ardron fit again and Capel again recalled, he had to wait until
the next season for an extended run.

The opportunities Lemon was then given were mainly at centre-forward while Ardron was recovering from a cartilage operation. A late
developer at soccer, having played rugby at school in his native Neath,
Lemon had encouraged talk of being a good prospect for a Welsh cap by

being a ready scorer in the Midland League, but his failure to find goals so easy to come by at the higher level soon made him a target for much barracking from small sections of the home crowd. Indeed, he was to score only one goal in his two dozen first-team games – and that in November 1953 against a Derby team in free-fall over three seasons from First Division to Third. The answer to the problem of finding an adequate successor to Ardron was most definitely not A Lemon.

Billy Walker, who completed twenty years in club management on 7 December 1953, had already said of Lemon that he 'would have to put him on the transfer list if he doesn't get a fair crack of the whip' when the criticism of this unfortunate young man took a very ugly turn. Shortly before the Forest team set out for a match at Rotherham on 16 January 1954, an anonymous 'letter of hate' was delivered by messenger to Lemon. Help was sought from the police in attempting to track down the writer, but without success. 'In all my experience,' said the Forest manager, 'I have never known a more dastardly attempt to put a player off his game. How can a boy be expected to do well when he gets a scurrilous letter just before an important match? It is enough to put off an experienced player, never mind a youngster who is making his mark this season.' Walker believed no regular Forest supporter would 'stoop to do such a thing.' He thought this poison-pen letter was written by someone who was determined to try to wreck the club's promotion chances.

Forest went into that match at Millmoor fourth in the Second Division table. Although beaten at Plymouth in the Cup the week before, they had been going strongly in the League, having lost only once (also at Plymouth) in five games since Ardron's scoring return in a home draw with Oldham early in December. The last three of those games had been won on the back of six more goals from Ardron – three of them at the beginning of a Christmas double over Leeds. For the visit to Rotherham Lemon was back at inside-left, where he was not alone in failing to find the target as unsettled Forest not surprisingly slipped to a 3-0 defeat that equalled their biggest of that 1953-54 season (the other at Hull).

Capel was once more recalled to the exclusion of Lemon as Forest immediately bounced back by knocking Leicester off their top perch with a 3-1 win in front of the City Ground's biggest crowd of the season, 34,271. And Capel was the scorer of Forest's first goal, though he was nearly beaten to it by little Hugh McLaren, a left-winger signed from Derby the previous day. McLaren, a noted goal poacher, almost found the net the first time he touched the ball, but he did not let that near-miss upset him. He played a part in Capel's goal, then scored the two others himself. It was a repeat of the two-goal debut he had made for Derby after his move there from Kilmarnock had enabled him to fulfil an ambition by partnering Scottish international Billy Steel. As a stand-in for Collindridge, and then briefly for Kelly at inside-right, McLaren maintained his flying start with four more goals in his next five matches, and he averaged almost a goal for every two of just over 30 games before his departure to Walsall after the following season. A poultry farmer away from football, he subsequently put in a couple of years at Gresley Rovers, but died at the early age of 39 in December 1965.

Shortly after signing McLaren, Billy Walker made it known that he was ready to negotiate for one of two centre-forwards who had been among the most prolific scorers since the war – Andy Graver, of Lincoln City, or Cecil McCormack, of Notts County. 'It depends,' he said, 'if either of those clubs is interested in players in our reserve team.' At the time, that reserve team was mainly an experienced one, with several seniors included either because they were coming back after injury or were needing to regain form. This was the line-up: Farmer; Whare, Clarke; Morley, McKinlay, Barclay; Wilson, Thompson, Ardron, Scott, Collindridge.

The only one of those players not to appear in the first team was Fred Barclay, a Dundee-born half-back who had been recommended by a Warrant Officer named Danny Long while serving with the RAF in the Middle East. Bill Farmer, a fearless 6ft-tall goalkeeper from Guernsey, had made his League debut earlier in that 1953-54 season in a 2-0 midweek defeat of Hull City. Billy Walker, who described him as 'a great discovery,' had signed him a couple of years before, in face of strong competition from Southampton and Tottenham, after a tip-off from Ted Malpas, a former Villa colleague who was also behind Bill Whare's move to the City Ground. Whare was born on Alderney but also lived on Guernsey, where he was educated – and from where he was deported to Germany during the war when the Channel Islands were occupied. He spent the rest of the war in an internment camp.

Farmer gained his first chance in Forest's League side because of an injury that ended a run of 68 League and Cup games by Harry Walker, and he stayed in for five more matches before himself going on the casualty list with a damaged shoulder. 'He took some bad knocks in a draw at Lincoln,' said his manager, 'and we have spent the week afterwards telling him how to keep out of trouble.'

Tempting though some of the men in Forest's reserve team might have been for would-be buyers when Billy Walker invited interest, neither Graver nor McCormack was to land up at the City Ground. Graver was still regarded as being 'in the England B team class' by Lincoln's manager, Bill Anderson, and it was obvious that he was out of Forest's reach in a straight cash deal when he was transferred to Leicester City for £30,000 after attracting interest from several other clubs. Within a few months he was back at Lincoln, dissatisfied with being in the Reserves while Leicester were heading for an immediate return to the Second Division. But he was soon on his way out again, to Stoke, and then to Midland League Boston United – from where, in 1958, he yet again returned to Lincoln. The diminutive McCormack was seen as Tommy Lawton's successor when Notts County paid £23,000 for him, but manager George Poyser said he wanted 'someone with more weight,' in putting him on the transfer list. No longer as ready a scorer as he had been with Gateshead and Barnsley, McCormack went into the Eastern Counties League with King's Lynn.

Billy Walker was looking for a new centre-forward midway through the 1953-54 season because Wally Ardron was then into his 36th year and becoming more prone to injury. Even so, Ardron was still in demand – from Oldham Athletic, whose manager, George Hardwick, the former Middlesbrough and England full-back, saw him as 'the ideal type of goal-getter we need' as the Lancashire club battled to avoid relegation from the Second Division. Hardwick 'phoned Walker for preliminary talks about Ardron on the eve of an early February home match with Fulham in which Colin Collindridge was restored to the Forest team as the latest leader of their front line, but the fee Oldham decided to offer after holding a special board meeting was unacceptable. With no real answer found to their goal famine, Oldham were unable to escape from the foot of the table and dropped back into the Northern Section of the Third Division from which they had emerged as champions only the year before.

Nottingham Forest, meanwhile, were pressing on with their attempt to get out of the Second Division at the opposite end. After their defeat of Fulham, based on a Capel hat-trick, they lost only two of their remaining dozen League games – both by an only goal, away to Bristol Rovers and at home to Blackburn – but had to be satisfied with a final fourth place for the second time in three years. The defeat by Blackburn, in their final home game, was the only one they suffered in the League at the City Ground all season – and it took a penalty by England winger Bobby Langton to obtain it. There were other winning visitors, but in a friendly match. Aston Villa, then a mid-table First Division side, won 2-0 on the date of the Cup's fourth round, from which they and Forest had been eliminated. The crowd, just over 8,000, was the smallest at the ground since about a thousand fewer had attended the last match of the previous season, when a defeat by the odd goal of three by Southampton had confirmed Forest in a final position of seventh.

Nine of Forest's fifteen victories at home in 1953-54 were gained in succession after they had opened that season by equally sharing six goals with Everton in an unusual midweek start made by 66 of the 92 League clubs. Also unusual was the fact that the return game with Everton at Goodison Park ended in another 3-3 draw. The most eventful of the wins in the successful sequence at the City Ground was gained by 5-4 against Stoke City. Alan Moore, in his right-wing mode, scored twice in a minute after the visitors had taken the lead, and he completed his only League hat-trick for the club as Forest, 4-1 ahead early in the second half, just managed to cling onto both points.

Forest's consistent home results offset their less impressive form away from home, where they gained only five wins against nine defeats, and kept them in the running for promotion right up to Easter. On Good Friday they were in fourth place, only two points behind the leaders with three games to go, after one of the four penalties Horace Gager converted in their last seven matches salvaged a hard-fought home draw with Birmingham City, the club immediately below them. The tension that afternoon built up to such a volatile level that two of the visitors' players, goalkeeper Gil Merrick and centre-half Trevor Smith, had to be given a police escort back to their dressing room at the final whistle. A crowd had formed on the field after Merrick and Capel had been involved in a goal-mouth incident.

The situation at the top was even more fraught. Leicester City went into the holiday programme back in the leadership they had wrested from Everton after shaking off the disappointment of losing to Preston in the second replay of an FA Cup quarter-final, but they were promptly dislodged again in losing 3-0 on Good Friday at Blackburn, who took over on goal-average. Blackburn, newly guided by future Forest manager Johnny Carey, tightened their grip next day with their away win over Forest while Leicester were held at home by the two goals Tom Johnston scored for Notts County – only for the top two positions to be reversed once more as Leicester won their return game with Blackburn 4-0 on Easter Monday. At that stage, with Leicester ahead on 54 points, Blackburn second on 53 (both with one match to play), and Everton third on 52 with two games left, any one of those top three could win the title or gain promotion as runners-up. Forest, who again shared the points with Birmingham when they met at St Andrew's, aided by another of Gager's penalties, were out of the running with 50 points from 41 games.

On the following Saturday, Leicester won 3-1 at Brentford, who were relegated with Oldham, to maintain their one-point lead over Blackburn, who scored the only goal of their final game at home to Swansea. But Everton defeated Birmingham at Goodison Park, also by 1-0, which meant that the second promotion place remained in the balance until the next Thursday evening. It was then that Everton had to travel to where Forest had wound up on that last Saturday with their twentieth victory of the season – Boundary Park, Oldham. And Blackburn hopes were dashed as Everton eased above them by scoring four times while keeping their own goal intact. Such a clear win was not quite enough, however, to snatch the title. Leicester took it by 1.62 of a goal to Everton's 1.59. Everton scored six goals against both Derby and Brentford, then eight against Plymouth; in successive home games Leicester scored nine against Lincoln and six against Brentford. These were the final leading positions:

Season 1953-54	P	W	D	L	F	A	Pts
1 Leicester	42	23	10	9	97	60	56
2 Everton	42	20	16	6	92	58	56
3 Blackburn	42	23	9	10	86	50	55
4 Nott'm For	42	20	12	10	86	59	52
5 Rotherham	42	21	7	14	80	67	49
6 Luton	42	18	12	12	64	59	48

With Leicester (though destined for immediate relegation) boosted by 36-goal Arthur Rowley, Everton by the twin strike force of John Parker (31 goals) and Dave Hickson (25), and Blackburn by 32-goal Tommy Briggs, Forest were clearly outgunned. Alan Moore was their leading scorer with 19 goals, one more than Tommy Capel. After having been the club's main marksman in each of his first four seasons following his arrival from Rotherham, Ardron still managed to get into double figures (just), despite making only fifteen appearances. He was brought back to lead the attack towards the end of the season, but missed the final match at Oldham, where Tommy Wilson became Forest's fifth player of the campaign to be tried there.

One of Ardron's goals, in a 2-2 draw at home with lowly Bury, was Forest's 3,000th in the Football League. They had conceded their 3,000th in their first game of the previous 1952-53 season, in a 2-1 home defeat by Blackburn.

CHAPTER SEVENTEEN

Major Team Rebuilding

With a rise to the First Division having again been tantalisingly just out of reach, the time had come for Billy Walker to do some major team rebuilding – especially after Forest had opened the 1954-55 season with five successive defeats, the first four without scoring a goal. One Sunday newspaper called for two minutes' silence to be observed for the club.

The process of reorganising the side's make-up had already begun in June 1954 with the sale to Coventry City of the Capel-Collindridge left-wing pairing, and the purchase of centre-forward Ronnie Blackman from Reading. Coventry's newly-appointed manager, the former Newcastle goalkeeper Jack Fairbrother, was also revamping his line-up, in the wake of a boardroom shake-up, and the Forest pair were his first important signings at a fee well into five figures – not a bad deal from Forest's view-point considering that Collindridge was then 34 and Capel only a few weeks from his 32nd birthday.

As when they had been injected into Forest's attack, both quickly made an impression back in the Third South, but 'the team that Jack built' faltered after leading the table and the dream of promotion had faded by the time Alan Moore also took the path from City Ground to Highfield Road a few days before Christmas. By then Fairbrother had left. Within a few weeks of taking the Coventry job in January 1954 he had become a widower with two young children after the death of his wife in an accident at home, and he resigned in the autumn of that year for 'personal reasons.'

In such harrowing circumstances, the partnership between Capel and Collindridge was soon broken up after the 1954-55 season. To the 72 goals he had scored in 162 appearances for Forest, Capel added 23 in 40 games for Coventry before making Halifax Town his sixth club in ten years; Collindridge followed his Forest totals of 156 games and 47 goals with 35 and six, respectively, for Coventry, then went into the Southern League with Bath City. Capel was later back with brother Fred at both Sutton, in Nottinghamshire, and the Derbyshire club Heanor Town. Collindridge and one of his new clubmates, Kevin Singfield, left Bath early in 1957 with the intention of hitch-hiking to Australia, where Collindridge's wife and baby daughter were on holiday, but they arrived back in England after getting no further than Marseilles in the south of France.

The signing of Ronnie Blackman was part of Billy Walker's main objective to put new life into the ageing spine of Forest's team – goalkeeper, centre-half and centre-forward. Harry Walker was 38, Horace Gager 37, and the increasingly injury-prone Ardron not far off 36. On past form Blackman, who was in his mid-twenties, looked the perfect replacement for Ardron, whose retirement from League football at the end of the 1954-55 season left only two double-century scorers still in it – Tommy Lawton, then nearing the end of his senior career with Arsenal, and Charlie Wayman, who had reached Middlesbrough by way of Newcastle, Southampton and Preston, and was soon to sign off at Darlington.

Blackman was a dockyard worker, playing for Gosport Borough, when Ted Drake, the former Arsenal and England centre-forward, took him to Reading in 1948. Southampton, Drake's first League club, had reckoned Blackman too frail on the evidence of one trial, but he had 158 goals to his name, a Reading record, when he was persuaded to change clubs by Billy Walker only a few months after refusing a move to Southend. His 39 League goals for Reading in one season, 1951-52, have also still to be bettered.

On those figures, it was quite reasonable to expect Blackman to carry on at the City Ground from where he had left off at Elm Park. But he utterly failed to fit in. Indeed, Ardron was back at the head of Forest's attack, if only temporarily, after that alarming opening losing sequence, and at the end of the 1954-55 season Blackman was offloaded to Ipswich Town. He had scored only three goals in his eleven League games for Forest – the first in a comfortable defeat of Derby during a brief recall, the others point-savers in isolated late appearances against Bury and West Ham.

That was the season in which Derby completed their rapid descent into the Third Division. And Ipswich Town, champions of the Southern Section only the year before, were their companions. Back in the division where he had started, Blackman scored a dozen goals in nearly 30 games as Ipswich finished a close third, then Third South champions again (on goal-average from Torquay United) under the new management of one Alf Ramsey. But the Suffolk club's remarkable rise to the First Division was too far way, in 1961, for Blackman to play a part in that too. After rejecting a transfer to Exeter City, he left for Tonbridge in the summer of 1958.

Billy Walker was eventually to appreciate that, in Tommy Wilson, he had an answer to the centre-forward succession ready to hand after all. Other players already on the staff more promptly filled the two other 'spine' positions. It needed no mastermind to see that Bobby McKinlay, exempted from National Service because of ear trouble, was just the man to take over from Gager, who yielded the automatic place he had held throughout the past six seasons after the first two matches of 1954-55. And Bill Farmer's patient wait for a regular place ended when Harry Walker was finally forced out the game by further injury in mid-October. Farmer, whose accurate distribution of the ball was a big asset, either through his strong kicking or throws-out to the wings, made an encouraging advance that season. After only three games of the following one, however, he dropped out injured and had the misfortune to become a deputy once more when 6ft 3in Harry Nicholson, obtained on a free transfer from Grimsby after impressing Billy Walker in a Midland League game against Forest's reserve team, played too well as his replacement to be kept out. Nicholson's debut, in a 2-0 home win against Leicester, coincided with a unique event. On his 279th appearance, Geoff Thomas scored the only goal he was to obtain in his 431 League and Cup games for Forest. He had moved out to the wing with an ankle injury.

As a result of Nicholson's intervention, Farmer had only just under 60 League and Cup appearances under he belt when, after six years with Forest, he signed for Brush Sports, a Loughborough works team. It was the first of three occasions in just over two years on which he left a Football League club. Within a month he was with Oldham Athletic, who hurriedly required a replacement when Derek Williams was posted overseas in the Forces.

From Oldham Farmer went to Worcester City, then had an unsuccessful trial with Coventry City before joining Corby Town. His younger brother Ronnie, a constructive wing-half with a penchant for scoring spectacular long-range goals and a sure-shot from the penalty spot, was also with Forest, whom he joined at the tender age of fifteen. Ronnie looked a particularly exciting prospect in the youth team, but, with more senior players in the way, he had few first-team opportunities before also going to Coventry, where he developed fully into the force Billy Walker had predicted. Whereas brother Bill had not got near the City's senior side, Ronnie was a key member of it in the club's zoom from Fourth Division to First, totalling more than 300 appearances before returning to Nottingham with Forest's neighbours. After some 70 games for Notts County he went to Grantham.

Shortly before Bill Farmer finally took over from Harry Walker in Forest's goal, Billy Walker failed with one £10,000 offer for a new forward but succeeded with another. The player who eluded him was Ron Stockin; the one he landed was Peter Small. Forest were the only club in

the League without a point or a goal when Walker agreed terms with
Wolverhampton Wanderers for Stockin on 3 September 1954, only to
find the former Walsall inside-forward unwilling to commit himself until
after he had been seen by representatives of four other clubs in the 'shop
window' with Wolves Reserves the next day. And one of those clubs,
Cardiff City, were a bigger attraction for him as members of the First
Division than a side struggling at the foot of the Second. Stockin went to
Wales for a fee said to be £12,000.

The signing of Small from Leicester City was completed in unusual
circumstances. The former Luton winger travelled to Walker's home in
the Nottinghamshire village of Ruddington, where the Forest manager
was ill with fibrositis, and completed the forms at his bedside. Taking the
place of McLaren at outside-left, Small scored on his debut in a 2-0 home
win against Ipswich Town that lifted Forest out of the relegation zone in
which they had spent all but one week of the season's first two months.
It was Ipswich's seventh successive defeat, and they were down at the
bottom of the table with Middlesbrough, who had also suffered a seventh beating in a row when Forest had halted their own shocking start by
doing a midweek double over them a little earlier. Boro, subjected to
boos, jeers and the slow handclap as Forest won 4-1 on their first visit to
Ayresome Park for 25 years, were newly relegated from Division One,
but they were to pull well clear of another descent. Fortunately for
Forest, the continued feeble form of Ipswich and Derby allayed real fears
of a return of Third Division fare to the City Ground, though a final
position of 15th was disturbing enough.

Small, adept at cutting into the middle for a quick shot, pepped up
Forest's attack from both wings besides scoring in both his games at the
head of the attack that season, but the inside-forward positions persisted
in posing particular problems during that period. Ten players were tried
at inside-right, just two fewer at inside-left. These included two, Keith
Turner and Malcolm Cluroe, who were given just the one senior chance,
and another, Alan Holder, who had only four. Turner, recently demobilised from National Service in the RAF after being spotted playing for
his station team at nearby Watnall, was discarded following the opening
defeat by an only goal at Luton. Cluroe, a boys' clubs international who
had not long turned professional, suffered the same fate after being in the
side trounced 5-1 by the Hatters in the return match on the last Saturday
before Christmas. – Forest's heaviest home League defeat for 24 years.

Holder hailed from Oxford, but came to Forest's attention while stationed with the RAOC in the Chilwell district of Nottingham. He was
signed on completing his Army service, and made his debut on the

October day of Bill Farmer's recall in a win at Plymouth, where Noel Kelly scored both Forest's goals with the aid of a penalty. Holder made one of his other appearances during a Cup run that provided some welcome relief from frequently disappointing League form. After the 3-1 third-round defeat at Bramall Lane of First Division Sheffield United, who were handicapped by an injury to their star man Jimmy Hagan, Holder deputised for the injured Kelly in a 1-1 draw at Hartlepools. Forest did not take their full allocation of tickets for that game, but the attendance of 17,200 set a ground record, which rose to 17,426 for Manchester United's visit in the third round two years later. Forest won the replay 2-1, but only after extra time, and that set the scene for a fifth-round tie with Newcastle that went to two replays and caused some off-field friction.

Newcastle were in the top half of the First Division, whereas Forest went into their first meeting at the City Ground with only five clubs below them in the Second. Yet Forest had the better of the play even when reduced to ten men by an injury to Small, who was taken to hospital for an x-ray after a tackle by 'iron man' Jimmy Scoular, but returned a quarter of an hour from the end. The 1-1 draw was therefore a somewhat lucky one for Newcastle, whose limbering-up exercises in preparation for the tie had been done in a hotel ballroom because of snow at their Blackpool training quarters. Snow covered much of the country from York to Swansea during a cold spell in which all bets on the football pools had to be cancelled for the first time in seven years, and it was because of the extremely bad weather that the dispute between the clubs arose.

The pitch for the first replay at Newcastle, where four goals were equally shared before extra time failed to find a winner on the last day of February, a Monday, was liberally covered with straw to protect it from twelve degrees of frost on the Saturday night after Sunderland had won there in a League game made possible by the clearance of snow. Even so, the ground was still so hard that Jack French, who had been brought back into the side at inside-right to the exclusion of Scott, was fit for the second replay, also at St James's Park, only after receiving treatment for a foot blister from David Davidson, a former Newcastle centre-half who was a physiotherapist at Whitley Bay.

There was nothing in the FA rules to say that a visiting club could be liable for any share of the cost of clearing a ground for play, so Forest refused to have anything deducted for that purpose from their percentage of the receipts from this Cup serial. 'We spent £1,400 to clear the pitch so that Saturday's League game with Sunderland and Monday's replay with Forest could be played,' said Ted Hall, the Newcastle secre-

tary. 'We don't expect Forest to pay the lot, but we think a good share
should come out of the gate.' To which Billy Walker responded: 'If
Newcastle spent all that money to get the ground fit it was so that they
could have a full house [62,835] against Sunderland on Saturday. We will
agree to pay any charges necessary for ground maintenance between
Saturday night and Monday's game, and from Monday until the second
replay [on the Wednesday], but nothing else.'

Total receipts amounted to £5,700, of which Forest's share was
£1,500, from a crowd of 38,573 at the first replay, and £5,500 from the
36,631 who watched the third meeting. More extra time was required to
resolve the issue, with the teams deadlocked at 1-1 after 90 minutes, and
the only goal it produced was Alan Monkhouse's second one for
Newcastle. That was the former Millwall centre-forward's only appearance in the nine ties Newcastle required (with further replays to overcome Huddersfield and Third Division York) to reach the final, in which
they carried off the trophy for the third time in five years by beating
Manchester City.

That Forest were not well off financially was already public knowledge. Only a few weeks before, Billy Walker had made five players available for transfer, saying that 'we have got to have new players to strength-
en the team and are forced to part with some men because we cannot go
into the transfer market on our present gates.' Attendances at the City
Ground had fallen as low as fewer than 11,000, and the crowd of just
over 25,000 for the home Cup clash with Newcastle had compared
unfavourably with the near-42,000 who had watched Notts County's
home tie with Chelsea on the same afternoon. None of the five players
listed – Blackman, Clarke, McLaren, Orr and Thompson – left before the
end of that season, but the money from the sale of Moore to Coventry
just before Christmas made it possible to bring in a player who was to
have a decided influence on the club's climb into the First Division within the next three years. But for a bad leg injury he might also have been
in the team that won the FA Cup in 1959.

This was Jim Barrett, an inside-forward snip at £5,000 from West
Ham's Reserves. He was signed on Christmas Eve, just a few hours
before the Hammers also sold winger Tommy Southren to Aston Villa,
who were then managed by Billy Walker's old playing partner Eric
Houghton. Next day, Barrett helped Forest to a surprise away win over
Birmingham. Small was the scorer of that game's only goal, but by the
end of the season Barrett was the club's leading marksman with ten goals
in 25 League and Cup appearances. He had scored 25 times in 87 first-
team games for West Ham after making his League debut as a 19-year-

old at Blackburn in the spring of 1950, and he was to total 69 in 117 matches for Forest before they recouped £7,000 from his transfer to Birmingham on the first day of October in 1959.

Barrett did not stay long at Birmingham, however. Back he went to West Ham, for whom his father, also Jim, had been a dominating figure, chiefly at centre-half, in nearly 470 games between the two world wars. Barrett Senior's international career was diametrically opposite to his club one. He was taken off injured only eight minutes into England's match with Northern Ireland at Goodison Park in 1928, and was never capped again.

It at first appeared that Barrett Junior would not be the only new-comer in Forest's team at St Andrew's on Christmas Day 1954. Alan Withers, a Nottingham-born winger, was reported to have been signed from Blackpool for £2,000, but that deal fell through when Forest could not meet his request for a house. Leeds United dropped out of the bidding for the same reason, and more than a year went by before Withers went to Lincoln City – after talking things over with his wife. He did eventually get back to his home city, with Notts County.

The away victory over Birmingham, who took the title in one of the closest finishes on record, was one of eight Forest achieved on their Second Division travels that season – a surprisingly high number in view of the fact that they never rose higher than fourteenth in the table. Only fourth-placed Leeds and Stoke (fifth) exceeded it in the section, both with nine. Luton and Rotherham were in the top two places with their fixtures completed, the Yorkshire club soaring to the runners-up spot with a result that makes very strange reading these days. They thrashed Liverpool 6-1, winger Ian Wilson scoring four goals. But Birmingham still had one game to play, and they won it 5-1 at Doncaster to snatch the championship and push luckless Rotherham out of the promotion reckoning. The first three each had 54 points – 15 more than Forest.

Another of Forest's away wins that 1954-55 season was their first at Ewood Park since 1908. Blackburn were the leaders when a second-half goal from Barrett was sufficient for both points on the first Saturday of March, the week before Horace Gager was brought back in McKinlay's absence through injury for his final League game in a home win against Plymouth. Later that month Forest added to their away tally (already augmented by the Cup win in Sheffield) by beating East Fife 5-1 in a friendly, their first game under floodlights, at the Bayview Stadium in Methil.

Tommy Wilson did the hat-trick in that match, but only a month later, four matches from the end of the season, his first decent run at centreforward was ended when he was concussed after half-an-hour's play in a narrow defeat by Bristol Rovers at Eastville – a match in which Peter Lay, normally a centre-half, made his League debut as Geoff Thomas's full-back partner. Lay, a Londoner who, like Fred Barclay, was recommended by Danny Long while they were in the same RAF team in the Middle East, was ideally built, at just over 6ft and almost 12st, for a defender, but that was his only appearance in Forest's first team. In the 1956 close season he returned to the capital with Queen's Park Rangers.

Wilson had greatly impressed Newcastle United officials as leader of Forest's attack during the Cup marathon between the clubs, but he was once more out of the reckoning when the 1955-56 season began. Five days before the big kick-off, he had a new rival for the centre-forward position finally vacated by Wally Ardron when Billy Walker paid Preston a substantial sum for 24-year-old Peter Higham, who led the attack for 38 consecutive Second Division games and one Cup-tie (lost at Doncaster Rovers) before dropping out injured. Even then Peter Small was his first deputy. Wilson, who had not got back into the League side until Christmas Eve – and then at inside-left, for half-a-dozen matches – led the line again that season only in the final fixture in early May at Fulham, where defeat, by the odd goal of seven, was Forest's first away from home in the League since a 5-2 mauling on a quagmire of a pitch at Anfield in mid-December.

The fast and lively Higham, who was born at Wigan, had a trial with Bolton before making his League debut as an amateur for Portsmouth, against Birmingham at Fratton Park in February 1950, while on National Service with the Royal Marines at neighbouring Southsea. Called upon after only two reserve games because of a spate of injuries, he provided the pass for one of the two goals with which Peter Harris gave Pompey victory on their way to retaining the First Division championship.

That, however, was his only senior appearance for the club. A torn thigh muscle put him out of action for a time, and, although Portsmouth wanted him as a professional, Preston met his preference for joining a team nearer his home after his demobilisation that summer. He was followed from North End to Nottingham by winger Eric Jones, who, dogged by injury, had limited scope with Forest before accompanying Higham to Doncaster Rovers near the March transfer deadline in 1958. Earlier that year Higham had refused to join Rotherham after the clubs had agreed terms, and the Millmoor club's manager, Andy Smailes, was again disappointed when he hurried to the City Ground to renew his bid, only to arrive just too late.

Higham was one of Forest's three new forwards on the opening day of the 1955-56 season, when he scored in a 3-1 home defeat by

Liverpool. The two others formed the left flank. Dennis Alexander was promoted from the Reserves to partner Stewart Imlach, a winger whose career revived in spectacular style with Forest after going into a sharp decline on leaving Bury for a season in the Derby County team relegated to the Third Division. In addition to being a prominent promotion and Cup winner with Forest, Imlach played four times for Scotland inside two months during the summer of 1958. And the last two of those international caps were gained in the World Cup Finals in Sweden, where Forest were also represented by Fay Coyle, a Northern Ireland forward from Coleraine. Whereas Alexander, later with Brighton after being linked with Exeter, was rarely seen in the first team after losing his place to Tommy Wilson, Imlach exceeded a double-century of appearances, scoring just under 50 goals, before leaving for Luton in the 1960 close season. His subsequent spells with Coventry and Crystal Palace took his aggregate of League games beyond 400. After that he was with Dover and Chelmsford City, then coached at Palace, Notts County, Everton (where he was also first-team trainer), Blackpool and Bury.

Imlach, who also operated on the right wing, had another new partner on the left towards the end of the 1955-56 season. On deadline day in March, Billy Walker signed Douglas John Lishman from Arsenal for £7,000. Next day, this well-built former Marine Commando did what Higham had also done – scored on his debut, but on the losing side. The visitors from Middlesbrough won 4-2, aided by a McKinlay own goal. Until that setback (on a day when Tommy Capel made a comeback for Halifax against his old club Chesterfield at Saltergate after being out for three months with a leg injury), Forest had been making a late challenge for promotion with only one defeat in eleven League games. They lost only twice more in their remaining ten matches, yet finished in seventh place – five points behind Leeds United, who went up with Sheffield Wednesday.

Victory over Wednesday at Hillsborough with goals from Barrett and Alexander was one of the season's highlights for Forest, though they were beaten by a £50 goal scored for the leaders in the icy conditions of the return game. That was the amount it had been agreed to pay Notts County each time Albert Broadbent scored that season after his transfer from the Magpies to the Owls. Notts County were Forest's opponents straight after each of those meetings with the Wednesday. Forest lost to their neighbours at the City Ground, but won at Meadow Lane as the result turned on a controversial equalising penalty – one of the six conversions during the season that enabled Barrett to edge one goal ahead of Higham as Forest's top scorer with a bag of 17.

Doug Lishman was a centre-half at his school before the war – in which he took part in the landing at Walcheren Island in the Netherlands and saw service in six other countries abroad – but after it he moved up to inside-forward and was Walsall's leading scorer for two seasons before costing Arsenal £10,500 in May 1948. Coached in the Gunners' style under the direction of manager Tom Whittaker and his assistant Jack Crayston, Lishman overcame illness and a broken leg to be that club's main marksman in five more seasons. Hat-tricks in three consecutive home games in 1951-52 earned him selection as a reserve for England against France at Highbury; he also played for England 'B' against Scotland in Edinburgh, won a League championship medal in 1952-53, and was in the injury-hit Arsenal team narrowly beaten by Newcastle in the 1952 FA Cup final.

On that imposing record he therefore looked even more of a bargain than Ronnie Blackman had appeared to be. And so he was to the extent of his high ratio of 22 goals in 38 games for Forest. But the fact that he was with the club for such a short time was the outcome of his response to an 'ultimatum' Billy Walker felt bound to deliver.

CHAPTER EIGHTEEN

Up to The Top Flight

The Lishman Affair came to a head on 10 January 1957, only ten months after the former Arsenal forward's arrival at the City Ground, when he was placed on the transfer list because Forest said he had failed to comply with their request to travel to Nottingham for full-time training.

Lishman had a part-time job as a salesman at Stoke, where he lived in the Fenton district. He had been training at Stoke City's ground, and explained that he was unable to accede to what he called Forest's 'ultimatum' because of travel difficulties mainly due to petrol rationing. He had been out of the first team since a defeat at West Ham on Christmas Day, when he had been recalled at inside-left after being absent for the first time that season on arriving too late, delayed on his train journey, for a match at Fulham on the previous Saturday.

Forest won that game at Craven Cottage with a second-half goal from left-winger Stewart Imlach, originally the only player to keep his place in an attack that had produced just three goals in the last six matches. The team first chosen by Billy Walker had Higham on the right wing in place of Small, Barrett as his partner in a move from centre-forward, where Wilson was reinstated, and Lishman switched from inside-right to link up with Imlach to the exclusion of Eddie Baily, the former Tottenham and England player who had been transferred from Port Vale early in October. With Lishman overdue, Baily was reprieved. This chirpy little Londoner had not missed a match since making his Forest debut in borrowed boots at Huddersfield on a day when a youngster named Bobby Charlton scored twice against Charlton Athletic in his first League game for Manchester United.

Baily remained at inside-left for much of that promotion-winning season until the last four matches. He then made way for Lishman, who was back in favour after the transfer fee demanded for him had been too high for both Stoke and Port Vale. Lishman was offered new terms at the end of the season, but after having a long talk with Billy Walker and thinking things over at his home, he notified Forest by letter that he had decided to give up football to concentrate on his business outside the game.

Baily stayed on for another season, helping Forest to establish themselves in the First Division to which they had returned for the first time since 1925. He then ended his playing career with Leyton Orient before going back to Tottenham as assistant to manager Bill Nicholson in the autumn of 1963. His 11-year stint in that post, after which he was West Ham's chief scout, increased his overall association with Spurs to 21 years. He had first played for the club as an amateur during the Second World War, and had been a key figure in the 'push and run' team that won the championships of the Second and First divisions in successive seasons from 1949 to1951. As Forest found, Baily was an asset for not only his one-touch creative skills but also his cheerful outgoing personality that was such a big booster of morale in the dressing room.

In complete contrast to their sorry start of the previous season, Forest got off to a flyer in 1956-57, going through their first seven matches before losing for the first time. With Whare and Thomas at full-back in front of the recalled Farmer, Morley, McKinlay and Burkitt in the half-back line, and Small, Barrett, Wilson, Lishman and Imlach up front, they had a well-balanced combination that followed a 4-1 win at Leyton on an opening day of gale-force winds with victories by 5-1 away to Bristol City and 3-1 at home to Fulham. Jim Barrett scored seven of their dozen goals in those games – two against Orient (including a penalty), two more at Ashton Gate, where Farmer saved a spot kick taken by City's record scorer John Atyeo (314 League goals from 1951 to 1966), and a hat-trick in the defeat of Fulham that lifted Forest to the top of the table on goal-average from Sheffield United and Swansea.

At that stage, just a week into the season, only two other clubs in the League had maximum points – and one of them, Luton in the First Division, lost 4-5 at Wolverhampton in their next game. The other, Brentford of the Third South, crashed 1-5 to Watford in their next home match. Swansea then surrendered their unbeaten record, at home to Barnsley, on the same Thursday evening in late August that Forest dropped their first point in the return game with Bristol City. Two days later, Forest also won at Swansea, by a 4-1 margin that was their biggest at the Vetch Field for 28 years, but it was not enough to regain the lead Sheffield United had taken over with a narrow win at bottom-of-the-table Fulham in midweek. The Blades, newly relegated from the First Division, but now revitalised under the management of former Arsenal skipper Joe Mercer, stayed one point ahead by trouncing Barnsley 6-1 at Oakwell.

The Bramall Lane club had no fixture during the following week, however, and Forest took advantage by regaining the leadership with a home victory against Blackburn in another Thursday evening match. Bryan Douglas, a winger soon to play for England, wiped out the first-half lead Peter Small gave Forest, but Jack Burkitt scored a spectacular winner from 30 yards with two minutes left. Harry Nicholson was back in goal for that game, in which Peter Watson deputised for McKinlay.

Watson, first spotted while playing for the local club Stapleford, had turned professional following his demobilisation from the RAF after assisting the club's Midland League and 'A' teams during his spells on leave. He had first stood in for McKinlay in an Easter Monday win at Lincoln the previous season, but, accomplished as he was, there were precious few further first-team chances for him at centre-half, such was the consistency of Gager's firmly established successor. In other emergencies Watson was also pressed into service at centre-forward, full-back and wing-half before leaving for Southend in the 1959 close season and proving himself a real bargain at £5,000. With Forest he was confined to thirteen first-team games; with the Essex club he played in more than 250, his career ending at the age of 31 when he suffered a broken jaw and double vision on his third appearance of the 1965-66 season.

The last of the three matches in which Watson replaced McKinlay during the 1956-57 season resulted in a home draw with Lincoln that left Forest still ahead of Sheffield United, who were also held at home, 1-1 by Leicester. And Forest still led a week later even after losing their unbeaten record away to Rotherham, who had sunk to the bottom of the table without a win in six matches. Sheffield United, having wasted their game in hand by losing 1-4 in midweek to a Swansea side freshly smarting from a 3-7 defeat at reviving Fulham, also shared two goals when visited by Bristol City. Two of Rotherham's goals in their shock defeat of Forest by the odd one of five came from a first-minute penalty and an own goal by Geoff Thomas. This was the match for which Freddie Scott, by then the club's official coach looking after the youngsters, was brought back for one last appearance as an emergency inside-right when Jim Barrett was out injured.

Only two points covered the top eight clubs after that day's programme, and on the Monday, in the only Second Division game played during the week, Leicester City became the new leaders by completing the double over Bury with a 5-4 win at Gigg Lane. Forest stayed a point behind the following Saturday, now themselves with a game in hand, by beating Port Vale 4-2 at the City Ground while three goals by Arthur Rowley helped Leicester to a 6-3 home win against Notts County. One more week on, a draw at Barnsley, where Lishman scored for the fourth successive match with his second-half equaliser, was sufficient for Forest to regain the lead as Leicester went without a goal in defeat by Liverpool at Anfield – only for the positions to be reversed once more at the next opportunity. While Forest were being beaten at Huddersfield in Eddie Baily's debut match, Rowley registered another hat-trick in Leicester City's 6-0 rout of Rotherham.

The lead changed hands yet again when Stoke City inched ahead of Leicester on goal-average by increasing their goals tally in their last four home games to 22 with a 3-1 defeat of Port Vale in the division's only fixture of the ensuing week. Forest, however, were only two points behind in third place, having played two games fewer than Stoke and one fewer than Leicester. The top three all won next time out, Forest keeping pace with a 5-1 home win against Bury in which both captains, Jack Burkitt and Stan Pearson, the former Manchester United and England forward, failed to convert a penalty. Peter Higham, reintroduced at centre-forward in the absence of the injured Wilson, was among the scorers.

A week later, Notts County, who had followed Fulham and Rotherham into last place with only one victory in a dozen games, welcomed back their key forward Ron Wylie, after a fortnight out with a dislocated left elbow, for their Meadow Lane clash with Forest, but he was kept off the score sheet in their 1-2 defeat. Meanwhile, Stoke's 3-3 home draw with Sheffield United enabled Leicester to regain the leadership with another six-goal romp, this time at Blackburn's expense (three more for Rowley).

Forest returned to second place by coming from behind at Doncaster to gain another 2-1 win while Stoke were losing at Fulham – only promptly to concede it again in a defeat at Stoke by the same score. Injury kept Bill Whare out of that game with the Potters at the Victoria Ground on the last Saturday of October, and he was not to appear in the first team again that season. Earlier in the month, his replacement for the match at Huddersfield had been Roy Banham, a former Nottingham Boys defender whose only previous senior appearance had been as McKinlay's centre-half deputy almost exactly a year before. This time the choice to take over from Whare fell on Jack Hutchinson, who stayed in as Thomas's partner for the rest of the season – and also for the first six matches of the next one before the Channel Islander was able to renew his hold on the right-back position. Banham, who had been signed straight from school at fifteen and been a boys' clubs international, was a prominent member of the Forest team that enjoyed a good run in the FA Youth Cup, but he did not get another first-team chance before leaving for Peterborough United following a trial with Sheffield United.

The match at Stoke was Forest's first in the League under floodlights. Back in 1951, the FA had decided that no more competitive games should be played under lights, even though they had been a great success in a Football Combination match between Southampton and Tottenham. A year later, official blessing was given for lights to be used at an FA Youth Cup-tie between Manchester United and Nantwich at the Cliff,

United's training ground, but it was not until November in 1955 that Carlisle's home match with Darlington became the first floodlit tie in the FA Cup proper. Encouraged by the fact that floodlighting saved England's game with Spain from abandonment at Wembley that month, the FA also gave permission for ties the next year to be completed under lights. The Scottish FA followed suit, and on 22 February 1956 (after the main fuse in the grandstand had blown out) Newcastle beat Portsmouth at Fratton Park in the first Football League game to be floodlit. A dispute that caused the Players' Union to ban such matches in their call for special payments then had to be settled before the League could sanction further fixtures, or part of them, under lights if clubs agreed.

But Nottingham Forest were among the clubs that, initially, did not agree. The big win gained in their first floodlit experience in Scotland might have been expected to have given members of the committee a taste for it, but it took them some months to cast aside scepticism that stemmed from their instinct that it was unnatural to play football out of daylight hours.

Billy Walker was quicker than they were to recognise the benefits, in bigger attendances, of not needing earlier kick-offs on Saturdays in the winter, and of not having to play on midweek afternoons – especially as the old custom of early closing times on Wednesdays or Thursdays was dying out. Some of the committee's doubts were dispelled after another friendly game under lights at Coventry (though Forest lost it 3-2), and they were therefore more amenable when the match at Stoke came along soon afterwards. At the start of that season a six-month delay in delivering steel held up the plans of at least a dozen clubs to install floodlighting, but Stoke were already well prepared, among the first to appreciate the potential of this new development.

From the lights of that part of the Black Country, however, Forest's fortunes dimmed as they slipped to sixth in the table, the lowest position they were to occupy all season. A 4-0 defeat at home by Middlesbrough, for whom Brian Clough scored the first of his League hat-tricks, was followed by a scoreless draw at Leicester and a struggle to share the points at the City Ground with Bristol Rovers after being behind at half-time. The clash with the leaders attracted a crowd of 40,930 to Filbert Street. That was just over 6,000 below the record for Leicester's ground, set for a Cup-tie with Spurs in 1928, but it was the biggest for a Second Division game there, and only about 1,500 below the League best for a First Division match with Arsenal two years before. Against Rovers, skipper Burkitt played his 100th consecutive League and Cup match, three weeks after making his 300th League appearance.

Another goalless game, away to Grimsby Town, left Forest with only Lishman's goal against the Bristol club to show from 360 minutes of football. In his search for a scorer, Billy Walker sprang quite a surprise by entrusting the leadership of the attack at Blundell Park to a 22-year-old salesman he had only just signed. It was the only time Ted Huddlestone, a 6ft local discovery who had recently completed his National Service, turned out in the League side. Barrett was back for the next match, but soon afterwards reverted to inside-right as Wilson was fit to resume at No 9 (as the centre-forward was labelled before the more confusing numbers of the squad system).

Some inconsistency crept into Forest's play as they strove to extricate themselves from their sudden lean spell. From a home win against Liverpool, who were to become one of their strongest challengers for promotion, they went to a home defeat by Leyton Orient, newly risen from the Third South, victory over Fulham at Craven Cottage on the day of Lishman's late arrival, and defeat by West Ham at Upton Park – all by the odd goal. Then, just as suddenly, they launched into a sequence of sixteen League and Cup games in which their only defeat was suffered by the lone goal that knocked them off the path to Wembley in a sixth-round replay.

After a snowy Christmas in which Forest's home match with West Ham was among those postponed (Torquay's players beat the weather by digging their motor-coach out of knee-high drifts on Salisbury Plain on their way to Brentford), that successful run for Forest began as they held out to beat their visitors from Swansea 4-3 after leading 4-1 at the interval. In their next home game, again in miserable conditions, they turned to the Cup with a 6-0 defeat of Goole Town, Yorkshire members of the Midland League who had reached the third round for the first time in their 44 years. Three of those goals, against a club beaten by Forest Reserves the week before, were credited to Barrett. The former Hammer was into a really hot scoring streak. He also did the hat-trick in a 7-1 away win over Port Vale and totalled 19 goals in 16 League games, in only two of which he failed to find the net. With the inclusion of his three against Goole, that gave him 22 in all during the period from late December to mid-April. And there would have been another if he had not blasted a penalty kick over the bar during a 3-1 home defeat of Rotherham that preceded the eclipse of Port Vale, who were battling unsuccessfully to avoid relegation after the resignation of manager Freddie Steele, the former Stoke and England centre-forward.

Five of the seven goals against those demoralised opponents came in a dozen second-half minutes. Their appetite whetted, Forest proceeded to dole out exactly the same punishment when they were at home to Barnsley a week later. Four of the seven that time went to Wilson. Barrett had to be content with just one. By a freak of the fifth-round Cup draw, Forest met Barnsley again the following Saturday, having reached that stage of the competition with a three-goal rally at First Division Portsmouth after being in arrears at half-time. Barnsley had their chance of some quick revenge at Oakwell, but were unable to take it. Imlach had his own, if less spectacular, goal glut to celebrate in Forest's more modest 2-1 win, scoring for the sixth successive game.

A settled side was one good reason for the improved form that kept Forest well in the running for promotion despite their Cup distractions. They alone of the Division Two pacemakers were still in the knock-out competition after the third round. For six League games and five Cup-ties from 7 January to 7 March. Billy Walker fielded the same line-up (Nicholson; Hutchinson, Thomas; Morley, McKinlay, Burkitt; Higham, Barrett, Wilson, Baily, Imlach). On the Thursday after knocking out Barnsley, Forest literally drew a blank in their home League game with Huddersfield, rearranged from the Saturday because of the Cup clash, but that was still good enough to get them back to second place. They then had 40 points, six behind Leicester (both from 30 matches) and were above Stoke, with a game in hand, on goal-average.

Two days later, two goals by Barrett, who had recovered from a cold in time to prevent the unchanged sequence being broken against Huddersfield, brought victory at Bury, who had full-back Robertson in goal from the 56th minute in which Roy McLaren had to go off injured. Stoke's goal figures remained inferior to Forest's even after Neville ('Tim') Coleman had set a League record for a winger with seven of their eight against lowly Lincoln, but a week afterwards the Potters again became Leicester's closest challengers by drawing with Sheffield United at Bramall Lane while Forest were away to Birmingham City in a Cup quarter-final.

Whereas in the fourth round no replays had been required in the sixteen ties for the first time in the Cup's history, three of the four in the sixth round were drawn – among them the goalless game watched by an all-ticket crowd of 58,000 (receipts £8,637) at St Andrew's. To begin with it was more of a battle than a game, some of Birmingham's tackling being described by John Davies in the *Daily Mail* as 'more than robust' in the first quarter of an hour before referee Jim Clough firmly stamped his authority. Full marks to Forest for not responding in kind. They never stopped trying to play good football, and would have won but for Barrett's mixture of bad luck and weak finishing. He brought Gil

Merrick, the moustached former England goalkeeper, to the save of the match, then (after Alex Govan had hit the foot of a Forest post) also made the miss of the match in heading over the bar from Imlach's pass in the last few minutes.

It might also have been Forest, the only remaining Second Division club in the competition, who won through to meet Manchester United in the semi-final at Hillsborough when the teams met again at the City Ground the following Thursday. They looked the more likely winners of the replay – until, that is, the 53rd minute in which they conceded a give-away goal described by *The Daily Telegraph*'s correspondent as 'a wretched affair of misunderstanding.' McKinlay started forward to protect his goalkeeper as Peter Murphy chased a pass from Gordon Astall into the penalty area, but the centre-half then hesitated in the belief that Nicholson would gather the ball without his aid. He was calamitously mistaken. Murphy lunged himself at the ball and toe-ended it into the net. Six minutes later, Higham headed what seemed to be a certain equaliser, but the ball bounced down off the underside of the bar to leave the referee with the difficulty of deciding that it had not crossed the line.

So remorselessly did Forest continue to attack, Birmingham might still have been made to regret not having taken advantage of originally being drawn at home for the first time in eight ties. But some magnificent defending, with Merrick excelling again to deny Wilson and Barrett, ensured that the losing finalists of the year before were the ones who joined Aston Villa and West Bromwich Albion as three Midland clubs reached the semi-finals in the same season for only the second time (the first in 1891-92). Once more, however, the Manchester obstacle proved too big for Birmingham. At Wembley in 1956 they had lost to City; in Sheffield in 1957 they were beaten by United, who were themselves to be the runners-up when they met Villa in the final.

For Forest, the ending of their dream to emulate West Bromwich's Cup and promotion double of 1930-31 was offset by the further finan-cial rewards from a gate of 36,486, although the alarming crowd scenes beforehand had made it appear likely that their then post-war record of 39,380, for a League game with Wednesday on Boxing Day 1951, would be broken (it now stands at 49,946 for a First Division match with Manchester United in 1967). The police, even those on horseback, were unable to keep order as fans fought to get into the ground. Many who gave up the attempt were accosted by spivs trying to buy their tickets, and it was fortunate that there were no serious casualties. During play, spec-tators crowded so close to the touchlines that corner kicks could be taken only after police had cleared sufficient space.

Neither did Forest come through the ordeal unscathed. For their next League game, drawn at Doncaster, they had to make their first team change since the start of the Cup run. Eddie Baily, who had played in that game against Goole only after needing treatment from trainer Les Gore at the Leyton Orient ground where he trained, reported unfit, and Doug Lishman had a one-match recall for the first time since his dispute with the club. The point gained at Belle Vue through a Barrett goal took Forest back above Stoke, who lost their unbeaten home record to Fulham. With Baily back, Forest pulled two points clear of Stoke by beating them 4-0 at the City Ground (two more for Barrett), but over the next three weeks a draw at Middlesbrough, after leading, was followed by defeats by the odd goal, at home to Leicester and away to Bristol Rovers, that pushed them down to third again. Until those rapid reverses, taking them up to early April, Forest had not lost in the League since Christmas Day – and only once, in the Cup, in sixteen games.

The biggest City Ground crowd of the season, 38,741, saw the narrow failure against Leicester, in which Barrett scored for the fifth successive League match. The runaway leaders, who the week before had lost at home for the first time, also to Fulham, then had 55 points from 37 games. Blackburn, 47 from 37, had slipped into second place by beating Stoke; Forest were on 46 from 35. At least Forest had the satisfaction of keeping that man Rowley quiet (Ian McNeill, after only ten seconds, and Derek Hines, in the second half, scored Leicester's goals), and the merit of that achievement was underlined when Rowley notched another hat-trick, his fourth of the season, at the very next opportunity. City made sure of promotion on 6 April, a fortnight before Easter, by beating West Ham 5-3 at Filbert Street while Forest were going under by the odd goal of five to Bristol Rovers at Eastville.

Forest got back on track the following Saturday with a home win over Grimsby in which Eric Jones replaced his former Preston clubmate Peter Higham on the right wing, and two days later they were back in second place with a 3-0 defeat of West Ham in the home game rearranged after being snowed off on Boxing Day. That put them on 50 points with four matches to play – eight behind Leicester and one ahead of Blackburn, who both had three fixtures left. Forest had no match on Good Friday, when Leicester clinched the title by coasting to a 5-1 victory at Leyton Orient, and Blackburn were held at home by a Notts County team struggling for survival.

Goal-average therefore preserved Forest's hold on the only other position by then available for promotion, but next day, with Lishman back in the side in Baily's absence, they surrendered it again in losing 1-3 at Anfield to a Liverpool side suddenly emerging as the major threat to their hopes of going up. Blackburn moved two points above Forest by winning in Bristol where Billy Walker's men had failed – but they had only one game remaining, whereas Liverpool had closed to within two points of Forest and, like them, had three matches to play. Stoke had dropped right out of the reckoning in suffering five consecutive defeats, without scoring a goal, since their drubbing of Lincoln.

So to Easter Monday, when a 2-1 home win against Sheffield United eased Forest back to second on goal-average from Blackburn, who were not to play their final match until 24 hours later. Leicester, meanwhile, were finishing with 61 points, denied another victory to celebrate the presentation of the championship shield as Orient unexpectedly extracted 4-1 revenge. Liverpool dropped a crucial point in a goalless game away to Bristol Rovers, putting them three behind Forest – both with two matches left. Next day, a large contingent of Forest fans cheered Notts County to the 2-0 victory over Blackburn at Meadow Lane that made the Magpies safe from relegation and dashed Rovers' last hopes of going up. Notts, for whom Jack Taylor, a former England 'B' forward from Luton, scored both goals, had entered the year with only ten points from 25 games. Since then they had gathered 17 from 15, consigning Bury, who completed their fixtures by losing at Stoke, to the drop with Port Vale.

That coincidental neighbourly good turn for Forest left Liverpool the last club with a chance to overhaul them – and such a tenuous prospect was emphatically swept aside at the end of the week by Forest's 4-0 defeat of Sheffield United at Bramall Lane that ensured the long-overdue return of First Division football to the City Ground. For Doug Lishman, two of whose goals in a hat-trick were laid on by Eddie Baily, it would have been a most fitting farewell if there had not been one more match to play, at home on May Day the following Wednesday – and if Notts County, of all teams, had not been shock 4-2 winners of it. Taylor again scored twice. Imlach equalised his first goal with a header from Lishman's pass two minutes into the second half, but Don Roby, a tricky winger, soon restored Notts' lead, and Taylor increased it before the last minute in which Wylie and Wilson netted for each side. Wilson was back on Forest's right wing, with Baily as his partner and Barrett at the head of the attack. On the same evening, Liverpool moved above Blackburn into third place with a home win against Bristol City.

Notts had revived under the direction of Frank Broome since the dismissal in January of manager George Poyser and trainer Vic Potts after the team then at the bottom of the Second Division had been knocked out of the Cup by Rhyl, a Cheshire League side. Broome, who had rejoined the club as assistant trainer, would have continued as manager if it had been up to the players to make the choice. Instead, Tommy Lawton was brought back to fill the post, only for him to strengthen the argument that good players do not necessarily make good managers. Notts, having had more than a dozen managers since 1934, might also have learned from the example Forest had set in keeping faith for so long with Billy Walker, one of the good players who did make a good manager.

These were the final positions at the top of Division Two:

Season 1956-57	P	W	D	L	F	A	Pts
1 Leicester	42	25	11	6	109	67	61
2 Nott'm For	42	22	10	10	94	55	54
3 Liverpool	42	21	11	10	82	54	53
4 Blackburn	42	21	10	11	83	75	52
5 Stoke	42	20	8	14	83	58	48
6 Middlesbrough	42	19	10	13	84	60	48

Billy Walker said that in leading Forest back to the First Division he had realised his last big ambition. But there was still that other Cup final win at Wembley to come.

CHAPTER NINETEEN

Vintage Game in Spectacular Start

Spectacular was a word rightly used at the time to describe Nottingham Forest's start to their first season in the top division of the Football League for 32 years. On Wednesday, 18 September 1957, a 7-0 home win against Burnley, to whom they had lost their unbeaten record at Turf Moor in the middle of the previous week, took them to the top of the table with thirteen points from six victories and one draw in their first eight games.

Of course it was too good to last, but Billy Walker's entertaining new-comers still finished just inside the top half, in tenth place. They won as many matches as they lost (16), and were only one point behind Manchester United, champions of the past two seasons. Too hot a pace after Forest's early hold on the leadership was set by Wolverhampton Wanderers, a club also set for a two-year hold on the title, but United might well have done the treble, or at least run Wolves very close, but for the disaster at Munich airport in which eight of their players were among the 23 people who lost their lives on the return journey from a European Cup-tie in Belgrade. They afterwards won only one League game in fourteen.

As it was, the runners-up for most of the season, and in the final reckoning, were Preston North End, who were Forest's visitors on the opening day, August 24, for the first Division One match to be played at the City Ground since 18 April 1925. The team with which Forest won 2-1, to the delight of most in a crowd of just over 33,000, included two new signings. During the close season, Billy Gray had been brought in from Burnley to fill the right-wing position mainly shared by Higham and Small in the winning of promotion; Charlie ('Chick') Thomson had arrived from Chelsea, a club for which Gray had also played, to take over in goal from Nicholson.

Gray, on the small side but nippy, built up quite a reputation as an amateur boxer before concentrating on soccer. For four years in succession he won a Northumberland schools boxing title, then enjoyed further success in the ring as a member of a boys' club. From starting to play football 'by kicking a can around' he progressed to being an amateur with the Dinnington Colliery team while doing his National Service as a Bevin Boy (as conscripts for pit work were named after Ernest Bevin, then the Minister of Labour and National Service). Although born in the North-

East, Gray entered League football down in London with Leyton Orient thanks to the discerning eye of Jimmy Richardson, the former Newcastle inside-forward who was on Orient's backroom staff. Richardson, who, as already mentioned, is best remembered for crossing the ball for Newcastle's notorious 'over the line' goal in the 1932 FA Cup Final, spotted Gray while back in the Tyneside area to visit friends, and arranged for him to have a trial.

So successfully did Gray grasp that opportunity, he was soon rated the best wing prospect since Arsenal's Cliff Bastin by Joe Edelston, Orient's chief scout. And it was also not long before he came to the notice of Stewart Davidson, Chelsea's assistant manager. Transferred to the Stamford Bridge club on the last day of March in 1949, much to the disappointment of, among others, Newcastle, Portsmouth and particularly Manchester United, Gray was a first-team regular for four seasons during which Chelsea twice reached the Cup semi-finals. There was genuine regret among many of their supporters when he was signed by Burnley in the summer of 1953. His fast and clever wing play had put him in line for an England cap, though he never got beyond one appearance for the national 'B' team, against Switzerland at Hillsborough, in which he had the misfortune to be forced off with a knee injury. He was top scorer in the first of his four seasons with Burnley, and, although he lost his place in the last of them, he became such a force for Forest in his late twenties that he made more appearances in their colours (223) than for any of his other clubs.

Perth-born 'Chick' Thomson followed his father as a goalkeeper in the Scottish League. He joined Chelsea from Clyde in October 1952, but was restricted to just over 50 League and Cup games in his four seasons at Stamford Bridge because for most of them he had to contend with competition from Bill Robertson, a fellow Scot. This was especially so during the 1954-55 season in which Chelsea were League champions for the first time in their Golden Jubilee year. Both qualified for a medal as Robertson kept goal for the first 26 League games, Thomson for the last 16. Like Gray, Thomson was to have most of his first-team experience with Forest, playing 136 times in League and Cup before leaving for Rugby Town. And, also like Gray, he collected a winner's medal at Wembley along the way (as we shall be coming to in due course).

The fact that Gray's filling of all five positions in the forward line of the contemporary formation while with Forest, as well as both full-back positions, became a source of some friction will also be detailed in its proper turn. His signing originally as a right-winger on 20 June 1957 led to the departure the following month of Peter Small to Brighton. More than six months went by before another contender for that position, Peter Higham, left for Doncaster in company with Eric Jones on the same March day of 1958 that Harry Nicholson left for Accrington and Roy Banham began a month's trial with Sheffield United.

Nicholson, who was later with Leyton Orient and Bristol City, did not add to his 78 appearances in Forest's first team after being supplanted by Thomson. For the only two matches Thomson missed through injury in his first season with the club, shortly before Nicholson's exit, Billy Walker looked first to Harold ('Harry') Sharratt, a Manchester schoolmaster, then to Arthur Lightening. Sharratt, an England amateur international who also played for two other professional clubs, Blackpool and Oldham, was the first amateur fielded by Forest in the League for 24 years, but he then resumed with Bishop Auckland in their quest for the Amateur Cup he had helped them to win at Wembley in each of the past three seasons. There was not, however, to be an extension of that sequence. The trophy in 1958 went to Woking.

Lightening, a South African, kept goal in just five more League games for Forest before moving to Coventry with Ronnie Farmer at a bargain joint fee of £6,000. Billy Frith, the Coventry manager, was so impressed when he saw these two 22-year-olds in a Football Combination game against Birmingham's Reserves at St Andrew's towards the end of 1958 that he clinched the deal straight after the final whistle. While Farmer also flourished at Highfield Road, Lightening was soon bearing comparison with Reg Matthews, who had won England caps with Coventry before going to Chelsea, and his value had increased to £10,000 by the time he moved to Middlesbrough in 1962. He went back to South Africa the next year to attend his brother's funeral, and never returned.

The 1957-58 season of Forest's reappearance in the First Division began on a new note of optimism for all clubs with their freedom from the abhorrent entertainment tax, and with a general improvement in gates after the loss of four million spectators over the past four seasons. But it was into only his first few weeks when there was growing concern over the number of bookings and dismissals, and the readiness of players to argue with referees (nothing new there nowadays then). There were deplorable incidents at some grounds, with bottles thrown and a referee smuggled away under police protection. Increased bonuses of £4 for a win and £2 a draw were thought partly to blame, plus the 'death or glory' demands of the Third Division set-up whereby clubs ending in the bottom halves of the North and South sections were to form the new Division Four. Further incentives were in the pipeline. The League Management Committee's new charter for footballers proposed a rise in the maximum weekly wage from £17 to £20, a 2.5 per cent share in 'safe-guarded' transfers, and a doubling of the signing-on fee to £20.

Billy Walker, a firm believer in fair play and discipline, commanded too much respect and authority for Forest to be caught up in the 'rough and tough' excesses, but it was not long before several of his players began to succumb in another respect. The first team's first victim of the influenza epidemic that swept through soccer that season was Bobby McKinlay, for whom Peter Watson was again a capable deputy in a 4-3 win at Tottenham and a 1-2 home defeat by Manchester United in early October.

One of Walker's finest discoveries made his League debut in the match with Spurs – and, like Gray on the opening day, he celebrated it with a goal (the winner as Forest rallied from being behind at half-time). John Quigley, a 21-year-old former Glasgow dock worker, had been plucked from the obscurity of junior football with the Clydeside club Ashfield. In the previous month he had scored twice in Forest's 4-0 defeat of a Managers XI at the City Ground, and once in their victory by the same score against an All Stars team in the testimonial match for long-serving Tommy Graham, Forest's trainer. Now he was thrust into First Division action in the absence of Jim Barrett, who had broken a bone in a foot.

For the game with Manchester United on 12 October 1957, an after-noon of fine autumn weather, the new East Stand at the City Ground was in use for the first time. Erected at a cost of £40,000, it accommo-dated 2,500, though it hardly came up to modern safety requirements with its bench seating and limited access. Even so, it enabled the atten-dance record to be broken. The 44,166 that had stood for 27 years, since an FA Cup-tie with the Wednesday, was raised to 47,654, the first few of whom turned up seven hours before the kick-off. And what a vintage game they saw, one hailed as 'a football rarity, a match between two great sides that exceeded expectation.' It was only three minutes old when winger David Pegg, deep in his own half, received a short throw-out from his goalkeeper, Ray Wood, and streaked 70 yards down the touchline before delivering an accurate cross from which Liam Whelan, better known as Billy, volleyed United into the lead. The two other goals, scored by Stewart Imlach in the 47th minute and Dennis Viollet in the 59th, were no less superb. There was not a weak link in either team. Wood and Watson were outstanding, but all were overshadowed by Duncan Edwards, who gave a display that, according to one critic, 'even this remarkable young man can surely not have achieved before.' What a great loss to football his death at Munich was.

Forest were again without Barrett, whose return was also delayed by influenza, but United were back to full strength after having had as many as six of their players stricken by the epidemic. Well as Forest played, they undoubtedly missed the sharp finishing of Barrett, who had scored for the seventh successive game in a 4-1 win at Portsmouth that had come straight after the crushing defeat of Burnley. It was after the next match, lost 2-0 at home to West Bromwich, that Barrett dropped out injured. Forest retained the leadership despite that defeat by Albion, with fifteen points from their first ten fixtures – but only on goal-average from Wolves, who moved two points clear at the top on the following Wednesday, when Forest did not have a match, by beating Spurs 4-0 at Molineux. And there the Wanderers were to stay – as many as eight points ahead at one stage, and with five to spare on the final day.

The narrow defeat by Manchester United was the first of four Forest suffered in a row as they stumbled down to eighth place in their leanest spell of the season. Barrett also missed a 1-3 setback at Leicester, where the home side, without the injured Rowley, profited from five changes after gaining only two wins in their previous dozen games. Skipper Jack Froggatt, soon to join Kettering as player-coach, was among those they dropped. McKinlay's return was Forest's only change; the unlucky Watson was to have only one other first-team chance all season, as left-half deputy for Burkitt.

Barrett was also back a week after the Leicester game, ending a three-match absence, but the goal from the penalty spot with which he gave Forest an interval lead was not enough to prevent another home defeat. Mid-table Blackpool hit back with two – one of them from David Durie, who earlier in that month of October had scored four, as a late deputy for Ipswich's injured Ted Phillips, in the FA's 5-2 victory over the RAF at Notts County's ground. Jack Burkitt, who was also in that FA team (with Tommy Wilson as a reserve), was among four Forest players who each received a second benefit cheque for £1,000 before the kick-off against Blackpool. The others were Jack Hutchinson, Bill Morley and Bill Whare. There was another happy event three days later, on 29 October. Billy Walker, the only manager still with the Football League club he had served before the war, cut a cake to celebrate his 59th birthday. It was in the form of an imitation rice pudding, a present from the Forest players who had been ordered by Walker to eat rice before each home match.

Considering that Forest's home form was mainly responsible for keeping them in a respectable position in the table in their first season back in the top sphere after such a long absence (ten of their sixteen victories were gained at the City Ground), perhaps the manager would have been well advised to have insisted on rice before away games too. After picking up both points at Tottenham, Forest had the best away record in the First Division, with five wins in six matches on their travels, but they defeated only one of the fifteen clubs they subsequently visited. That lone success away from home after the initial spurt was achieved by the convincing margin of 4-1 at Newcastle in the last fixture Forest ever fulfilled on a Christmas Day – though next day they failed to 'rice' to the occasion in losing 3-2 in the return game back at home.

By then Barrett was again out of action. The season ended for him on the first Saturday of December, when he tore ligaments in his right knee after 26 minutes of a 2-0 home win against Sunderland in which Burkitt made a 150th consecutive appearance. It was a cruel blow for the former Hammer, who was play only three more times in the first team before the move to Birmingham that did not work out well for him. Until injury and illness took their toll, he was in brilliant form in Forest's assured start to First Division life.

Barrett's consistent scoring during that period made him a reserve for the Football League against the League of Ireland at Leeds and earned him a place in the England 'B' team that defeated a Sheffield Combined XI of United and Wednesday players by 5-4 in the Sheffield FC centenary match under the Hillsborough floodlights (Notts County, formed in 1862, are the oldest League club, but Sheffield FC came into existence five years earlier). Barrett did not find the net in that match at Wednesday's ground – the West Bromwich pair, Bobby Robson (3) and Ronnie Allen (2), shared the 'B' team's goals – but he gave a good account of himself and might well have won further representative recognition if he had been able to keep fit.

Robson, who scored twice on his England debut against France shortly after his hat-trick for the 'B' team, was also among the goals for Albion against Forest in both League and Cup that season. The future England manager netted both in the victory that ended the Nottingham club's opening sequence of four home wins, scored one of the five with which West Bromwich stormed to a fourth-round FA Cup replay victory at the City Ground on the last Wednesday of January, and then obtained another just over a week later as Albion won the return League match by the odd goal of five.

Such a heavy Cup defeat at home was a huge shock, and not only because Forest had appeared to have done the hard bit by drawing 3-3 in the original tie at the Hawthorns, where the biggest crowd of the day, 58,000, saw all six goals scored in 15 second-half minutes from the 58th on a pitch lightly covered with snow. Albion went into the replay without the injured Allen, and it was only 25 minutes old when they lost another key player, the hard-tackling Maurice Setters. Allen, who, along with Robson and Derek Kevan, another international team-mate, scored more than twenty goals that season, was out with the ankle injury that had left him limping from the first minute of the thrilling stalemate at West Bromwich. Setters, a Cup winner with Manchester United five years later, was carried off with badly strained ligaments in his right ankle a minute after Robson had wiped out the ninth-minute lead Wilson had given Forest with what was to be their only goal. Major H Wilson Keys, Albion's chairman, said afterwards that Setters 'spent the whole interval trying to persuade me to let him go back into the game.' The club's doctor advised against giving the pain-killing injections the player requested.

So the ten men carried on with a comeback that was described as 'a miracle' in next day's *Birmingham Post* and *Daily Mirror*. They went ahead in the 33rd minute with a powerful shot from Frank Griffin, scorer of Albion's winning goal in the 1954 final. Brian Whitehouse, Allen's deputy, made it 3-1 just before the hour, Kevan almost burst the net with a piledriver four minutes later, and Forest fans in the crowd of 46,477 (a City Ground record for a midweek game) began streaming away twenty minutes from time when Don Howe, England's current right-back, completed the scoring from the penalty spot. 'Chick' Thomson revealed that he 'strained a thigh muscle after half-an-hour, and could only hobble about,' but Albion were full value for a magnificent performance. 'When Setters went off,' said skipper Ray Barlow, 'I told the lads to use the long ball, leaving Whitehouse upfield. It worked wonderfully.'

Billy Walker was not alone in saying: 'We've seen the Cup winners today. Albion were brilliant.' Joe Mercer, the former Everton, Arsenal and England wing-half who was there as manager of Sheffield United, West Bromwich's next Cup opponents, said: 'This was one of the greatest club performances I have ever seen. It was a fantastic victory.' The trophy did indeed seem set for that part of the Midlands when Albion won another replay with ten men in the next round, beating the Blades 4-1 despite losing Griffin with a broken leg – especially as they were then paired with a Manchester United side stricken by the Munich disaster.

But it was not to be. Again they went to a replay, but were beaten by the only goal, scored in the last minute by one of United's replacements, Colin Webster, a young Welsh international winger who described it as 'the softest I've scored for a long time'. Victory for United at Wembley, which they reached with another replay win (over Fulham at Highbury), would have been an emotional epic in adversity, but once more the fates decreed otherwise. Bolton, aided by a controversial goal for which their centre-forward, Nat Lofthouse, barged both ball and goalkeeper Gregg over the line, made them losing finalists for the second successive year.

Manchester United were Forest's first opponents in the League after Munich. A post-war record crowd of 66,123 packed Old Trafford that day, 22 February, and paid silent tribute to the dead at a memorial service held on the pitch before kick-off. The game was drawn, Alex Dawson equalising a first-half goal by Stewart Imlach, who earlier that month, in a trial game in Edinburgh, had staked his claim for inclusion in Scotland's World Cup party by making two goals and scoring another in a Scottish FA XI's 3-2 defeat of a Scottish League side. Billy Walker was there to see his winger make a big success of his first representative appearance, but Forest's manager then hurried off to Belfast in his quest for new players – a trip that resulted in the signing of Fay Coyle, a centre-forward from Coleraine, and Eddie Nash, an outside-left from Derry City.

Coyle won a fourth Northern Ireland cap while with Forest, but made only four appearances in the club's first team. Nash did not feature at all. Florence was the uncommon venue for Coyle's senior debut. Forest were without a League game on 22 March because Villa Park, where they were to have been the visitors, was required for the Cup semi-final in which Fulham earned their replay with Manchester United. So during the preceding week Billy Walker took his men off to Italy, where they played a scoreless draw in Florence with Fiorentina, then one of that country's leading clubs. A contingent of sailors from Royal Navy vessels anchored at Leghorn gave Forest strong vocal support – and they saw Coyle almost make a scoring start in shooting inches wide from a pass by Chris Joyce, a young Scot who was given a brief run in the side around that time, either on the wing or at inside-forward.

There were also no goals when Coyle first led the attack in the League, at Chelsea on Good Friday. The only one of his next game, at home to Luton, was scored by Wilson, switched to become one of Barrett's inside-right successors. It was Forest's 67th of the season in the League, then a club record in the First Division. Coyle was omitted after a 0-3 defeat at Roker Park by Sunderland, a club sliding towards Division Two for the first time in League membership dating back to 1890. Newcastle, Portsmouth and Sunderland all finished with 32 points (ten fewer than Forest), and it was only on goal-average that Sunderland lost their proud record in going down with Sheffield Wednesday.

Ken Simcoe, a young reserve, was the other centre-forward Billy Walker tried that season, in two consecutive matches for which Wilson was unavailable. Simcoe scored in the second, a defeat at West Bromwich, but there was no further call for him before he took the familiar path to

Coventry. The one other match Wilson missed while Simcoe was with Forest was the first of the next, 1958-59, season. The attack was then led by a new player, normally a winger, who features in the next chapter.

That game was the only one from which Wilson was absent in what would otherwise have been a sequence of 80 in League and Cup. The most regular members of Forest's team during the two seasons of promotion and the first one back in the First Division were Geoff Thomas, who played in all but two of the club's 92 matches in that period, and Jack Burkitt and Stewart Imlach, who were both out of just three. Burkitt's run of successive games ended at 154 when Watson stood in for him in a 5-2 home win against Sheffield Wednesday on the last Saturday of 1957, but it was almost halted nearly two months before that. He had a narrow escape when the taxi in which he was travelling from Nottingham to the BBC television studios in Birmingham after a home game with Arsenal skidded on the wet road near Ashby-de-la-Zouch and went into a ditch. He was shaken, but uninjured – as was the driver – and when the vehicle was put back on the road they were able to return to Nottingham.

The interview Burkitt was prevented from giving as captain was to have been about the Baily-inspired 4-0 victory with which Forest had stopped the rot of four defeats on the Gunners' first visit to the City Ground for 33 years. To mark the occasion, the match programme contained a tribute of one and a half pages to the late Alex James, one of the most famous and talented players ever to wear an Arsenal shirt. And it was because of Forest that red was the colour of that shirt. When the Gunners were renamed Royal Arsenal FC in 1886 it was decided to wear red shirts, no doubt as an economy measure, because several of their players already possessed them after having played for Forest. A full set was subsequently presented by the Nottingham club.

Bill Morley followed Burkitt to a century of consecutive appearances. He reached 104 in a 2-0 Cup win at home to Third Division Gillingham that led to the fourth-round meetings with West Bromwich, but then dropped out injured from a drawn game against Manchester City at Maine Road. Ronnie Farmer made his League debut as his deputy. That was also Forest's only other match without Burkitt in those two seasons, and his place was then filled by Jack Hutchinson, who had been on the sidelines since having to give way to Bill Whare as Thomas's partner.

For Thomas, however – and for Baily and Morley too – time was also running out as a regular choice. The new winger just referred to, who began as a centre-forward for one match, and at inside-right for the next, was but one of three costly close-season signings who were to play a leading part as Billy Walker again guided a team to an FA Cup final triumph.

CHAPTER TWENTY

A Wembley Preoccupation

The three important additions Billy Walker made to his playing staff in July 1958 were, in order of arrival, full-back Joe McDonald from Sunderland, winger Roy Dwight from Fulham, and wing-half Jeff Whitefoot from Grimsby Town. Dwight, a cousin of the entertainer Elton John, was the costliest at £14,000. Whitefoot commanded a fee of £10,000. McDonald had been on the transfer list at £5,000, but it was understood that Sunderland accepted a slightly lower sum to speed his return to first-team football.

McDonald had played some 150 First Division games for newly-relegated Sunderland since joining them from Falkirk at the age of 23 on 15 March, 1954. Bill Murray, then Sunderland's manager, had planned to sign John Paterson from Hibernian, but Paterson, an Englishman, had refused to leave Edinburgh and, with the transfer deadline looming, Murray had therefore made a snap decision to go for McDonald instead.

For more than two years that proved a wise second choice. In 1955 McDonald played for Great Britain against the Rest of Europe in an Irish FA anniversary match at Windsor Park, Belfast, and early the following season he was capped by Scotland against Wales and Northern Ireland. But he first became unsettled at Roker when he was suddenly switched to outside-left (with Billy Elliott, a former England left-winger, paradoxically put in his place at left-back), and his dwindling appearances back in the first team's defence as Sunderland stumbled into the Second Division made his wife more amenable to the move further south she had refused after he had earlier been put on the transfer list. McDonald repaid Walker's judgment with 124 League and Cup appearances in three seasons before leaving for Wisbech. He was afterwards player-manager at Ramsgate and later emigrated to Australia, where he died in 2003.

The capture of the Dartford-born Dwight was a coup for he had been Fulham's top scorer in each of the past two seasons. He had made up for lost time after having to wait almost five years for his League debut after joining the Cottagers from Hastings in the summer of 1950 – and then being kept in the background until a regular place in their attack opened up for him with the injury-enforced premature retirement of the free-scoring Bedford Jezzard. Dwight's 26 goals in 1956-57 included hat-tricks against Swansea (home and away), Notts County and Port Vale. In 1957-58, four goals against Sheffield United helped him to a total of 24.

Whitefoot very nearly signed for Forest eight months before he did agree to join them. Early in November 1957, when he was with Manchester United but unable to get back into their League side because of the fierce competition for places, he motored down to Nottingham from his home at Sale, on the Cheshire side of Manchester, where he was in partnership with an uncle in a landscape gardening business. 'I am just deciding,' he said before setting out, 'whether it would be worth giving up my part in the business to move to another club. With a club nearer Manchester this would not have arisen. I am very keen to get into League football regularly, and if my wife and I decide it is worth giving up this business interest I would definitely like to join Forest.' On arrival, he expressed a liking for Nottingham, the club and the type of house offered him – but then refused to sign because he could not be guaranteed an immediate first-team place.

A week later, after again turning out for United's reserve team, he said he had 'finally decided to join Forest,' adding: 'I have heard that Leicester, Sheffield United and Cardiff are also interested, but I will definitely be going to Forest.' The transfer was agreed, Whitefoot was prepared to accept Forest's terms – and then he again prevaricated, saying that he wanted more time to think things over. An exasperated Billy Walker, having spent several days negotiating with United, declared himself 'very upset when he started dithering.' He was even more upset a few days later when Whitefoot went to Grimsby Town, whose manager, Allenby Chilton, was a former Manchester United clubmate. The Mariners paid £8,000 for the privilege, but only seven months later Whitefoot became their third player in seven days to ask for a move, following centre-half Roy Player and goalkeeper Colin Tinsley. He said his family could not settle down in Grimsby, so the request was granted and Forest finally got their man.

Whitefoot, a former schoolboy international who was one of the original 'Busby Babes,' learned the fundamentals of football from his father outside their home in the cobbled cul de sac of Platt Street, Cheadle. A tough little tackler, he became the youngest to play in the League for Manchester United when he made his debut against Portsmouth in April 1950 at the tender age of 16 years 105 days. He gained a First Division championship medal in 1955-56 and won an England Under-23 cap against Italy in Bologna, but lost his place to Eddie Colman when only five appearances short of 100 for United in League and Cup. With Forest he made not far off 300 more in a stay of ten seasons before, having had to give way to Henry Newton, he retired through injury in 1968. Billy Walker was amply justified in not letting his annoyance at the drawn-out failure of his initial approach deter him from again going after Whitefoot at the next opportunity.

Dwight and Whitefoot went straight into Forest's team on the opening day of the 1958-59 season (McDonald's debut was delayed until the fourth game), and a most sobering experience they found it. The fixture list could scarcely have given Forest a more difficult start. They began away to Wolverhampton Wanderers, who were to be champions for the second successive season, and were thrashed 5-1. Four days later, they were at home to rebuilt Manchester United, set to be runners-up for the title, and were beaten 3-0. Dwight, leading the attack with Quigley and a youngster named Bob Morrison (in his only League game for the club) on either side of him, scored Forest's goal at Molineux, where Bobby Mason spurred Wolves with a hat-trick. Bobby Charlton, who that afternoon scored three times against Chelsea, was twice on target for United at the City Ground. The crowd of 44,971 was a Forest record for a midweek evening home League game.

With no points gained, eight goals conceded, and the season not yet a week old, some team reorganisation was called for. Walker supplied it by recalling Lightening in goal, moving Dwight to the outside-right position he was to occupy in all his other games for Forest, and reinstating Quigley as his partner. The other change was enforced by one of Imlach's rare absences through injury, Gray crossing from right to left to deputise. The outcome was Forest's biggest League win of the season, by 5-0 at home to Portsmouth. Quigley and Wilson both scored twice, the other goal coming from Dwight.

Four days later Pompey handed out similar treatment to Aston Villa. Peter Harris, like Dwight restored to the right wing, after being an experimental inside-right (against Forest), scored all their goals as they got off the mark with a 5-2 victory at Fratton Park. Although the season had still not reached its third Saturday, there had been two five-goal men before him: Brian Clough, for Middlesbrough, and Chelsea's Jimmy Greaves. Harris's feat did, however, give him a unique distinction. It took him to a total of 187 in First Division matches, beating the record for a winger set by Billy Meredith 34 years earlier. The tooth-picking Welsh international spent 30 years, from 1894 to 1934, amassing his 184 for the two Manchester clubs; Harris exceeded it in thirteen post-war seasons.

Portsmouth, however, were set in a course very different from Forest's. The League champions of two successive seasons from 1948-50 were on a slippery slope that took them out of the First Division, straight after twice narrowly escaping relegation, and eventually plunged them into the depths of Division Four before their fortunes revived. For

Forest, the path in 1958-59 led to their first visit to Wembley and a famous victory in their first FA Cup Final for 61 years. For a time, too, League honours also looked a distinct possibility. At the end of November, Forest were only three points behind leaders Arsenal, with a game in hand, after a hat-trick by Dwight in the space of 25 second-half minutes had given them their first win at Leicester for 50 years in conditions so foggy that the referee almost abandoned play. But they were not to rise higher than the sixth position they then occupied in the table. Although they remained in the top half until as late as March, the Cup became their absolute priority, and the consequent concentration of eight First Division matches into the last month before the final could only be viewed as an unwanted distraction.

Indeed, the undue dip in League form of both Forest and the other finalists, Luton Town, between the semi-finals and Wembley caused a complete about-face among critics who, while looking somewhat askance at two such 'unfashionable' clubs, had welcomed the break in the Lancashire, North-East and London monopoly of most of the post-war finals. One of them, Frank Coles, wrote in *The Daily Telegraph*: 'When Nottingham Forest and Luton Town qualified for the Cup Final it was realised that Wembley this year must, in the absence of Wolves, Manchester United, Newcastle and other giants of the Midlands and North, lack some of its usual lustre. Unfortunately, neither Forest nor Luton have made much attempt in the meantime to whet the appetite of the soccer public by their performances in the League. On the contrary, both have made it abundantly clear that nothing now matters from their viewpoint except the final.'

While Forest were going well in the League after their off-putting start, and before the Cup effect really began to bite, they had a run of ten games in which their only defeats were by clubs in the top four, at Highbury and at home to Preston. McKinlay helped Arsenal to the 3-1 win that maintained the one-point lead they then held over Wolves by uncharacteristically hitting the ball into his own net from all of 25 yards. North End were without their star man, Tom Finney, who had a recurrence of the strained thigh muscle that had handicapped him in England's big victory over Russia at Wembley during the week, but they still had a match-winner in another international forward, Tommy Thompson

Jim Barrett, who had been out of the side since his serious injury nearly a year before, had a one-match recall against Arsenal in another of Imlach's infrequent absences (Gray switched to the wing). In the next game – won 2-1 at home to Everton, who hit the goal's framework three times – Eddie Baily was brought back as Quigley's deputy for what would be his last League appearance before his Christmas move to an Orient side he helped to escape relegation from the Second Division. The fee was about a tenth of the £30,000 Orient had received from their recent transfer to West Ham of Phil Woosnam, the Welsh international who was among his new club's scorers when Forest, by then preoccupied by the Cup, were beaten 3-5 by the Hammers in London at the end of January.

That match brought an isolated return for Bill Morley because a groin injury kept out Whitefoot, whose impressive form since joining Forest had already earned him selection for an FA XI against the Army at Newcastle. It was the first change Billy Walker had made for ten games, much of the team's success during that period having been due to the manager's adherence to a settled side. Thomson had soon regained his place in goal from Lightening, with Whare and McDonald the full-backs, Whitefoot, McKinlay and Burkitt at half-back, and a forward line of Dwight, Quigley, Wilson, Gray and Imlach. That was also the line-up fielded in the Cup run, right through to Wembley.

Willie Fraser, a goalkeeper twice capped by Scotland, was signed from Sunderland on Christmas Eve, but he played only twice in Forest's first team – and what traumatic experiences they were. On his debut in March Forest suffered their biggest defeat of Billy Walker's twenty years in charge, losing 7-1 at home to Birmingham City – the club they had thrashed 5-0 in a Cup replay only a dozen days before. In April, Fraser was given his second chance in the League match at Luton, and this time Forest were beaten 5-1. On both occasions Thomson was not the only regular member of the team to be out of it. Against Birmingham, the three other changes from the Cup side brought in Watson for McKinlay, Morley for Burkitt, and Younger for Quigley. Against Luton there were three other changes in Cup personnel: Thomas for McDonald, Palmer for Burkitt, and Barrett indirectly in place of Dwight (Gray reverted to the right wing from the inside-left position that Barrett filled in his last first-team game for Forest).

It was a first League appearance for Billy Younger, a youthful reserve from Whitley Bay whose progress had been held up by an ankle injury for which he had had an operation at about the same time as Barrett had undergone surgery on his right knee shortly before Christmas the previous season. Younger was to have only a dozen more senior outings before his transfer to Lincoln City in October 1960, whereas Calvin Palmer, a signing from Skegness, exceeded a century – just. Palmer made his League debut in a home draw with Arsenal on the Saturday before the Thursday evening match with Luton. His 101st senior game for the club in September 1963 (won with a Quigley goal) was played at Stoke, the club to which he was then transferred for £30,000. By early 1968, when he moved to Sunderland, Palmer's value had gone up to £70,000. Four years later, he went to Hereford United, whose player-manager, Colin Addison, had been a clubmate with Forest.

There was a tragic sequel to the match in which Birmingham gained such emphatic revenge for their Cup defeat. Only just over a fortnight later Jeff Hall, City's 29-year-old England full-back, was struck down by polio, and he died on 4 April. He was on the losing side only once in his seventeen successive internationals, in most of which his partner was Roger Byrne, one of the Manchester United players who perished at Munich the year before. Four of Birmingham's League games over Easter were postponed on medical advice when Hall was taken ill, making it necessary for special permission to be given for an extension that enabled them to complete their League programme two days after the FA Cup Final. As it turned out, the FA agreed to the season lasting for another full week after the Wembley showpiece, their decision influenced by the serious disruption of the fixture list by unusually bad weather in January.

Forest, however, preferred to get their League games out of the way before the final, even though that meant cramming so many into April, and they played their last one with a week to spare before the big day. They were in a safe position around the middle of the First Division table, with no longer any chance of challenging the leaders, and once a place in the final had been secured Billy Walker's only concern was to steer clear of serious injuries. The changes he and managers of other Cup-conscious clubs made for League matches in the later stages of the knock-out competition led to some sections of the Press recalling that Arsenal and Newcastle had been fined in the past for fielding weakened teams in such circumstances.

But Walker needed no reminding of the Football League's Regulation 23, which stipulated: 'Each club shall play its full strength in all League matches unless some satisfactory reason is given. In the event of the explanation not being deemed satisfactory, the Management Committee shall have power to impose such penalties as they shall think fit.' He had valid reasons to offer for having to leave out key players as the big day neared. Tommy Wilson, who played in all 50 of Forest's League and Cup games that season after missing the first one, was joined by only John Quigley in being a Forest finalist to appear in all thirteen League matches the club played between winning their semi-final and turning out at Wembley. Whitefoot and Dwight both missed one, the others two each. Burkitt was troubled by a sore toe and swollen knee, the rest by ankle knocks. Gray and McKinlay were the last of the doubts, declared fit after receiving treatment for, respectively, a sore toe and sprained left ankle.

Forest were below strength in only five of those thirteen games, however – and in giving priority to the Cup they lost half of the eight others when they had a full team out. Spirits revived when the first-choice side scored five goals in a win at Preston within days of the Birmingham debacle, though the concession there of three more goals renewed doubts that deepened when the same players were beaten in the next two matches – by 2-1 at home to Burnley and 3-0 away to Blackburn, two sides just above them in the table. Much concern arose in mid-April when, again at full strength, Forest lost at the City Ground to lowly Chelsea and even lowlier Leicester in the space of four days.

After Chelsea had departed convincing 3-1 winners (Forest's goal was a Gray penalty), Billy Walker declared that the time had come for his men to recapture their Cup form for the visit of Leicester, who were struggling with Manchester City and Aston Villa to avoid falling into the Second Division with already-doomed Portsmouth. But for once his rallying call went unanswered. The margin of defeat widened to 1-4 for a fifth setback in nine games since the victory at Deepdale. Forest were described as 'decidedly deflated' as Leicester moved two points clear of both their companions in distress despite leaving out Roy Stephenson, a recent £8,000 buy from Blackburn. His inside-right replacement, Ken Keyworth, a six-footer who usually played at wing-half, scored one of the goals. Bill Whare put one of the others into his own net.

On the same day, Luton crashed 5-0 at Molineux as Wolves made sure of emulating the post-war achievements of Portsmouth and Manchester United by winning the League title for a second successive season. Like Forest, the Hatters had then won only twice since clinching their place at Wembley, and both clubs were blamed for 'a casual approach that discounted form completely as a pointer to the outcome of the Cup final.' It was even said that they were making 'a laughing stock of the championship'.

With three League games left, Forest were down to 13th with 38 points, nineteen behind the champions but ten clear of the drop zone. Their next match, on the Monday after losing to Leicester, was at home to Aston Villa, and a side that showed only one change, Watson for McKinlay, pushed Billy Walker's old club nearer relegation with first-half goals from wingers Dwight and Imlach that were to be the club's last in the League that season. Villa were then above Manchester City only on goal-average, but Leicester still looked the better bet for going down because two of their last three games were against Wolves and the runners-up, Manchester United. Leicester duly lost at Molineux, but unexpectedly beat United before ending with a defeat at Maine Road that saved Manchester City. The draws with which Villa wound up away to City and West Bromwich were not sufficient to prevent their loss of First Division status for the second time.

Two days after their victory over Villa, Forest had a fourth consecutive home match, against Leeds, in which they fielded three newcomers. It was a lone appearance for one of them, James Martin, a Glaswegian from a Scottish junior club who deputised for Imlach. Another, Bernard Kelly, was retained as Dwight's partner, with Quigley switched to inside-left in place of Gray, for the last League game of the season, away to West Bromwich at the end of that week (the last Saturday before the final), but he left for Aberdeen after also playing twice in Spain during a close-season tour, and in an FA Charity Shield match. The third man, goalkeeper John Armstrong, stood in for Thomson, and then for his successor, Peter Grummitt, on almost two dozen occasions over the next four seasons.

Kelly, previously with Raith Rovers, joined Forest from Leicester City earlier in April, shortly after they had given their best League display of the lead-up to Wembley by winning 3-1 at Everton with a team restored to full strength two days after the heavy defeat at Luton that was to prove a most misleading Cup Final 'rehearsal'. Armstrong arrived from Barrow a few days after Arthur Lightening's departure to Coventry, becoming the eleventh Scot on Forest's books in a total professional strength of 33. The fee of £3,000 gave Barrow, then a Fourth Division club, a nice little profit on the £300 they had paid to take him from Bellshill Athletic, a Scottish junior side, along with full-back Jimmy Fraser. From Forest, just before Christmas in 1962, Armstrong went further from his Airdrie birthplace by moving to Portsmouth.

Forest were beaten in both their last two League matches before going to Wembley. Alan Shackleton, formerly of Bolton and Burnley, scored all three Leeds goals to which there was no reply; a side unsettled by five more changes let in two more without response at West Bromwich, where Bill Morley played in his 282nd and last League game for the club. With the addition of Cup-ties, Morley left for Wisbech Town with a truly grand total of 301 first-team appearances.

A final placing of 13th with 40 points (three more than Luton, who finished 17th) was disappointing after the fine showing Forest had initially given in their first season back among the League elite, but cause for celebration was still to come

CHAPTER TWENTY-ONE

Cup Final Triumph with Ten Men

The twin towers of the old Wembley were rapidly diminishing dots on the horizon of the mind's eye for Forest and their fans when the half-time whistle sounded in the third-round FA Cup-tie at Tooting and Mitcham's tight little Sandy Lane ground on 10 January 1959. On a deeply rutted and frozen pitch, the last amateurs left in the competition were two goals up against their First Division visitors from Nottingham on what they had hailed as 'the biggest day of our 70 years' history.'

Cup history was then in the making. As was pointed out in the match programme, no First Division side had ever lost to amateurs in this annual knock-out tournament. And in modern times only one other amateur club, Bishop Auckland, had progressed as far as the fourth round (their run was ended by York City in 1955). But the prospect of one of the biggest of all the upsets began to fade seven minutes after the interval when Murphy, scorer of one of those shock first-half goals for the Isthmian League side, had the cruel misfortune to put the ball into his own net. That was the turning point, though Forest had to rely on a hotly-disputed penalty, converted by Gray, to force a replay. They were the better footballers, but there was no denying that they were very lucky to survive. As one critic put it: 'An untidy way of saving a game.'

This was a first appearance among the big boys of the third round for Tooting and Mitcham, a club formed in 1932 by the amalgamation of Tooting Town and Mitcham Wanderers. In the first round proper, after the 'special preparation' of one evening's extra training, a team that included a stonemason, quantity surveyor, salesman, coachbuilder, draughtsman and machine setter matched Third Division Bournemouth for stamina and bettered them in finishing off attacks by three goals to one. On first reaching the second round two years before, Tooting and Mitcham had lost 2-0 at home to Queen's Park Rangers. This time they were drawn at home again – to Fourth Division Northampton Town, who the previous season had sprung the big surprise of the third round by knocking out Arsenal. David Smith, the Cobblers' manager, was under no illusions about the strength of Isthmian League football after admitting his men had been given 'a very hard match' by Wycombe Wanderers in negotiating their first Cup hurdle, and his worst fears were realised when his injury-ridden side, level 1-1 at the interval, went out to a second-half goal scored by Paddy Hasty, an Irish amateur international.

The Sandy Lane ground, which was packed by a record crowd of 14,300 for Forest's visit, was a market garden before Tooting Town took it over in 1922, and the sale of 7s 6d worth of onions from the grounds appeared on the club's balance sheet for the following season as the first money towards their development fund. A new grandstand was in the process of being built when Forest played there, with only the centre section then in use. Proceeds from the Cup were going towards its completion at an estimated total cost of £15,000, the project envisaging the inclusion of a gymnasium, bars and committee rooms. In that last respect Tooting and Mitcham felt they had something in common with Forest. To quote again from the match programme: 'The Midland club is the only one in the four divisions of the Football League which is not a company, and whose affairs are governed by a management committee quite similar to our own set-up.'

Disappointment at throwing away a two-goal advantage against Forest was assuaged by the healthy share of receipts to be expected from the replay. In any case, as team manager George Dring pointed out, the Amateur Cup was Tooting and Mitcham's main objective. Indeed, he was becoming concerned that their chances of reaching the final of that competition for the first time might be affected by the clashing of cup dates. A first-round visit to Winchester had already had to be postponed because it was originally scheduled for the day of the match with Forest that was given its double meaning of a home draw. There was also the icy grip of winter to be taken into consideration. Five third-round FA Cupties had to be postponed from their original date, and the need for seven replays complicated the problem – especially when widespread fog, snow and frost allowed only three of the eight matches rearranged for the following Wednesday to be played.

Forest's replay was among those called off. About 100 Tooting and Mitcham supporters, along with the club's players and officials, learned of the postponement while they were waiting for their train at St Pancras. The new date for the game, on the Monday of the next week, 19 January, posed immediate problems because several of the amateur players would then have difficulty in obtaining leave from their jobs. One of them, John Harlow, the right-back and captain, said he would definitely not be available. 'I am starting a new job on that day,' he said, 'and cannot ask for time off.' Norman Pilgrim, who had deputised for him against Bournemouth, was again put on stand-by after hopes of bringing the game forward to the Saturday, 17 January, had been dashed by the Football League's ruling that Forest must fulfil their home First Division fixture with Aston Villa that afternoon.

But Pilgrim was not needed, and neither were Forest able to face Villa. The weather again saw to that. A record number 28 out of 46 Football League games, and ten out of eighteen in Scotland, could not be played on the Saturday, and Forest's replay was once more impossible on the Monday – one of four of the eight rearranged for that day to be postponed as a thaw set in. At least Tooting and Mitcham were able to get their Amateur Cup-tie out of the way a week later than intended. They defeated Winchester City 5-1.

Another complication arose from a misunderstanding the previous summer between the Football League and FA Cup fixture-makers. Because of this, there were only two weeks between the third and fourth rounds instead of the customary three. As a result, Forest's replay with Tooting and Mitcham eventually took place, after the two postponements, on the Saturday of round four, 28 January. And even then the City Ground pitch was so heavy after overnight rain on top of melted snow that until very late in the week there was a real danger of yet another delay. Forest, who had to do their training on the car park outside the main stand, were unchanged for the ninth successive game, Imlach making his 150th first-team appearance for the club. The amateurs were restored to full strength by the return of goalkeeper Wally Pearson, hero of their defeats of Bournemouth and Northampton, who had fractured his jaw in a league game lost 1-6 to Bromley on Boxing Day. His stand-in for the original tie, Ray Secker, a 21-year-old engineer's labourer from Barking, had been out of action for two months while on Barking's books the previous season, and then sidelined for another month after being injured again in his first reserve game for Tooting and Mitcham.

The kick-off for the replay, watched by a crowd of 42,320, was brought forward to 2pm to allow for extra time, but none was needed. By the interval Forest were two goals ahead through Dwight and Wilson, and Imlach was the only scorer of the second half. The two other remaining non-League clubs, Peterborough United and Worcester City, were also eliminated that afternoon. Peterborough, champions of the Midland League, lost their third-round replay at home to Fulham by a lone goal; Worcester, high fliers in the Southern League who had beaten Liverpool's Second Division promotion challengers under the captaincy of former Welsh international Roy Paul, went out in the fourth round, conceding two goals at home to Sheffield United without reply.

One week later there was another sad sequel for Tooting and Mitcham. They were beaten 2-0 in the second round of the FA Amateur Cup at Hendon. Crook Town were the winners of the final of that competition at Wembley, but to Tooting and Mitcham went the honour of being deservedly voted Amateur Team of the Year on the strength of their FA Cup achievements. Before overcoming two League clubs and then taking Forest to a replay, they had romped through the qualifying rounds with wins over Bromley by 5-1 (in a replay), Redhill 7-1, Sutton United 8-1, and Horsham 4-0. And they rounded off their season by carrying off the London Cup with a 5-2 revenge victory over Hendon in the final at Highbury.

After finally disposing of those Isthmian League upstarts, Forest were hurried back onto the Cup trail in the middle of the next week for their rearranged fourth-round game against Grimsby Town. In common with Tooting and Mitcham, the Mariners had drawn their third-round tie at home after leading 2-0 at half-time, but they had caused a big upset by winning their twice-postponed replay with Manchester City at Maine Road by 2-1. Forest might therefore have been expected to face another tough test, but they went in at half-time three goals to the good and won easing up by 4-1. Grimsby had good reason to regret releasing Whitefoot. He opened his Forest account with a wonder effort from some twenty yards against his former club. And for Grimsby the end of the season provided a marked contrast to the cup celebrations both Forest and Tooting and Mitcham enjoyed. They went down from the Second Division with Barnsley.

Birmingham City, at St Andrew's, were Forest's fifth-round opponents. Both clubs went into the match fresh from heartening First Division victories. On the Saturday before, Birmingham won 5-1 at home to Preston, and Forest, helped by another Whitefoot goal, defeated Bolton 3-0 at the City Ground. Bolton went into that game third in the table, four points ahead of Forest, but both had remarkably similar records in the League. Forest had goal figures of 50-37, Bolton 50-38, and both had won exactly half of their 26 matches. Forest, however, had lost ten times to Bolton's six, and the Lancashire club were generally fancied to get the better of them – especially as Nat Lofthouse had just shown that he was in his best form with a hat-trick against Luton. But Lofthouse became an influenza victim, and he was badly missed by Wanderers in a confident display by Forest.

The Cup balance was also seen in Birmingham's favour, and not only because they had home advantage. They were running into form after a deplorable start to the season, having won eight and drawn one of their last ten games under the new single management of former England winger 'Pat' Beasley (he had been joint manager until the resignation of Arthur Turner, the other half of the partnership). Forest were not doing too badly themselves, with six wins and a draw in eight matches since

Boxing Day, but it was not exactly surprising when, urged on by the majority in the all-ticket crowd of 55,300, Birmingham went into the lead. 'Chick' Thomson, who had been a doubtful starter with a throat infection (Willie Fraser almost faced the club against which he later let in seven goals when he made his League debut for Forest) was beaten in the first half by former Plymouth winger Gordon Astall. And that was how the score remained until the last 45 seconds, when Tommy Wilson grabbed a headed equaliser.

Billy Walker took an optimistic view of the replay. 'We should win next time,' he said. 'We played the wrong type of football – Birmingham didn't. If we can snatch it as late as that, what can come between us and Wembley? I have my best team for 25 years, better than the Sheffield Wednesday side that won the Cup in 1935. We shall be at Wembley.' Four days later, however, Forest again went desperately close to going out. In front of nearly 39,500 at the City Ground, they fell behind in the thirteenth minute of extra time to a goal scored by Johnny Gordon, a signing from Portsmouth earlier in the season, and only five minutes were left for play when they were saved once more by a late header – this time from Roy Dwight. 'Tommy Wilson headed the ball through to me about eight yards out,' said the winger. 'I could not see the goal because Gil Merrick had come out, so I more or less shut my eyes and lobbed it over his head to where I thought the far post was.'

At the end of that week Forest looked leg weary when the only change from their Cup team was Thomas for the injured Whare in defeat by an only goal at Blackpool, but on the Monday, back to full strength, they were a revelation with a 5-0 broadside against Birmingham in the second replay before a crowd of almost 34,500 at Leicester. Sweet revenge indeed for their exit at Birmingham's hands two years before. Dwight did what he had done against Leicester City at the same ground in the League at the end of November – scored three goals. Gray got the two others, one from the penalty spot.

Impressive as that display was, an even more demanding effort was required five days later. Bolton Wanderers, the Cup holders, were then back at the City Ground for one of the quarter-finals, having won the second replay of their fifth-round tie with Preston at Blackburn with a solitary goal by the recovered Lofthouse at the same time as Forest were outplaying Birmingham. And, despite the imposing presence of their talisman, Bolton were again defeated – if by the narrower margin of 2-1. It was their first Cup defeat for 25 months. In a storming start, Quigley hit an upright within seconds of the kick-off and Wilson gave Forest a third-minute lead. Wilson also scored in the third minute of the second half, during which Bolton were limited to a 63rd-minute reply by right-winger Brian Birch when Thomson over-reached in trying to try to punch clear a free kick from full-back Leslie Hartle and went heavily to ground. There had been a gate of just under 30,000 for Bolton's League visit in February; the lure of the Cup now raised it not far short of a sell-out 44,500. Outside the ground on the Friday before the game touts found ready buyers for tickets they were offering at five times their face value of two shillings (10p). To help ease congestion on the terraces, a number of wooden forms borrowed from Nottinghamshire CCC at Trent Bridge were placed inside the boundary wall around the pitch.

Forest looked forward to their first semi-final since 1902 (when they lost 3-1 to Southampton at Tottenham) with well-earned praise from Bolton's manager Bill Ridding. Anticipating favourably on Forest's behalf, he said: 'We could not wish to hand the Cup over to a better bunch of footballers and sportsmen. This was their day, and I hope it's the same at Wembley.' With the Wanderers out, and Blackpool, three times finalists since the war, facing a replay at Luton, Forest were installed as the new favourites. There was overdue recognition among the pundits that, to quote one of them, 'Billy Walker has built a team of talented ball players worthy of the best traditions of soccer's show day.' And although that view tended to be modified when Forest's League form suffered as their Cup quest became the priority, it could not be denied that their then 61-year-old manager had made a great success of combining the five players who had cost no more than the signing-on fee (Whare, McKinlay, Burkitt, Quigley and Wilson) with six of experience who had been unkindly, but with some justification, described as cast-offs from their previous clubs (Thomson, McDonald, Whitefoot, Dwight, Gray and Imlach).

Of the four sixth-round Cup-ties, Forest's was the only one that did not go to a replay. Blackpool were in luck at home to Luton, who went ahead through Billy Bingham five minutes from time, only for full-back Ken Hawkes to let in Ray Charnley for the equaliser with an attempted back pass to his goalkeeper instead of making a straightforward clearance. The referee blew the final whistle before play could be restarted. Third Division Norwich, away to Second Division Sheffield United, came from behind in also salvaging a 1-1 draw – despite goalkeeper Ken Nethercott's having only one undamaged arm for the last half-hour after dislocating a shoulder in falling awkwardly at the feet of Willie Hamilton, the Blades' inside-right. The other match, the all-First Division clash of Aston Villa and Burnley at Villa Park, was goalless. These drawn games increased the number of replays for the first six rounds to 42, compared with 29 for the whole of the competition proper the previous year. This meant that Cup receipts would surpass the record takings of the 1957-58 season, the first following the lifting of entertainment tax.

The draw for the semi-finals paired Forest with Villa or Burnley, prompting Billy Walker to say that he and his players were not worried which of them they played. He added, however: 'Personally, I would prefer Villa, my old club. On our form last week, when we beat Birmingham so easily and then disposed of Bolton, the Cup holders, I think Forest can beat anybody.' Form also pointed to a Forest victory. Not only had they won eleven of their last thirteen League and Cup games, they had also mastered both Villa and Burnley away from home that season. Billy Gray, who had been converted into an inside-forward so effectively by Walker, would have preferred his former club Burnley as semi-final opponents, but it was the manager who got his wish as fortune favoured Villa at Turf Moor. Burnley, just below midway in the League table, dominated play but failed to score; Villa, dumped at the foot of the First Division by Portsmouth's draw at Leeds while they were being taken to their replay, had precious few chances in an undistinguished display, yet scored twice through their Irish winger Peter McParland.

The other replays resulted in victory by the odd goal for the home sides. A goal scored fittingly by Allan Brown seventeen minutes from the end shattered Blackpool's dream of a fourth Wembley appearance and put Luton into the last four for the first time. More sensationally, Norwich did likewise, edging out Sheffield United 3-2 after an exhilarating opening half-hour had thrust them into a two-goal lead. The Yorkshire club, also to be frustrated in third place behind promoted Wednesday and Fulham in Division Two, twice reduced their deficit, but were undone by the glorious third Norwich goal scored by the prolific Terry Bly with twenty minutes to go. Scottish international Brown's goal against his old club was fitting because it kept alive his hopes of getting to Wembley after having four times been foiled in that aim by injury – twice in the Cup, twice for his country. His winning effort was remarkably similar to the one he had scored for Blackpool in the sixth round at Highbury six years earlier – with, fortunately, one vital difference. Against Arsenal he had broken a leg in the act of shooting as he had tripped over Jack Kelsey, the Gunners' Welsh international goalkeeper.

Back at the Hillsborough ground Billy Walker knew so well, Forest put behind them the grisly intervening League thrashing by Birmingham to reach their second FA Cup Final after an interval of 61 years – but they needed the pep talk the manager gave them at half-time. Villa were the better of two scrappy teams up to that point, thanks to their deep defensive system. The deciding goal was scored in the 65th minute by Johnny

Quigley, the only Forest forward who had not previously found the net in that season's competition. He not unnaturally described it as 'the most wonderful moment of my life.' In a little over a year he had travelled in story-book fashion from the obscurity of Scottish junior football to the gates of Wembley. It was also quite a change for three of his team-mates who had been on a losing semi-final side with other clubs – Gray with Chelsea in 1950 and 1952, McDonald with Sunderland in 1956, Dwight with Fulham in 1958. Villa, whose 16th appearance in a semi-final set a record, were undone when their centre-half Jimmy Dugdale, a Cup winner with West Bromwich in 1954 and Villa in 1957, uncharacteristically failed to control a bouncing ball and enabled Wilson to break away down the left. The centre-forward's speculative cross fell luckily between Doug Winton, Villa's former Burnley left-back and Vic Crowe, a Welsh international wing-half who served Villa for seventeen years as player, coach and manager. Quigley, who went close on two other occasions, brought the ball down as he went through the gap and calmly beat goalkeeper Nigel Sims from about eight yards.

In a game well below expectations, too-intricate Forest could not have reasonably grumbled if Villa had at least forced them to a replay. Indeed, within six minutes of Quigley's goal referee Ernie Crawford controversially whistled for a handling offence as McParland ('I could have blown the ball in') prepared to hit the ball home from close range. The Irish winger also twice brought out the best in goalkeeper Thomson, and Forest were thankful to weather a late onslaught in which Villa forced three successive corners. 'We just about deserved to win,' said a less-than-pleased Billy Walker, 'but we played badly in the first half and must do much better at Wembley.' Villa's subsequent relegation made the failure to defeat them more convincingly all the more disappointing.

The other semi-final, between Luton and Norwich, did go to a replay. It was originally due to take place at Stamford Bridge, but was switched to White Hart Lane after protests by Fulham, who had a Second Division game at Craven Cottage the same day, and Norwich, who thought the Chelsea ground unfair because Luton had only recently been there in the League. Luton had not yet played at Tottenham that season, and although Norwich had drawn at the Lane in the fifth round the FA said that was 'sufficiently long ago not to make any difference.' No objection was raised by Arsenal, Spurs' North London neighbours, who had a match at Highbury on semi-final afternoon.

Luton, who during September had briefly topped the First Division – one of seven clubs who set the pace before Wolves clinched the title after being knocked out of the Cup by Bolton – took the lead against Norwich through Brown, but Bobby Brennan, a former Luton player, scored the equaliser on his 34th birthday. Brennan, capped five times by Northern Ireland, was in his second spell with Norwich. They had released him to Great Yarmouth in the Eastern Counties League, then paid £2,000 to get him back. The draw took Norwich's run with only one defeat to twenty matches, yet only two seasons before they had gone through 25 without a win and finished last in the Third Division South.

Buoyed by this dramatic improvement under the management of former Scottish international Archie Macaulay, they had realistic hopes of becoming the first Division Three club to reach the final, but in the replay at Birmingham City's ground on the following Wednesday afternoon they shared the semi-final fate previously suffered by Millwall (1937), Port Vale (1954) and York City (1955). Just one goal, slammed home from five yards in the 56th minute by Billy Bingham, brought their march on Wembley to what was described at the time as 'a sad and outrageously unjust end.' Luton, very much second best, were fortunate indeed to keep their goal intact, especially in the last minute of the first half when, to quote another contemporary report, the boot of full-back Brendan McNally 'somehow got in the way' of a bullet-like header by inside-left Hill.

So Luton were in the final without a manager following the departure of 'Dally' Duncan to Blackburn (chairman Thomas Hodgson led the team out at Wembley) and luckless Norwich were left to face an intimidating backlog of League fixtures after 16.5 hours of Cup football that had included the prized scalp of Manchester United as well as Tottenham's. It had left the East Anglian club with too much to do to have a hope of overhauling promoted Plymouth, behind whom they finished by five points in fourth place. Luton's unimpressive display in the replay made Forest more favoured to win at Wembley despite their below-par showing against Villa and slump in League form – even after their 5-1 'rehearsal' defeat by a Luton side that otherwise also showed First Division fragility. In fact, that reverse could be seen as a benign finger of fate. In fielding a team below full strength at Kenilworth Road, Forest repeated what they had done in a League match with Derby County on the Easter Monday of the week leading up to their 1898 final against the Rams. Five of their first team had sat out that 0-5 beating at the Baseball Ground. At the Crystal Palace, with those men back, Forest defeated the same Derby side 3-1.

One man particularly pleased to see Forest and Luton in the final was Jack Clough, the referee appointed for the Wembley showpiece. For at least three years it had been an open secret that he was in line for this honour, but the regularity with which clubs from his part of the country (Bolton) reached the final had spoiled his chances. Not since 1952, when Newcastle defeated Arsenal, had there been a Wembley without a Lancashire club. Now Clough had his opportunity, also made possible by the FA's extension of the age limit for outstanding officials. Clough, a senior clerk with the North-Western Electricity Board at Bolton, had reached 47, the normal retiring age for referees, in 1958. He had taken up refereeing twenty years before after breaking a leg as a player on Bolton's ground, and was in his eleventh season on the League list. In 1956 he refereed the Amateur Cup Final between Bishop Auckland and Corinthian Casuals, and a year later had the rare distinction of being appointed for the French Cup Final. He had officiated in more than twenty international matches, and in the Central American championships in Honduras.

During Cup Final week, Forest played a lighthearted six-a-side game at their training headquarters at Hendon. Billy Gray lapped the track alone, anxious not to aggravate the sore toe that had caused him to miss the club's last two League matches, but he was never a real doubt for Wembley. As in all the previous rounds, Billy Walker announced this line-up: Thomson; Whare, McDonald; Whitefoot, McKinlay, Burkitt; Dwight, Quigley, Wilson, Gray, Imlach. Luton were also able to field a first-choice team: Baynham; McNally, Hawkes; Groves, Owen, Pacey; Bingham, Brown, Morton, Cummins, Gregory. Syd Owen, Burkitt's opposite number as captain, was the new Footballer of the Year, having beaten Billy Wright. who was ending his distinguished career with Wolves, by 137 votes to 134 in the closest ballot since the Football Writers' Association had initiated the award eleven years ago. Next, quite a way behind, came Manchester United's Bobby Charlton, who was to follow Wright to a century of England appearances.

The 36-year-old Owen had already declared his intention to retire as a player after the final (he filled the Luton managerial vacancy and was later a first-class coach with several other clubs, notably Leeds). He obviously hoped to bow out in the grand manner by going up to receive the trophy, but was thwarted for two very good reasons. The first was Forest's spectacular spurt of two goals in the opening fourteen minutes; the other their heroic defence with only ten men for almost the last hour of the game after Roy Dwight had been carried off with a broken right shin bone. 'The boys were magnificent,' said Billy Walker. 'It was our defenders who won the day. They were great,' Dwight was the scorer of the first goal in the tenth minute, placing his left-foot shot perfectly after moving into the middle to meet Imlach's low pulled-back centre. Wilson headed the second from Gray's diagonal cross towards the far post.

The injury that made Dwight the sixth player to be seriously hurt at Wembley in seven years occurred in the 34th minute, when he collided with Brendan McNally. 'We both went for the ball,' said the Luton right-back, 'and Roy was a bit late in the tackle. I did not think he was serious-ly hurt, and as he was taken off on a stretcher I said to him "Hard luck, Roy." He told me "It's OK, Brendan. It was my fault".' Dwight, who described it as 'a complete accident', watched the last 25 minutes of the match on television in a Wembley hospital. Billy Walker and skipper Burkitt took his winner's medal there that evening, along with a match programme signed by the Luton players bearing the message: 'Bad luck. But now all the best. You deserve it.' A nice touch.

Inevitably, after the Wembley injury jinx had struck yet again, up again went the cry for substitutes in Cup and League games. But again it was unanswered – even after another final was spoilt as a fair contest when Leicester's right-back Len Chalmers was an early casualty at Wembley in 1961. Clubs had to wait until the 1965-66 season to use substitutes in competitive matches, and then originally only for injuries. Dwight, inter-viewed at his hospital bed while his team-mates and their wives were at Brighton before returning home, thought that injured goalkeepers should be replaced, but was 'not sure it would be a good thing for other players.' Billy Walker had not the slightest doubt on the matter, declaring that 'sub-stitutes should be allowed for any position; it spoils the biggest game of the season as a spectacle when one side is reduced to ten men.'

McNally himself was almost a stretcher case in the 1959 final. He dis-located his right knee when he twisted sharply as his studs caught in the holding turf late in the second half. Luton were then desperately press-ing for an equaliser after Dave Pacey had halved the deficit 25 minutes from the end when presented with a straightforward chance from a Hawkes centre following a short corner taken by Bingham. McNally col-lapsed in agony, but was able to carry on, limping tentatively, after being helped to the touchline and having the knee steadied back into position by trainer Frank King. Next day it was discovered that the Eire interna-tional had strained ligaments of the knee from which he had had two car-tilages removed two years before. He missed Luton's close-season tour of Germany, Belgium and France, and Eire's game with Czechoslovakia in Bratislava the following Sunday.

Jack Burkitt was in the wars at Wembley too. He put his shoulder out in a heavy fall, but pluckily continued playing – as did Billy Gray, who was badly affected by cramp in the last quarter of an hour. Forest just man-aged to hold out for their 2-1 victory, surviving their most alarming scare when, with four minutes left, Allan Brown headed a Bingham cross inches wide. 'If the ball had been six inches to the left it would have been my most memorable goal,' said the future Forest manager.

Jim Barrett, who had been out of the Cup reckoning with Jack Hutchinson, scored his last first-team goals for Forest on the tour of Portugal and Spain they made as Cup holders – in a 1-0 win before a crowd of 75,000 at Valencia, and in a 1-6 defeat in Madrid. In other games, a Gray penalty beat Sporting Lisbon as rain fell throughout, and Thomson saved a penalty in a 1-0 defeat by Oviedo. Hutchinson's last contract with the club ended that summer; Barrett left for Birmingham in the autumn.

Never again did Forest field the team that made them winners of the FA Cup for the second time in their long history. Dwight took some time to recover from his injury, and he played in just three more League games, scoring one goal (taking him to respective totals for the club of 53 and 27) before drifting off to Gravesend in March 1961. Soon afterwards his former Fulham clubmate Jimmy Hill took him to Coventry, and he later also played for Millwall.

CHAPTER TWENTY-TWO

Walker's Last Season as Manager

Billy Walker had only one more season as Nottingham Forest's manager after the Wembley win of 1959. In October that year an inscribed memento was presented to him at a meeting of the club's committee to commemorate the twenty years he had completed at the City Ground the previous March. He was beginning to feel jaded, however, and he resigned in June 1960. Three months later, shortly before his 63rd birthday, he became a member of the committee on which he extended his service well into a 25th year until shortly before his death in Sheffield in November 1964. His health was often not good towards the end of his life, especially after he suffered a stroke in October 1963.

Sadly, the Cup triumph did not prove the springboard to more success. Forest went desperately close to relegation in Walker's last season as manager, finishing 1959-60 in 20th place – only one point above Leeds United, who went down with the other faded finalist, Luton Town. Forest also made an early exit in their defence of the Cup, losing 0-3 away to Sheffield United of the Second Division after edging to a slender home victory over Reading, then a mid-table Third Division side. The scorer of the lone goal that defeated Reading in the third round was Jim Iley, who became the club's latest costliest player when £16,000 of the money from the Cup run was expended on his transfer from Tottenham Hotspur the month before the season began.

Iley was also Forest's only scorer in his first League game for the club, lost away to Manchester City on the First Division's opening day, but his debut had been made the week before in the annual FA Charity Shield match between the First Division champions and the FA Cup holders. That, too, had ended in defeat for Forest, Wolves winning 3-1 after Tommy Wilson had headed the opening goal despite being handicapped by injury. Iley's inclusion at left-half for Burkitt was one of three changes for that match from the Wembley line-up. Bernard Kelly, in his last first-team appearance before returning to Scotland with Aberdeen, was at inside-left in place of Gray, who reverted to the right wing in Dwight's enforced absence.

Wilson recovered in time to continue at centre-forward at Maine Road, but there was still a place there for the young man who had taken over from him during the game with Wolves. Peter Knight, a 22-year-old signed during the close season after being given a free transfer by

Southend United, was the surprise choice at outside-right when Gray reported unfit, but he was to have few further calls for first-team duty before going to Oxford United.

With Burkitt available again, Iley was also in the forward line against Manchester City, moving into the inside-left position to which Spurs had also tried him for just one match after he had failed to hold down the left-half berth in which he had first come into prominence with Sheffield United. Iley graduated to the Blades from their nursery club, Oaks Fold by way of Pontefract, and gave up his job as a miner to become a full-time professional only the month before he entered League football at the age of 18 at Charlton Athletic a few weeks before Christmas in 1954. Cynics would say he is most remembered at Sheffield for missing two penalties in four minutes against Notts County, but he was a stylish performer, clever and constructive, who made just over 100 appearances before his transfer to Tottenham, also for £16,000, at the end of August in 1957 restored him to the First Division from which United had been relegated.

Spurs bought him to replace Tony Marchi, their captain, who had gone into Italian football, but he soon lost his place to John Ryden, who had been signed from Accrington Stanley as a centre-half. Although reinstated for much of another season, Iley then again had to take a back seat when a Scottish driving force named David Mackay breezed in from Hearts, and it was this that precipitated his move to Nottingham. With Forest, he completed another century of League and Cup games, in both wing-half positions besides centre-forward, inside-left and on the left wing, before leaving for Newcastle in September 1962. He was afterwards a manager who had to make do on shoestring budgets and consequently experienced difficulty in satisfying either directors or supporters.

Roy Patrick was the next newcomer Billy Walker drafted into the team in his last season as Forest manager. A full-back from Derby County, Patrick had been the youngest to play for the Rams in the League when introduced at Sunderland at the age of 16 years 277 days in September 1952, but had been given few other opportunities while Derby dropped two divisions before he was twenty. He had his best run in their side when they were runners-up in the Third North in 1955-56, but was back in the Reserves when Walker sought him. In his two seasons with Forest Patrick topped the half-century of appearances, mainly as right-back successor to Whare, then moved to Southampton. He was later with Exeter before returning to the Midlands with Burton Albion.

Walker really put the emphasis on youth when he chose a teenage right wing for a match at Fulham early in October. Calvin Palmer was recalled as partner for Geoff Vowden, then still an amateur, who was the latest addition to the club's recruits from the Channel Islands (he was born at Barnsley, but moved with his family to Jersey at the age of four). It would have been Palmer's fourth first-team game instead of his third if he had not been at the centre of a City Ground mystery during the lead-up to the FA Cup Final the previous April. Shortly before Forest's penultimate League game that season, lost at home to Leeds, Jack Burkitt reported unfit with leg and thigh injuries, so Billy Walker decided to play the 18-year-old Palmer in his place. The youngster had been at the ground in the morning, but now could not be found. A hurried search of the premises revealed no trace of him, contrary to the club rule that all members of their staff not playing had to report to the ground an hour before the start of a senior home match. Burkitt therefore turned out after all, took a knock, and finished limping, a knee badly swollen.

With Wembley imminent and the captain crocked, it was a very serious business, demanding disciplinary action. Palmer reported as usual the next day, and when asked by Walker to explain his absence he said he had been unable to leave his lodgings because of a stomach disorder. This was confirmed by his landlady, leaving the fair-minded manager with no option but to let the matter drop. The consequences, however, could have been considerable if Burkitt had been unable to lead his team out for the final. Fortunately, he responded to treatment, and his confident prediction that he would be fit in time was borne out.

For Vowden, also eighteen, the match at Fulham was his fourth in Forest's first team. He had made his League debut in a 2-0 home win against Bolton a week earlier, and had also played home and away against St Mirren in midweek meetings of the reigning Cup winners of England and Scotland on either side of the game with Bolton. Forest lost 3-2 to St Mirren at the City Ground, Vowden scoring both their goals on his first senior appearance, and drew 2-2 with them in the return match at Paisley with the aid of a Gray penalty.

The win over Bolton on the last Saturday of September took Forest to eighth in the table, the highest position they were to occupy all season. Near the end of the following month, during which Vowden played for an FA Amateur XI against Cambridge University at Eastbourne, Forest were down to 17th after Tottenham, then the leaders, had sent them to a fourth successive defeat. Drastic action was called for, and Billy Walker supplied it by going back into the transfer market with a £20,000 splash that brought in Colin Booth from Wolverhampton Wanderers.

Here was an inside-forward who scored nearly 150 goals in 300 games for his four League clubs – 41 for Forest in 98 appearances. He had been a consistent scorer since schooldays in which he had captained Lancashire Boys, played for his home city of Manchester against Swansea in the English Schools Trophy Final of 1950, and been chosen for an England schools trial. While at Molineux he had featured in two title-winning seasons and won an England Under-23 cap. The 1959-60 season was almost into its fourth month when he joined Forest, but he still finished it as their second highest scorer behind Wilson (if with modest respective totals of eight and eleven), and he was their leading marksman in each of the next two before departing to Doncaster. Two years later he cost Oxford United their then record fee of £7,500, and he spent three seasons with them before injury compelled his retirement.

Booth did not get straight off the mark for Forest, but they ended their losing sequence on his debut with a 3-1 home win against Chelsea. He had still not scored when, on his fourth appearance, Forest crashed to their heaviest defeat of Billy Walker's reign as the 1-7 beating by Birmingham was overtaken by the concession of eight goals without reply at Burnley. Bobby Robson had been enough of a problem for Forest with Fulham and West Bromwich. This time it was his unrelated namesake, Jimmy, who did most of the damage. Five times he put the ball into Thomson's net. What a bleak November afternoon that was, with a team containing all but three of the Wembley winners. Those missing besides Dwight were McDonald and Burkitt, whose places in the riddled defence were taken by Patrick and Iley.

Burnley themselves were later on the wrong end of a thrashing, 1-6 victims of Wolves, but they went on to deny those opponents a title treble by succeeding them as champions – and also cost them the first League and Cup double of the twentieth century. Wolves had another big win in their final League game, by 5-1 at Chelsea, but Burnley did not complete their programme until two days later, when they took over at the top – for the first time that season – by narrowly beating Manchester City at Maine Road. Wolves, foiled by one point, defeated Blackburn in the FA Cup Final at Wembley at the end of that week.

Booth scored his first Forest goals in the game that followed the trouncing at Turf Moor. He got two of them in a 4-1 home win against relegation-bound Leeds United – but that score was promptly reversed in defeat at West Ham, where Billy Walker produced his sixth newcomer of the season. Tony Barton, listed by Fulham at his own request, was signed for £10,000 on the recommendation of his best friend from Craven Cottage days – none other than Roy Dwight, whose return to training a few days later, though still limping, meant that in due course they might be competing for the right-wing position. 'We have always been pals,' declared Barton. 'Now we are rivals too, but it doesn't make any difference.'

That prospect, however, never properly developed. It was from Barton that Dwight took over for his belated and brief comeback, but by then his pal, who stayed with the Dwights when he travelled up to Nottingham from London for home matches, was as uncertain of a regular first-team place as he had been during his in-and-out existence at Fulham. Barton found it hard to settle after again being in a well-beaten team, by 5-1 against Manchester United, on his City Ground debut, and he altogether added only two dozen League and Cup appearances to the 49 he had made in five seasons with the Cottagers before going to Portsmouth near the end of 1961. With Pompey he had contrasting fortune, helping them to the Third Division title that season, going on to take his total of League games just beyond 200, and then giving further service as senior coach.

From Fratton Park, Barton rejoined his former Portsmouth teammate Ron Saunders as assistant at Aston Villa, and on succeeding him as manager steered them to victory in both the European Cup and European Super Cup. Two seasons later failure to qualify again for Europe cost him his job, and he gave up his next post, at Northampton, following a heart attack after helping to build the side that won promotion from the Fourth Division. He recovered to become assistant to Chris Nicholl, a former Villa player, at Southampton, only to be laid low again by ill health. He underwent a quadruple heart by-pass the year before he died, aged 57, at his Hampshire home in 1993.

Billy Walker's failing health also took its toll as his hitherto sure touch began to falter during the 1959-60 season in which Forest slipped into such a startling decline so swiftly after his career had scaled another peak with the success at Wembley. Six more goals were let in at Everton, where John Armstrong was the goalkeeper who had to do the back-bending during his longest sequence of appearances in the side (and that a mere eleven games) while Thomson was sidelined. Of their sixteen games after that sobering visit to Goodison Park, Forest won only four – almost half as many as they lost, with the five others drawn.

It was hereabouts that Billy Gray was tagged a 'troublemaker' after forcibly expressing his objection to the frequent changes of position he was required to fill in the forward-line. Centre-forward was the only one of the five he did not occupy. The situation deteriorated to the point where he demanded a transfer, and he withdrew his request only after he had been asked to do so at a committee meeting to which he was summoned, and which the manager was also required to attend.

Forest entered April, the season's last month, four points clear of Leeds United, who were next to the bottom of the table, after a win by the only goal at Leicester, but that advantage was down to a single point on Easter Monday just over a fortnight later – and the Yorkshire club had a game in hand. From their three Easter matches Forest gleaned just two points, in draws at Chelsea and at home to Wolves, whereas Leeds beat Bolton and took three points from Preston.

Nerves in both relegation-threatened camps were jangling, but that was as bad as it got for Forest. On the penultimate Saturday they gained one of their best victories of the season, by 3-0 at home to Newcastle, while Leeds lost away to Everton. Even so, although there was only one Saturday of the League season left, Leeds still had it in their own power to escape going down at Forest's expense. Not only did they have that game in hand to play during the week, they also were at home on the final day to none other than the Nottingham club. But Leeds lost in midweek, by 3-2 away to Blackburn, a team not far above them in the table, and that meant Forest were safe no matter what the outcome of their visit to Elland Road. It was all the more galling for Leeds when they did wind up with a victory on the day they had been hoping to celebrate staying in the First Division, though they needed a penalty to score the only goal of the match. This was how it all worked out down in the depths:

Season 1959-60	P	W	D	L	F	A	Pts
16 Everton	42	13	11	18	73	78	37
17 Manchester C	42	17	3	22	78	84	37
18 Blackburn	42	16	5	21	60	70	37
19 Chelsea	42	14	9	19	76	91	37
20 Birmingham	42	13	10	19	63	80	36
21 Nott'm For	42	13	9	20	50	74	35
22 Leeds	42	12	10	20	65	92	34
23 Luton	42	9	12	21	50	73	30

The team Billy Walker sent out at Leeds for what turned out to be his last League match as a football club manager was: Thomson; Patrick, McDonald; Whitefoot, McKinlay, Burkitt; Barton, Quigley, Iley, Younger, Gray. A year after Wembley, Bill Whare alone was missing from the defence fielded in the Cup final, but Quigley was the only member of the forward line to be in the position he had occupied in that match – and he had been moved to the other inside berth for half of his appearances in the meantime. Whare, whose omission after the debacle at Burnley left him just two games short of 300 in the League (he totalled 321 in all), retired when his contract expired at the end of the season. So did his old partner Geoff Thomas, who had been in the Wembley party as reserve.

Thomas brought down the curtain on sixteen years of exceptional service in a scoreless home draw with Wolves on Easter Monday. That was his 403rd League match, a total increased to 429 with the inclusion of cup-ties. And there would have been a good many more but for injuries and the strong competition for a place that he had to face when fit again. While Whare, who had revisited the Channel Islands each summer for his favourite pastime of fishing, went to Boston United, Thomas became player-manager of Bourne Town and later owned a greengrocery business at Woodthorpe.

Stewart Imlach had also been in Forest's League side for the last time by the end of the 1959-60 season, and Tommy Wilson was to be seen in it only once more soon after the start of the next one. The careers of both had blossomed under Billy Walker's astute direction, Imlach having scored 48 goals in his 204 League and Cup games for Forest, Wilson 89 in his 217. Imlach, along with Dwight, made his First Division exit for the club in the return match with Burnley, who were confined to merely one goal in completing the double, but there was one more match for him after that before his transfer to Luton Town. He was among the scorers in a 5-1 win at King's Lynn in a testimonial game for two of the Norfolk club's players, Mick Manning and Jock Henderson.

The move to relegated Luton did not work out for the Scottish winger. Within four months he was on his way again, to Coventry City. After two years there he joined Crystal Palace, then ended his playing career in 1967 with spells at Dover and Chelmsford. The clubs with which he subsequently coached before going into retirement in 1980 included Notts County (while Billy Gray was manager there), Everton, Blackpool and Bury.

Tommy Wilson had a final scoring spurt of a goal in each of six successive games straight after the Cup defeat by Sheffield United, through February into May, but lost his place at centre-forward after a home draw with Preston in which Dwight made his short-lived, but scoring, comeback. Wilson's only other first-team game in Billy Walker's last season as manager was his only one at outside-left, in an Easter defeat at Wolverhampton in which Billy Younger scored his first League goal. Early the following September Wilson made his farewell appearance, back at the head of the attack, against Newcastle at the City Ground, but was again on the losing side. Two months later to the day, 3 November 1960, he was transferred to Walsall for £4,000, and he spent two seasons there before retiring from League life.

Billy Walker moved 'upstairs' to the committee room with a record behind him of which he had every reason to be proud. Two promotions and a Cup win, and the legacy of a number of proven players who still had much to offer. Two of them, Bobby McKinlay and Jeff Whitefoot, were still regular members of the first team at the time of his death, over four years since he had handed over the reins. Another, John Quigley, had only recently lost his place, and he played a few more times after that before moves that took him to Huddersfield, Bristol City and Mansfield. Quigley, who was later Mansfield's assistant manager, then a coach in the Middle East, totalled more than 500 League and Cup appearances for his four clubs – 270 of them with Forest, for whom he scored 58 goals.

The vast experience Walker had gained in some 40 years at the top of the English game as player and manager made him one of its most respected and influential figures. In his youth he was an accomplished cricketer, but Association football was always his first love. It could be said that he literally gave his life to the game, wearing himself out in the cause. The fact that he handed over when the club's fortunes were at a low ebb was to be regretted. It was ironic and inappropriate that Walker, Forest's most successful manager up to that time, should step aside after a season in which relegation was only narrowly avoided. And even more so when, 33 years later, Brian Clough, the club's most successful manager of all, stood down after a season in which relegation was inescapable.

Billy Walker was somewhat austere in comparison with the amiable, pipe-smoking George Poyser, his opposite number over the river at Meadow Lane during part of his long reign with Forest, but when he had something to say it was well worth hearing. For some years he expressed those views to the benefit of listeners to BBC radio's Midland Home Service, in discussions on soccer topics with other experts such as Stan Cullis, manager of Wolverhampton Wanderers' Cup and League winners, and the very forthright Harry Storer, manager of promotion-winning teams at Coventry, Birmingham and Derby.

One of the subjects on which Walker had a very definite opinion was coaching. 'I am not anti-coaching,' he stated, 'but I oppose most strongly the type of coaching which convinces youngsters that everything the coach says is 100 per cent right and, consequently, original ideas from the pupil must be wrong. It is essential that young footballers should be permitted to express their individual talent, and that the era of the mass-produced, coached, robot should end.'

It was that willingness to let players express themselves that made Nottingham Forest one of the most attractive teams in the country to watch during his many years at the City Ground.

CHAPTER TWENTY-THREE

Andrew Beattie Takes Over

Nottingham Forest were nine matches into the 1960-61 season before they played their first game under Billy Walker's successor as manager – and during that time they introduced two more new players to their ranks. Len Julians, a centre-forward signed from Arsenal for £8,000, had scored twice on his debut for Leyton Orient after being an amateur with Walthamstow Avenue. For Forest he had to be satisfied to start with one goal in a 2-2 home draw with Manchester City on the new season's opening day, 20 August 1960. The other newcomer, in a 3-1 win at newly-promoted Cardiff five matches later, was winger Dick ('Flip') Le Flem, the latest to come off the production line from the Channel Islands in the wake of Bill Whare, Bill Farmer, Geoff Vowden and Ray de Gruchy, a winger turned full-back who was with Grimsby and Chesterfield after failing to break into Forest's first team. Le Flem, best remembered for a 'wonder goal' against Burnley (he beat five men in a run almost half the length of the field and scored with a perfectly-placed shot), arrived as an apprentice from Jersey, but, like Vowden, he was not born there. Bradford-on-Avon, in Wiltshire, was his birthplace.

Le Flem was in the side to stay that season, and he remained a first choice for nearly 150 games before his transfer to Wolves early in 1964. Julians, however, was dogged by injury right from the time he broke his nose in only his fourth appearance for Forest, in a 1-1 draw at home to Blackburn, and when he went to Millwall, at about the same time as Le Flem's departure, he had played in only just over 60 League and Cup games since leaving the Gunners – if with the respectable return of 25 goals. Le Flem, who was later with Middlesbrough before joining Orient, left Forest in exchange for Alan Hinton, a fellow left-winger. Hinton played for England while with both Wolves and Forest, but was never fully appreciated at the City Ground. Some of the club's committee members, by then lacking the wiser counsel of Billy Walker, were heard to suggest that Derby would be asking for their money back when he moved to the Rams. They were made to think again when he was in Derby's two championship-winning teams of the 1970s after helping them back to the First Division.

Julians' arrival spelled the end of Tommy Wilson's days as a Forest first-teamer. Wilson was restored to the head of the attack for just the home match with Newcastle when Julians dropped out with his nose injury. For the other games Julians missed that season – and there were almost 40 of them – the leadership was entrusted first to Vowden, and then Colin Addison, a £12,000 import from York City.

Vowden, by then a burgeoning professional, scored three goals in Forest's last match before the new manager took over, in a 4-2 home win over Fulham on 21 September 1960. It was the only hat-trick among the 45 goals he scored in 105 games before his £25,000 sale to Birmingham in October 1964, but one of the two he registered while at St Andrew's gave him a unique distinction. Against Huddersfield Town in September 1968, it was the first by a substitute. Vowden netted 94 times in just over 250 appearances for Birmingham before losing his place to Trevor Francis, who eight years later became Britain's first £1 million footballer when Brian Clough signed him for Forest. From St Andrew's, Vowden moved the short distance to Aston Villa, with whom he won a Third Division championship medal in the course of increasing his aggregate of goals beyond 160. He then became Kettering Town's player-manager and afterwards coached in Saudi Arabia as well as back in England.

The fee paid for Addison was then a record for York City, but it proved as excellent an investment as those for Freddie Scott and George Lee from the same source. Addison, who was born in Somerset but moved to York with his family at an early age, was Forest's top scorer in three seasons out of four, falling only just shy of 70 goals in 176 games before following a leaner spell at Arsenal (who paid £45,000 for him) with a more profitable one at Sheffield United. After that he had a very varied managerial career that was most notable for piloting Hereford to a giant-killing FA Cup run in the 1971-72 season – a leap into the spotlight that promptly led to their election to the Football League.

Addison was the first major signing Forest made after the appointment of Andrew Beattie as Walker's successor. Forest had hoped Harry Catterick would fill the vacancy, but 'as a result of proposals made by the board' he decided to stay in charge of Sheffield Wednesday. 'We are really very unhappy about this,' said Walker. 'I don't blame Harry Catterick for not taking the job. He's got a better offer, and that's all there is to it. One thing is certain. None of the applicants we looked at before will do. We've scrubbed the lot. So now we'll have to start right again from scratch. I certainly won't carry on. I have had 27 years, and that is enough for any one man. It will be no use expecting me to just go on indefinitely.' A Forest official said the club had become 'a bit of a shambles,' and that points had been lost 'simply because there was no direction.'

Another key figure preceded Addison into the team. In May 1960, the month before Walker resigned as manager for health reasons but then welcomed the opportunity to join the club's committee, goalkeeper Peter Grummitt was taken on from his home club Bourne Town. It spelled the end of 'Chick' Thomson's hold on the position, after 136 games, when the 18-year-old Grummitt was given his first senior chance at home to Bolton Wanderers early in November after creating a big impression in the Reserves.

The youngster could hardly have made an unhappier start. The first time he touched the ball was to pick it up out of the net after Jim Iley had put it there with an own goal in the very first minute. There was a plague of Forest own goals around that time, four of them in six matches. But Grummitt did not let that deter him. From the day of his debut he was an undisputable first choice – for just over 350 further League and Cup games over nine seasons. Subsequent service with Sheffield Wednesday and Brighton took him to around 600 overall. Although denied a full cap, he played for England's Under-23s, and in the Football League XI.

The only Forest matches Grummitt missed before dropping out of the side with a broken arm after the first 90 of his appearances were in the first and second rounds of the League Cup in 1961-62 and two friendly games. With Thomson having left for Rugby Town, Noel Wood, a Retford-born trialist from the Army, was Forest's first-team goalkeeper for the only time in a 4-1 defeat of Gillingham in the first-round League Cup-tie for which the City Ground floodlights were switched on for the first time. John Armstrong kept goal on the three other occasions. Forest won in the second round of this new knock-out competition at Queen's Park Rangers, but then, with Grummitt back, lost at home to Blackburn. Grummitt was an ever-present in the First Division in both that season and 1966-67, and was absent only once in three others while with Forest.

Forest recovered to draw with Bolton when Grummitt made his League debut, thus ending a sequence of seven defeats with which Andy Beattie had the misfortune to begin his inevitable task of following Billy Walker. Beattie, who won seven Scotland caps before the Second World War and played five more times for his country during it, was a one-club man with Preston as a full-back, twice an FA Cup finalist, but was with nine others as manager in either full, assistant or caretaker capacities. Forest, who had also been among the nine clubs for which he had played as a guest in the war, were fifth on his managerial list. To concentrate on his job at the City Ground he resigned from his second spell as Scotland's team manager – a post he had first held in reaching the World Cup finals of 1954 in Switzerland.

Beattie brought two other young players into the Forest team for the club's entry into the inaugural League Cup on 6 October 1960. They were

Barry Wealthall, a Nottingham-born full-back from Hyson Green Boys' Club, and John Rowland, an outside-right from the Derbyshire village of Ironville. They shared in a home win over Halifax Town, gained with a couple of Younger goals, that provided the one bright spot during the new manager's opening run of League defeats, but neither established himself before leaving – Wealthall for Grimsby Town, Rowland for Port Vale. A crowd of only 3,686, the smallest at the City Ground for a first-team game since the war, saw Forest also win in the second round with two goals from Quigley against Bristol City, but their first League Cup venture ended in the next round at Burnley.

There were two more fresh Foresters at Turf Moor, though one of them, Billy Cobb, had made his League debut a fortnight earlier, in a Boxing Day victory that completed a Christmas double over Beattie's old club Preston. Cobb, a forward from Ransome and Marles, a works team in his home town of Newark, scored his first senior goal in the defeat at Burnley by the odd one of three. For the other new recruit, Beattie went back to Scotland for Doug Baird, a full-back from Partick Thistle. Both these players got into the mid-thirties for Forest appearances, then both moved to Plymouth Argyle in October 1963 – Baird for the £10,000 he had cost.

Another Scot, Brian Grant, became the 25th player of the 1960-61 season in Forest's first team, and also their youngest in the First Division, when he deputised at left-back for the injured McDonald in another drawn home game, against Leicester City, towards the end of April. He was 17 years and 347 days old. Taken on as an apprentice from Coatbridge, Grant was another to find limited scope while at the City Ground, but he was into his fourth year there before he left for Hartlepool.

With Grummitt's commanding presence instilling new confidence into the defence, Forest went straight from their losing League run under Beattie's management to an unbeaten sequence of nine games. Leicester would have broken it but for a penalty save by Grummitt in a draw at Filbert Street, and Manchester City might have avoided a 1-2 defeat at Maine Road if they had not had to play the whole of the second half without the injured Denis Law. It was no coincidence that Forest had their most settled side of the season during that successful period, with Patrick and McDonald at full-back in front of Grummitt, Palmer and Burkitt able wing-halves on either side of McKinlay in the absence of Whitefoot and Iley, Gray back on the right wing as Booth's partner, Vowden leading the attack, and Quigley linking up with Le Flem on the left.

Burkitt had his last sustained spell in the team before Iley's return for the last few matches that season. Brought back briefly in the following one after a torn cartilage had again put Iley out of action, the former skipper made the last of his 464 League appearances almost exactly thirteen years since his first at Coventry as a 22-year-old – in an away match with Manchester City on 21 October 1961. Just over two weeks later he finally turned out in the first team for his well-deserved testimonial game against Malmo, the Swedish club Forest were to defeat in the European Cup Final of 1979. Forest also mastered Malmo for Burkitt's benefit, but play had to be abandoned twelve minutes from time because of fog when they were leading 5-1. One goalkeeper named Svensson was beaten four times in the first half – by Addison, Quigley, Vowden and Le Flem, in that order – and, because of injury, was then replaced by a namesake who was beaten by Booth midway through the second half. So all Forest's forwards scored – and Burkitt missed the chance to join them by failing with a penalty at 2-0.

At the end of that season Burkitt gave up playing to take up a coaching post with the club. In April 1966 he was appointed manager of Notts County, but the stress of that job so quickly impaired his health, with Forest's neighbours near the foot of the Fourth Division, that he was allowed leave of absence in December.

Suffering from nervous strain owing to overwork, Burkitt resigned during the following February. Seven months later, he had recovered sufficiently to make a comeback as Derby County's trainer, and during his two years in that post the Rams romped to the Second Division title under the direction of Brian Clough and Peter Taylor, a management team that was also to inspire a dramatic turnabout in Forest's fortunes. Burkitt was in his 78th year when he died at Brighouse, Yorkshire, in the autumn of 2003.

The undefeated run with which Forest followed their losing sequence in Andy Beattie's first season as their manager ended on the last day of December, when David Herd did the hat-trick for Arsenal in their 5-3 away win. A bad start was then made to 1961 with defeat in both the knock-out competitions. Birmingham City paid their thirteenth successive unbeaten visit to the City Ground with victory in the FA Cup; three days later, Cobb's first goal and Baird's first appearance could not prevent the League Cup exit at Burnley. But Birmingham were beaten by a Booth goal when they next visited Nottingham a few weeks later for a League match that marked McKinlay's 300th appearance, and the only setback for Forest in their first seven First Division games of the new year was inflicted by a lone Sheffield Wednesday goal at Hillsborough.

There was a significant development in that match. Baird was injured early on, and Gray dropped back into defence so successfully that he would no doubt have been kept at full-back for the rest of the season but for breaking his collar bone on the brink of half-time at Everton. After the completion of the League programme he reappeared in that position in the County Cup final against Notts County, and also during the club's close-season tour of Czechoslovakia. Then he extended his career in the top flight into his mid-thirties as a full-back for most of his last two seasons with Forest before Millwall made him their player-manager. After leading the Lions from Fourth Division to Second in successive seasons, and also managing Brentford and Notts County, he was back at the City Ground as groundsman for a few years.

Extra time was needed for Forest to win both their County Cup semi-final with Mansfield and final against Notts County in May 1961. An Addison goal put paid to the Fourth Division club, and Notts, then in Division Three, conceded an own goal in losing 3-4 after scoring three times in the last 19 minutes of normal time. It was somewhat disquieting to experience so much difficulty in disposing of opposition from lower regions of the League after having also been in some danger of relegation until a late stage of the season. Not until five games from the end did a home draw with West Ham ensure safety, after which only one further point was picked up. Earlier, two goals in the last seven minutes had snatched a 3-2 victory against visiting Manchester United; now, on the run in, two conceded in the last ten minutes brought a 3-1 defeat at Bolton. And on the final day Forest were undone despite themselves scoring three goals in another away match. Jimmy Greaves netted all Chelsea's four.

A final placing of 14th, one of four clubs on 37 points (Newcastle and Preston went down with 32 and 30 respectively) was far from reassuring, and in the next season, 1961-62, Forest fared even worse. Down they dropped to 19th, this time leaving it as late as their penultimate game, won 2-0 at home to Aston Villa, to make sure of staying up. They also again failed to get past the third round of the League Cup, and fell at their second fence in the FA Cup, back at Billy Walker's old football home at Hillsborough. And there was another knock-out competition in which they were thoroughly trounced. Competing in Europe for the first time, they did well to hold Valencia to a 2-0 lead in the first leg of their Inter-Cities Fairs Cup-tie in Spain, but crashed to a 1-5 defeat in the return game played at the time of October's annual Nottingham Goose Fair. Machado Waldo, a Brazilian centre-forward, took just thirteen minutes to double the deficit, and winger Nunez added a hat-trick.

There were four more newcomers in Forest's team during that season. First in was Trevor Hockey, an 18-year-old outside-right who cost £15,000 from Bradford City. He made his debut in late November, in a home defeat by Bolton that left Forest sitting uncomfortably only two points above the bottom club. John Winfield, the next to be brought in by Beattie, had joined the club in 1959 and signed full-time professional forms the month before Billy Walker stepped down as manager. He was also on the losing side at home on his first appearance, in February, but scored from wing-half against Blackpool. Two games later, Nottingham-born David Pleat, a name since made more familiar as manager of Luton and Tottenham, and as a pundit on television and radio, became another home debutant – and he, too, was a scorer, but this time in victory, against Cardiff City. The fourth man was Joe Wilson, a hard rock of a full-back from Workington, who came in for the last ten games.

Hockey, who had gone to Bradford City straight from school and made his League debut at sixteen, was a soccer nomad, his head swathed in a mass of black hair and beard, whose career embraced five other League clubs and more than 600 matches. He stayed with Forest long enough for almost 80 of those games, then left for Newcastle United, and from there for Birmingham. Although born in Yorkshire, he was capped by Wales through ancestry while with Sheffield United, Norwich and Aston Villa before returning to Valley Parade. In April 1987, the month before his 44th birthday, he was back at his home town of Keighley, taking part in a five-a-side tournament, when he suddenly collapsed and died.

The first-team door was rarely opened to Pleat even though he was on Forest's books for more than four years, yet he still brought in a fair-sized fee when he first joined Luton as a player. Joe Wilson held his place for the best part of two more seasons, and the first dozen or so games of a third, before moving to Wolves, but the biggest bargain in that batch of newcomers eventually proved to be Winfield, the longest lasting legacy from the Walker era. When the chance of a regular place opened up for him at left-back after five seasons with the club, he grabbed it so enthusiastically and efficiently that he was off the team sheet for only five of the 242 League and Cup games Forest played in the next five. He was with the club for thirteen seasons altogether, and in the last one, 1973-74, he was absent from just four of their 56 matches in talking his total of appearances to 410. After a final spell at Peterborough, where John Barnwell, a former Forest team-mate, was manager, he was back on home territory (he hailed from Draycott, just over the county border into Derbyshire) as a newsagent in Nottingham city centre.

Forest improved to finish ninth in 1962-63, Andy Beattie's third season as their manager. They also reached the FA Cup quarter-finals before being well beaten by Southampton in a second replay at Tottenham, but for some time there had been rumblings of discontent because many regarded Beattie as too defence-minded. At one point he experimented unsuccessfully with a double centre-half plan, putting Peter Hindley, originally a centre-forward, alongside Bobby McKinlay. Hindley, son of a former Forest player, later struck up a far more profitable partnership at fullback with Winfield, and, like him, exceeded 400 appearances.

In another match, Beattie so unsettled the side that only Grummitt and McKinlay kept their places, while eighteen team changes were made in three consecutive games. This followed the ending of the Cup run that had begun with victory in the most dramatic climax to a Forest match that season. In the third round at home to Wolves, both sides scored in injury time, through Le Flem and Barry Stobart, to end the game 4-3. There was a new left-back in that Forest team. Dennis Mochan, a former East Fife defender who cost £7,000 from Raith Rovers, made his competitive debut, but had earlier played in a friendly at Stockport.

It was ironic that Forest's committee came to feel that the time had come for another change of manager considering that only one defeat was suffered in the last ten games of that 1962-63 season. That strong finish included the completion of the double over Liverpool and Aston Villa, a draw with Manchester City despite injuries to Hindley and Whitefoot that reduced the side to nine fit men, and, on the last day, a home win against Manchester United in which Mochan's goal was the only one he scored in some 120 games before going to Colchester.

The successful run that took Forest into the top half of the table was also notable for the first appearance of Ian Storey-Moore, an Ipswich-born winger discovered in Scunthorpe junior football. He made it in a defeat of his home club, the winning goal debited to Ipswich's goalkeeper Roy Bailey, whose son Gary followed him between the sticks for Manchester United and England. Storey-Moore was also to play for England and the Old Trafford club, but it was not until beyond the scope of this book that he became a first-team regular at the City Ground.

The confident manner in which Forest rounded off their 1962-63 League programme made them favourites to win the County Cup they had retained at the end of the previous season only after extra time against Mansfield Town. But again more than 90 minutes were needed to decide the final, and this time it produced the winning goal for Notts County. Less than two months later, Andy Beattie, sensing the tide of opinion running against him, resigned.

CHAPTER TWENTY-FOUR

Last Legacy with Carey in Charge

Johnny Carey, the second and last manager of Nottingham Forest while Billy Walker was on the club's committee, arrived at the City Ground with two promotions to his credit since ending his distinguished career as a player with Manchester United.

In 344 games for United, Carey was a League champion and FA Cup winner, yet it was only by chance that he joined the Old Trafford club. Chief scout Louis Rocca travelled to Dublin to look at another player, but Carey was the one who most impressed him. The versatile and gentlemanly Irishman went on to play for United in every position except on the wing. He captained not only club and country (capped by both Northern Ireland and the Republic) but also the Rest of Europe against Great Britain, and in 1949 he was Footballer of the Year.

In his first managerial post he piloted Blackburn Rovers back to the First Division in 1958; in his third, in 1962, he took Leyton Orient to that level for the first time. In between, fifth in 1960-61, then Everton's highest final position since the war, was not enough to save him from being sacked by the Goodison club – in the back of a London taxi on the way from a Football League meeting. A similar fate was not in store for him when Orient were immediately relegated, but it was shortly afterwards, in July 1963, that Nottingham Forest invited him to fill the vacancy left by Andy Beattie. He had no hesitation in accepting. As he said, if not with any originality, 'They made me an offer I couldn't refuse.'

Forest's first League game under Carey's control was at home to Billy Walker's first love, Aston Villa. And they lost it to a goal scored by Tony Hateley, a centre-forward who had come to the fore with their city rivals at Meadow Lane. His opposite number in the Forest line-up was Frank Wignall, who was making his debut after being signed from Everton during the month before Beattie's resignation. The fee of about £20,000 made Wignall the club's latest costliest player, an outlay he amply justified with just over 50 goals in nearly 180 games well into a fifth Forest season before completing his League career with Wolves, Derby County and Mansfield Town. While at the City Ground he recovered from breaking a leg in a County Cup final defeat of Mansfield to catch the attention of England's manager, Alf Ramsey, who late in the same year of 1964 awarded him a couple of caps. He scored twice on his debut against Wales.

The first of Wignall's goals for Forest came on the Wednesday after the losing start against Villa. An unchanged Forest team (Grummitt; Wilson, Mochan; Whitefoot, McKinlay, Winfield; Hockey, Addison, Wignall, Quigley, Le Flem) ventured into Anfield, which was becoming a fortress under the dynamic management of Bill Shankly – and came away with both points. The only goal scored by Liverpool, who went on to win the League title for the second time in three seasons, was an own goal by McKinlay. Neither did any of Liverpool's players score in the drawn return game, but in the meantime, on the second Saturday, a hat-trick for Tottenham by Jimmy Greaves caused Forest to come another cropper.

Three weeks later, however, Carey had a start for which he could scarcely have hoped. Forest were at the top of the table after a fifth successive win. But that height was too dizzy for them. The competition up there was so keen that the dropping of a home point to Blackburn a week afterwards was sufficient to send them down to fifth, and they were never serious contenders for a championship that Liverpool carried off with four points to spare. Forest had their moments, but tailed away to finish Billy Walker's final full season with the club 13th in the table, 16 points off the pace. Compensation in the Cup eluded them too. Drawn at home in the third round to Preston, who were then a Second Division side, they were held to a goalless draw and lost the replay by an extra-time goal in a Deepdale snowstorm.

The second newcomer to the Forest team that season was Henry Newton, a Nottingham-born former Nottingham Boys player who qualified by six months as another Walker legacy because he was first signed as an amateur in January 1960. He turned professional during the summer of the following year, but had to wait for his first League chance until 8 October 1963, when, at the age of 19, he deputised for Whitefoot, whom he was eventually to displace, in a 2-0 home win against Leicester City. There were to be 315 Forest games in all for Newton before his move to Everton merely postponed his preferred transfer to Derby that led him to a League championship medal in 1974 as the last big signing for the Rams by Brian Clough. Forest blocked his direct route to Derby as they felt that enough of their talent had already gone there – Hinton, Wignall (by way of Wolves) and Welsh international Terry Hennessey.

Arthritis finally caught up with Newton while he was with Walsall, forcing his retirement. At his peak he was well worth the England call that never came, though he played for the Under-23 side and was on the verge of the 1970 World Cup squad.

Carey's first entry into the transfer market on Forest's behalf took him back to Leyton Orient for Billy Taylor, but this Scottish wing-half was preceded into the first team by West Countryman Mike Kear, a winger from Newport County who was signed a couple of months after Taylor. Both made only intermittent appearances before leaving – Taylor for Lincoln City, Kear for Middlesbrough. Carey also negotiated the Le Flem-Hinton exchange deal, but struck the biggest transfer bargain of his first Forest season by taking John Barnwell from Arsenal, even though he had to raise the club's record outgoing fee to £30,000.

Barnwell, who had first attracted attention in Bishop Auckland's successful side, spent some six seasons at the City Ground, during which he added 200 appearances to the 150 he had made in eight seasons with the Gunners. In his deep-lying role, linking defence with attack, he was one of the first players to be termed a midfielder. Wolves were among the clubs he later managed, and in 1980 he guided them to victory against Forest in a League Cup final.

Another player who gave Forest superb service also made his debut in Carey's first season. Sammy Chapman, who shared a Wednesbury birthplace with Billy Walker, was signed as a forward from junior football in Walsall, and it was at inside-left that he was introduced at the age of 17 in a scoreless home draw with Stoke City in mid-January. He was not called up again for first-team duty while Walker was still at the City Ground, and made only rare appearances over the next few seasons, but his career then took off with an emergency switch into defence. He became an automatic choice at wing-half, and had more than 400 games under his belt by the time he moved across to Notts County in 1977.

Forest's Meadow Lane neighbours provided the first silverware of Carey's reign, Wignall scoring three in the 5-1 win that reclaimed the County Cup. Wignall ended the League season as Forest's top scorer with a modest total of 16 goals that included his first senior hat-trick in a 3-2 victory at Bolton, but, in addition to enjoying himself at the expense of Notts County, he increased his overall tally for the season to 22 with three more goals in the 8-0 defeat of a New Zealand touring side. Forest's own tour at the end of the season took them to Berlin, where Addison scored all three goals of the game with the Hertha club, and Switzerland. The Continental tours to which Forest were now becoming accustomed were a far cry from the more homely days of Billy Walker's management when winding-down charity soccer matches had been played with a rugby ball against the Nottingham Rugby Union club.

Three days before the start of the 1964-65 season, Forest's committee sanctioned another fee of £30,000 for the transfer of Chris Crowe, a winger or inside-forward, from Wolves. Crowe played for Scotland as a schoolboy, having moved from his Newcastle birthplace to Edinburgh with his family, but for England at youth, Under-23 and senior level (one full cap against France at Hillsborough in 1962). He was with Leeds and Blackburn before Wolves, and with Bristol City after Forest.

Crowe and his new team-mates got off to a winning start at home to Birmingham City, but it was a mighty close thing. Forest scored three times in the last seventeen minutes to snatch both points by the odd goal of seven. Addison, who had notched another hat-trick in a pre-season friendly at Brentford, again led the way, netting twice. Barnwell, the other scorer along with Hinton, obtained two more goals in another narrow win, in a Friday evening game at West Ham, and Hinton was the two-goal man in the following midweek home victory over Everton that avenged a defeat suffered at Goodison Park the previous Tuesday. Crowe took thirteen games to get off the mark, then scoring both goals in a home draw with Chelsea that was made most memorable for the piglet that ran across the pitch in a university rag week stunt.

It was obvious in these last months of Billy Walker's long time at the City Ground that Johnny Carey had assembled a team comparable with some of the best that Walker himself had built. Forest were to finish fifth, then the second highest final position in their history, but in those opening weeks alone they achieved several results that stamped them as a force to be reckoned with as goals flowed with some regularity from Addison, Wignall and Barnwell. Their 2-1 win at Elland Road, for instance, ended Leeds' run of 30 unbeaten home games on the last Saturday of September (Leeds were deprived of the title by Manchester United that season only on goal-average). Impressive victories were also gained away to Arsenal and at home to Sunderland and Aston Villa. The match at Highbury was the only one Grummitt missed all season, giving James Cargill, who had joined as an apprentice, the first of his few opportunities in the first team's goal. He kept a clean sheet. Addison did the hat-trick against Sunderland; Wignall likewise against Villa.

On the afternoon of the day Billy Walker died, 28 November 1964 (also the day of the death of Jimmy McMullan, the former Scottish international who succeeded him as manager of Sheffield Wednesday), Forest were at Blackpool with this team: Grummitt; Hindley, Mochan; Newton, McKinlay, Whitefoot; Crowe, Addison, Wignall, Barnwell, Hinton. They won 2-0, Addison and Barnwell scoring. Although more than four years had elapsed since Walker's resignation as manager, and his effectiveness as a member of the committee had declined over the last few months because of his ill health, this was the definitive ending of the Walker Era. For it to coincide with a victory was a most fitting climax to one of the truly magnificent footballing careers, as both player and manager.